D1592656

DISCARDED

DISCARDED

The Multiculturalism of Fear

The Multiculturalism
of Fear

JACOB T. LEVY

OXFORD
UNIVERSITY PRESS

OXFORD
UNIVERSITY PRESS

Great Clarendon Street, Oxford OX2 6DP

Oxford University Press is a department of the University of Oxford.
It furthers the University's objective of excellence in research, scholarship,
and education by publishing worldwide in

Oxford New York

Athens Auckland Bangkok Bogotá Buenos Aires Calcutta
Cape Town Chennai Dar es Salaam Delhi Florence Hong Kong Istanbul
Karachi Kuala Lumpur Madrid Melbourne Mexico City Mumbai
Nairobi Paris São Paulo Shanghai Singapore Taipei Tokyo Toronto Warsaw

with associated companies in Berlin Ibadan

Oxford is a registered trade mark of Oxford University Press
in the UK and in certain other countries

Published in the United States
by Oxford University Press Inc., New York

© Jacob T. Levy 2000

The moral rights of the author have been asserted
Database right Oxford University Press (maker)

First published 2000

All rights reserved. No part of this publication may be reproduced,
stored in a retrieval system, or transmitted, in any form or by any means,
without the prior permission in writing of Oxford University Press,
or as expressly permitted by law, or under terms agreed with the appropriate
reprographics rights organizations. Enquiries concerning reproduction
outside the scope of the above should be sent to the Rights Department,
Oxford University Press, at the address above

You must not circulate this book in any other binding or cover
and you must impose this same condition on any acquirer

British Library Cataloguing in Publication Data

Data available

Library of Congress Cataloging-in-Publication Data
Levy, Jacob T., 1971–
The multiculturalism of fear/Jacob T. Levy
p. cm.
Includes bibliographical references and index.
1. Ethnic relations—Political aspects.   2. Social conflict—Political aspects.
3. Fear—Cross-cultural studies. 4. Political violence. 5. Nationalism. 6. Multi-culturalism.
I. Title.
GN495.6.L495 2000   323.1′01—dc21   00–031356

ISBN 0–19–829712–2

1 3 5 7 9 10 8 6 4 2

Typeset in Sabon by
Cambrian Typesetters, Frimley, Surrey

Printed in Great Britain
on acid-free paper by
T. J. International Ltd
Padstow, Cornwall

To
Shelley Dawn Clark

ACKNOWLEDGEMENTS

While writing this book, I was fortunate enough to be part of two, over-lapping but separate, stimulating intellectual communities.

The first of these was the community of political theorists at Princeton University, the faculty and graduate students in the Program in Political Philosophy and the University Center for Human Values. Much of this book was presented to the graduate student Political Theory Luncheon, the seminar of Mellon Graduate Fellows at the University Center, the Research Seminar in Political Theory, and the seminar of Woodrow Wilson Society of Fellows. I benefited greatly from discussion and comments from both members of the faculty and my graduate colleagues. Jonathan Allen, Oliver Avens, Clancy Bailey, Aurelian Craiutu, Patrick Deneen, Suzanne Dovi, Denise Dutton, Jeffrey Herbst, Elizabeth Kiss, Walter Murphy, Alan Ryan, Roy Tsao, and Maurizio Viroli each provided me with a sounding board, useful insights, and/or written comments on some part of this project.

My greatest debts at Princeton are clearly to my faculty advisors, Jeremy Waldron, George Kateb, and especially Amy Gutmann. Professor Waldron suggested ideas and lines of reasoning that reshaped much of my understanding of my own arguments; most of Part III has been affected by these conversations. Much of Part I was written in a kind of dialogue with Professor Kateb. I have tried to show that even the morally individualistic liberalism he powerfully and frequently defends had to accommodate itself to the facts of ethnic pluralism and ethnic loyalty in the world. Professor Gutmann—in her comments on this work and related projects, in her course on Ethics and Public Policy, and by the example of her own work—has taught me lesson after lesson about political theory that engages with politics and policy. She has assisted, supported, and improved this work in any number of ways.

The other intellectual community has been made up of political theo-rists and philosophers who think and write about ethnicity, nationalism, and multiculturalism. Brian Barry, Joe Carens, William Galston, Steven Grosby, Steven Macedo, David Miller, Margaret Moore, Jeff Spinner-Halev, Yael Tamir, Iris Marion Young, Patrick Macklem, Wayne Norman, Oonagh Reitman, John Tomasi, and Melissa Williams have all read and commented on parts of the following, or provided ideas that helped me to understand some issue more clearly.

I owe Chandran Kukathas and Will Kymlicka extraordinary debts of gratitude. Dr Kukathas advised me during my year as a Fulbright Scholar at the University College, University of New South Wales, Canberra. He provided structure and direction at an early stage of my study of multiculturalism in general and the rights of indigenous peoples in particular. In the years since he has been a frequent commentator on my work and a good friend. Professor Kymlicka has never served as my advisor in any formal sense but has been amazingly generous with his time and energy. He has commented on most of what I have written on multiculturalism at one time or another, dating back to the extensive comments he provided on my undergraduate thesis on multiculturalism and education. His encouragement, and his ideas, have made all the difference in my work. I have come to learn that his generosity extends to many graduate students and faculty to whom he owes no institutional duty but whose work interests him. I do not know how he finds the time both to be a productive scholar and to provide so much to so many other scholars, but I am happy that he does. If I very often disagree with Professor Kymlicka's work in the pages that follow, this is only because his work has done so much to structure the problems and define the questions which this book addresses. Without his work, this book simply could not exist in anything like its current form.

Others who have provided useful commentary include Shelley Clark, John Gould, Walter Grinder, Roderick T. Long, Patchen Markell, Jamie Mayerfeld, Andrew Norton, Tom Palmer, Jeremy Shearmur, Nancy Rosenblum, and Mark Warren. The earliest ancestor of this project benefited from supervision from Nancy Rosenblum, Ed Beiser, and the late Eric Nordlinger. Dimitriy Masterov provided valuable research assistance while I was completing the manuscript. Dominic Byatt and Amanda Watkins at OUP have been enthusiastic, supportive, patient, and extremely helpful. My new colleagues at the University of Chicago helped me through the final stages of writing with useful conversations, questions, and answers, and the Department of Political Science provided time and institutional support for which I am quite grateful.

I owe debts of more disparate kinds to Kathy Anderson, Christine Blundell, Michael Drummey, Peter Furia, Arthur Gilcreast, Sanford Gordon, Vartan Gregorian, Walter Grinder, Jane Hale, Elaine Hawley, Barbara James, Stephanie Jenks, Mildred Kalmus, Valerie Kanka, Naomi Lamoreaux, Bertrand Lemmencier, Heidi Parker, Michele Penner-Angrist, Canio Petruzzi, Stephanie Resko, Chandra Sriram, Anthony Theille, David Weber, and Daryl Wiesen.

While writing this book or engaged in related research I have been supported by a Fulbright Scholarship, a National Science Foundation

Graduate Fellowship, a University Center for Human Values Mellon Graduate Fellowship, a fellowship from the Woodrow Wilson Society of Princeton University, and a Hume Fellowship and a Lambe Fellowship from the Institute for Humane Studies, George Mason University. Nuffield College at Oxford University graciously hosted me for a time while I was completing the book, and I received extremely useful comments when I presented a chapter to the Nuffield Political Theory Workshop. Funding to allow me to present this research at scholarly meetings was provided by The Princeton University Dean's Fund for Scholarly Travel, the Department of Politics at Princeton University, the Lichtenstein Project on Self-Determination at Princeton's Center for International Studies, a Mentor Grant from the Spencer Foundation, the Institute for Civil Society, the Canadian Centre for Philosophy and Public Policy, and the Institute for Humane Studies' Hayek Fund. I have presented parts of this research at, and am grateful to audiences at, the Institute for Economic Affairs in London, the American Political Science Association Annual Meetings of 1995, 1996, 1998, and 1999, The Northeastern Political Science Association conference in 1997, the International Network of Philosophers of Education conference in Johannesburg in 1996, a conference on multiculturalism at the Hebrew University of Jerusalem in 1997, and conferences sponsored by the Institute for Civil Society and the Institute for Humane Studies.

Part of Chapter 1 was previously published as 'The Multiculturalism of Fear,' *Critical Review* 10 (1996), 271–83. An earlier version of Chapter 5 was published as 'Classifying Cultural Rights,' in Ian Shapiro and Will Kymlicka (eds.), *NOMOS XXXIX: Ethnicity and Group Rights* (New York: New York University Press, 1997). Chapter 6 has been published as a chapter of Will Kymlicka and Wayne Norman (eds.), *Citizenship in Diverse Societies: Theory and Practice* (Oxford University Press, 2000). And a very small part of Chapter 7 was previously published in my review essay of M. A. Stephenson (ed.), *Mabo: The Native Title Legislation, Policy* 12:2 (1996), 41–4.

J.T.L.

University of Chicago
February 2000

CONTENTS

PART I

Political Theory in a Multiethnic World

Introduction

Political Theory, Multiculturalism, and Nationalism

POLITICAL THEORY AND FACTS

Since long before Rousseau put it so pithily, political theorists have thought that their task is to discuss 'men as they are and institutions as they might be.' This dualism creates a tension within every normative theory about politics. Which facts about the world are to be taken as inescapable givens, and which as correctable accidents or reformable mistakes? Which social problems are to be accommodated and which are to be overcome? The division between ideal and non-ideal theory does little to answer such questions. John Rawls, for instance, takes as given certain facts about modern individuals—that they possess limited altruism toward one another, for example—and certain facts about modern societies, such as the permanence of reasonable disagreement about religious and other fundamental questions of the good life. Yet given these constraints he sets about constructing a theory which assumes away a variety of other complications, such as the possibility of a culturally heterogeneous society, migration of persons or capital, and permanent disagreement about the right as well as of the good. Such complications he leaves for later, 'non-ideal' stages of theorizing. A cursory look at the world around us, however, suggests that ethnic and cultural pluralism are as inescapable as religious pluralism, that disagreements about justice are as prevalent as disagreements about the good life. Why are some of these taken into account in an 'ideal theory' and others not?

I say this not to criticize Rawls but to illustrate the problem at hand, and to suggest that it cannot be evaded by labeling a theory 'ideal' or 'non-ideal.' Any theory which is not foolishly utopian must assume that there are some human limitations and some aspects of the human condition which cannot be overcome, at least not in the foreseeable future. Any theory which is to have any normative bite must suppose that some social problems are reformable, some human tendencies meliorable.[1]

John Gray has suggested that 'meliorability' is one of the cardinal assumptions of liberalism in whatever guise, presumably to be contrasted with both utopian assumptions of perfectibility and conservative assumptions of unchanging human nature.[2] But I am not sure that the trichotomy still holds, if it ever did. Meliorability does not distinctively mark out *liberal* political theory; it marks out normative political theory as such, at least in an age in which utopianism is discredited and conservative believers in an unchanging human nature are filled with plans for the reform of states and policies. Not all political theory is normative, of course; and by this I do not only mean what is sometimes called 'positive political theory,' the application of rational choice and game theory to political analysis. Much history of political thought and some analytic political philosophy lack overt normative implications; and much theorizing in the continental tradition about the world or the human condition seeks to enrich our understanding rather than to morally guide our practice. This book, however, is a work in normative political theory.

Normative theories and theorists can and do disagree over *which* facts about the world are to be taken as given and which are to be viewed as subject to change; but they do not disagree that there are some facts of each kind. I doubt that they ever did, even if yesterday's conservatives seem from today's perspective to take everything about their world as unchangeable and yesterday's utopians seem to regard humanity as infinitely malleable.

So the theorist has no choice but to stipulate givens and subjects for criticism, and to offer reasons for the choices. Those reasons can probably not be irrefutable, though the fact that a given problem *has* been overcome in this or that time and place is surely a good reason for treating it as subject to change, and the fact that a given problem seems *never* to have been overcome, or at least never to have been overcome in a wide society, is a good reason for treating it as permanent. A record of disastrous attempts to overcome it also seems a good reason for taking it as given. Rawls offers the record of the Wars of Religion as justification for

---

[1] A more useful contrast is drawn between idealistic and realistic theories—not 'stages' of the same theory—by Joseph Carens in 'Realistic and Idealistic Approaches to the Ethics of Immigration,' *International Migration Review* 30: 1 (1996), 156–70, Carens's continuum between realistic and idealistic approaches, between smaller and larger gaps, between is and ought, is in the terms I use here a continuum from taking more of the world as given to taking more of the world as open to reform.

[2] John Gray, *Liberalism* (Minneapolis: University of Minnesota Press, 1986).

taking religious pluralism as given. Similarly, every large-scale and systematic attempt to overcome the conditions of modernity and modern liberty as described by Constant has been a failure, and typically a bloody failure.

Yet Constant himself argued that that does not mean private interests and pursuits must be allowed *unmitigated* priority over public ones, or that there is *no* place in modern society for the republican liberty of the ancients. What one person says we must accept, another says we can mitigate. Whoever says what he or she accepts as given is open to criticism by those who insist that the resulting theory is therefore blind to this or that possibility. Yet the attempt must be made.

THE FACTS OF NATIONALISM AND MULTICULTURALISM

This book is about multiculturalism, ethnicity, and nationalism.[3] It lays out a normative theory regarding such subjects as how states should respond to the fact of cultural pluralism, how and when they should make special accommodation for ethnic minorities, when secession is justifiable, and what demands can and cannot rightly be made on behalf of cultural communities. As a work of normative political theory, it must take some of the world as given and some as subject to reform.

Responsible normative theories about multiculturalism must therefore take some aspects of life in a multiethnic world as given—'must' because attempts to deny or radically alter them have systematically been bloody failures, and 'must' because they are true, as well as 'should' for reasons I will return to below.

First, we need to take seriously the enduring power of group loyalty and attachment, and the durability of ethnic and cultural groups. Ethnocultural identities are strongly felt, and experienced by many people at many, perhaps most, times to be permanent and immutable.

---

[3] Among the many terminological muddles in debates about ethnicity and politics are the word 'multiculturalism,' the word 'pluralism,' and the relationship between them. Both are sometimes used descriptively and sometimes used normatively. In both senses, sometimes 'multiculturalism' is taken to mean a rigid separateness of ethnic identities and 'pluralism' something more fluid, and sometimes precisely the opposite is taken to be the case. When I use 'multiculturalism' or 'cultural pluralism' without modifiers, I refer to a description of the world. Normative positions are specified with modifiers—'the multiculturalism of fear,' 'multicultural accommodation,' 'the multiculturalism of recognition.' I do not take there to be much inherent difference between 'multiculturalism' and 'cultural pluralism,' but I will sometimes use a phrase like 'hard pluralism' to connote less fluid, more rigid arrangements and situations.

Persons identify and empathize more easily with those with whom they have more in common than with those with whom they have less. They rally around their fellow religionists; they seek the familiar comforts of native speakers of their native languages; they support those they see as kin against those they see as strangers. They seek places that feel like home, and seek to protect those places; they are raised in particular cultures, with particular sets of local knowledge, norms, and traditions, which come to seem normal and enduring. These feelings, repeated and generalized, help give rise to a world of ethnic, cultural, and national loyalty, and also a world of enduring ethnic, cultural, and national variety. Nations are felt (if not always thought) to be ancient in origin, continuous in history, and unified in spirit. These feelings are powerful, sometimes latent but easily and quickly mobilized, and ignored at our peril.

A corollary is that ethnocultural pluralism is an enduring characteristic of most modern states. Nearly every state is ethnically and culturally heterogeneous, and the various identities affirmed by members of those states do not and will not readily fade. Walker Connor famously suggested that there were only seven examples in the world of states that met the nationalist test of one state per nation, one nation per state: Denmark, Iceland, Japan, Luxembourg, the Netherlands, Norway, and Portugal. The Koreas are basically ethnically homogenous, but the 'one nation' is divided into 'two states'; for current purposes they should be included. But Japan, despite its self-image, faces issues of multiculturalism with regard to both a Korean minority and the Ainu; and Norway has a Saami minority, albeit one smaller than Sweden's or Finland's.[4] More recently, looking only at countries with populations over one million, the Minorities at Risk research project under the direction of Ted Robert Gurr has identified 268 politically salient minority groups making up almost a fifth of the world's population.

But we also have to acknowledge that these feelings of permanence in ethnic identity are false. Nations are modern and imagined communities.[5] Cultural communities are constantly interacting and influencing one another, and are internally heterogeneous to begin with. Cultural identities are fluid, though not infinitely so; traditions are contested;

    [4] Walker Connor, 'Eco- or Ethno-Nationalism?', in *Ethnonationalism: The Quest for Understanding* (Princeton: Princeton University Press, 1994), 155.

    [5] See, of course, Benedict Anderson, *Imagined Communities* (London: Verso, 1983; 2nd edn. 1991). See also Anthony Smith's and Ernest Gellner's contributions to 'The Warwick Debate,' and Smith's subsequent Ernest Gellner Memorial Lecture, all printed in *Nations and Nationalism* 2: 3 (1996), 357–88, for reflections on the considerable agreement between reasonable views of nationalism that are usually thought of as modernist (Gellner) and non-modernist (Smith).

and individuals make decisions about which if any of their ascriptive identities to emphasize over others. The cultural variety of the world endures, but the particular cultural communities into which it seems to be organized do not.[6] This reality is also ignored at our peril, for reasons I will begin to describe below and to which I return throughout the book.

One result is that—like ethnic pluralism—cultural hybridity, mélange, metissage, mestizaje, the processes of blending and melding and change under whatever description, are facts of the world, facts of our condition, and they always have been. They are not new; they are not distinctively modern—much less distinctively post-modern—and, most important, they do not somehow offer a solution to the problems associated with life in a multiethnic world. Hybrid cultural communities (as all cultural communities, in some sense, are) are themselves particular. A blending of two or more cultural traditions does not yield humanity as a whole; it yields a particular combination. And, over time, that particular combination can itself come to feel natural and given; it can become a source of personal and communal identity in its own right; it can become a new object of loyalty; it can become a new bounded community, from which outsiders are excluded. A particular process of metissage may result in the defusing of a particular conflict (though it may not, and even if it does it may only do so over a very long period). But it does not somehow defuse cultural or communal conflict as such.

This book does not celebrate ethnic and cultural identities, the beauty or diversity they add to the world, or the meaning they add to the lives of many. One recurrent theme is that the preservation or perpetuation of any one cultural identity or community is not, by itself, a political goal of high moral importance. But neither does this book advocate or even look toward the transcendence of ethnic or cultural identities in favor of a cosmopolitan ethic. Encouraging the abandonment of particular cultural identities is also not a political goal of high moral importance. We should recognize the meaning and order that cultural and linguistic communities give to persons' lives; we should also recognize the countless evils that have been committed in the name of ethnicity and nationality. In this book, therefore, attachment to one's own ways and one's own kind (in all the various and contradictory ways in which those are defined or constructed) is treated neither as a virtue to be praised nor as a vice to be condemned but as a fact of the world. The

---

[6] See Elizabeth Kiss's first thesis: 'We should conceive nationalism as a lasting feature of our world but not as a fixed, primordial, or pre-political phenomenon.' 'Five Theses on Nationalism,' in Ian Shapiro and Russell Hardin (eds.), *NOMOS XXXVII: Political Order* (New York: New York University Press, 1996), 301.

communitarian celebration of cultural communities as such slips too quickly from is to ought, while the position that no accommodation can be made to ethnicity because it ought to be left behind has forgotten that ought requires can.

Contrasting what we could today call the ethnic group and the state, Lord Acton wrote that 'our connection with the race is merely natural or physical, whilst our duties to the political nation are ethical. One is a community of affections and instincts infinitely important and powerful in savage life, but pertaining more to the animal than to the civilized man; the other is an authority governing by laws, imposing obligations, and giving a moral sanction and character to the natural relations of society.' The contrast is overdrawn, but that is not the point at hand. Even as Acton draws this distinction, he proposes to make use of the 'community of affections' in political life. Although he thinks that 'the nationality formed by the State' is 'the only one to which we owe political duties,' he assumes that the feeling of connection to 'natural' communities will endure. He indeed hopes that these feelings of national attachment will be strong enough to rival attachment to the state, so as to check 'the servility which flourishes under the shadow of a single authority.' A diversity of nations 'in the same State is a firm barrier against the intrusion of the government beyond the political sphere.'[7]

  John Stuart Mill, Acton's antagonist on the question of nationalism, also sought to put national sentiment to the service of liberty. He thought it 'in general a necessary condition of free institutions that the boundaries of governments should coincide in the main with those of nationalities.'[8] Their disagreement was not on the question of whether such sentiment could be transcended or defeated; neither even entertained the possibility. Their disagreement was only on the question of whether a national or a multinational state most effectively made use of national sentiment in the pursuit of freedom. Acton and Mill share what seems to me something importantly sensible in normative theorizing about ethnic politics and conflict. Neither celebrates ethnic and national attachments or seeks to preserve, perpetuate, or extend them. Nor do either of them suggest any general project of advancing beyond ethnicity. Both take ethnic attachments as a given, a fact to be channeled

[7] 'Nationality,' in *Selected Writings of Lord Acton*, i: *Essays in the History of Liberty* (Indianapolis: Liberty Fund, 1985 [1862]), 425–9.
[8] John Stuart Mill, 'Nationality,' in *On Representative Government*, in *Utilitarianism, Liberty, and Representative Government*, ed. A. D. Lindsay, (New York: E. P. Dutton and Company, 1951 [1861]), 489.

productively if possible and constrained if not. This is, I think, an appropriate position.

Both the durability and the fluidity of ethnic identity are sometimes forgotten, and sometimes moved into the category of meliorable conditions. Too much emphasis on the constructedness of identity and cultures perhaps leads some postmodernists to forget how real they can feel and how much they matter in the decisions people make, the actions they take.[9] I think Eric Hobsbawm—not a postmodernist but a Marxist—has been misled in this way in his important work on nationalism.[10] Hobsbawm has pointed to the invention of national traditions, the fact that putatively ancient beliefs were deliberately fostered at a moment in the not-too-distant past, and supposed that someday soon people will reject nationalist fictions in favor of the reality of class interests. But—to take a simple example—when a contemporary speaker of French realizes that it is not in fact the language of his ancestors, that a handful of generations ago they were Alsatian or Provençal-speaking peasants and not 'Frenchmen,'[11] that their languages were deliberately discouraged in a coercive assimilationist French nationalist project, he remains a speaker of French. He typically remains more comfortable in a Francophone milieu, and is perhaps unwilling to see that milieu undermined by the encroachments of English, eager for political action to bolster the position of his own language. Learning that the francophone national state was an invention, an imagined and created community, does not make him any more willing to see it uninvented or replaced by another imagined community. Similarly, the fact that the Hutu and Tutsi identities as they exist now—biological, racialized, and fixed—were more or less creations of the Dutch colonial government does nothing to diminish their terrible power in the Great Lakes region of contemporary Africa. In short—and I think this is true throughout the social sciences, not only in the study of nationalism—we must remember that simply because something is an invention or a construction does not mean it can be remade or unmade at will.

The same criticism applies to those theorists, typically liberal or socialist, who hold that the overcoming of national and ethnic loyalties

---

[9] On this point see See Tariq Modood, 'Anti-Essentialism, Multiculturalism and the "Recognition" of Religious Groups,' in Will Kymlicka and Wayne Norman (eds.), *Citizenship in Diverse Societies* (Oxford: Oxford University Press, 2000).

[10] Eric Hobsbawm, *Nations and Nationalism Since 1780* (Cambridge: Cambridge University Press, 1990).

[11] Eugene Weber, *Peasants Into Frenchmen: the Modernization of Rural France, 1870–1914* (Stanford: Stanford University Press, 1979).

is a valid normative political project. Certainly, truth is an important normative value, and exposing the untruths which many nationalists and ethnic advocates tell about their groups' virtues and histories is a worthy project. So is blunting hatred of outsiders, which sometimes requires working to diminishing the intensity of loyalty to insiders. This book is largely about the normative political project of blunting the edges of ethnic collisions, diminishing the violence and cruelty which are too often characteristic of ethnic politics.

But some propose to solve the problem of ethnic violence by transcending ethnicity and ethnic sentiment. I want to suggest that this is analogous to proposing to do away with material self-interest as the solution to poverty; both are misguided and utopian. Reasonable people disagree on how to alleviate poverty, and on what it would mean to do so; but reasonable solutions propose either to marshal and channel self-interest in particular ways or to limit and constrain it in particular ways (or, usually, both). They do not propose to abolish it. Perhaps even more apropos of the topic at hand is Madison's famous treatment of the problem of faction. 'The latent causes of faction are [. . .] sown in the nature of man.' Human diversity, basic self-interest, and fallibility mean that we will always be divided in our opinions. Abolishing the liberty which allows those diverse opinions into public would be like 'the annihilation of air . . . because it imparts to fire its destructive agency.' So if we wish to control the 'mischief' of faction, 'relief is only to be sought in the means of controlling its *effects*.' Faction cannot be done away with, so it ought to be made use of or constrained, as the case may be. This is how I propose to treat ethnicity.[12]

Teaching people not to, as Mill put it, 'like in groups,' convincing them not to feel more comfortable around those they perceive as their own kind, inducing them to abandon the moral and social ties they feel to their ethnic and cultural communities—this is utopian at best. At worst, it is the deceptive rhetoric of civic nationalism, trying to persuade people to abandon their particularistic identities and identify solely with the state—but that is a particularistic identity, too.

But the fluidity and constructedness of ethnicity can be forgotten,

---

[12] To be precise, Madison calls liberty one of the 'causes' of faction and supposes that abolishing liberty would abolish faction (and not merely its expression), albeit at far too high a cost. I doubt that this is quite right. Perhaps a tyranny can suppress open factional strife, but it cannot actually do away with the partiality and the diversity of interests that are the stuff of faction. It can only give power to one faction and then pretend that that faction is the whole. Similarly, as we have learned many times, tyrannizing over an ethnic minority and abolishing the liberty to belong to it only suppresses—it does not end—the underlying diversity. Madison, Federalist #10, in Clinton Rossiter (ed.), *The Federalist Papers* (New York: Mentor Books, 1961), 78–80.

too, and not only by partisans of one or another group but by scholars and policymakers as well. If there were no possibility of such individual decisions, then in fact many of the dangers of multicultural life would be lessened. There would be no need to tyrannize over members of one's own group in order to keep them within, and there would be no point in the violence against minority cultures to try to make them give up their old ways and assimilate. But the malleability, and the dangers, do in fact exist.

This fact will surface a number of times in the pages that follow. In Chapter 1 I discuss consociational and hard-pluralist regimes for multi-ethnic states, and argue that they depend on (as well as reinforce) the immutability of the various ethnic identities; In Chapter 3 I show that arguments for universalized nationalism rely on an assumption that we know which collectivities in the worlds are nations and who belongs in which one. Chapter 6 is about the recognition of indigenous and religious legal codes in the general law of the state, and draws attention to the dangers of treating either minority communities or their traditions and rules as constant. In these and other cases, one source of danger is the tension between political and legal imperatives for rigid categories and the more fluid underlying ethnic and cultural realities. Boundaries between cultural groups are blurred; boundaries between states need to be clear. Cultural traditions evolve continuously; legislation about those traditions changes only discretely.

THE MULTICULTURALISM OF FEAR

I have already several times mentioned one or another 'danger' of ethnic politics. It might be thought odd to begin a work of normative theory with so much attention to what can go wrong in the world. All normative theories take some account of dangers and evils, even if only to offer utopian remedies for them. Most normative theories shy of utopianism recognize that social and political life inescapable has some Scylla-and-Charybdis moments. But the theory described and defended in this book, 'the multiculturalism of fear,' places perhaps an unusual degree of emphasis on recurrent social and political dangers which must be avoided but cannot be escaped.

Liberal normative theory is characteristically concerned with the liberties and powers of individuals and, sometimes, the distribution of material resources among them. In the recent normative and philosophical literature, liberal political theories of multiculturalism and nationalism have been constructed with reference to the status of cultural member-ship as a primary good to which individuals have a right,[13] or the right of individuals freely to join or exit from cultural associations,[14] or the right of individuals to give public and joint expression to their national identities.[15] Liberal criticisms of multiculturalism and nationalism have focused on the possibility of individuals forming cosmopolitan identi-ties,[16] or the moral irrelevance of particular memberships to questions of justice, or the moral deficiencies and pathologies of communal loyalty.[17]

But perhaps another kind of political theory is appropriate to discus-sions of culture and ethnicity, one that begins with special attention to certain kinds of wrongs and dangers in the world rather than with the analysis of individuals and their rights.[18] Much of this book aims to offer social theory in the tradition of Montesquieu, Madison, Tocqueville, Mill and Acton rather than philosophy in the tradition of Kant and Rawls, though of course none of those thinkers simply falls on either side of such a crude dichotomy.

In particular, I aim to develop a political and social theory of multi-culturalism and nationalism which pays primary attention to the dangers of violence, cruelty, and political humiliation which so often accompany ethnic pluralism and ethnic politics. Judith Shklar famously argued that the essence of liberalism was that it is a political doctrine aimed at preventing cruelty and the terror cruelty inspires, especially (though not only) political cruelty and political terror. Liberal political theory, she argued, is centrally about how to prevent this *summum malum,* how to avoid these greatest of political evils. She called her liberalism a liberal-ism of fear. In this book I argue for a political theory of multiculturalism which is centrally concerned neither with preserving and celebrating ethnic identities nor with overcoming them, but which instead focuses on mitigating the recurrent dangers such as state violence toward cultural minorities, inter-ethnic warfare, and intra-communal attacks on those

[13] Will Kymlicka, *Liberalism, Community, and Culture* (Oxford: Oxford University Press, 1989).

[14] Chandran Kukathas, *The Liberal Archipelago* (Oxford: Oxford University Press, forthcoming).

[15] Yael Tamir, *Liberal Nationalism* (Princeton: Princeton University Press, 1993).

[16] Jeremy Waldron, 'Minority Cultures and the Cosmopolitan Alternative,' 25 *University of Michigan Journal of Law Reform* 25 (1992), 751–93.

[17] George Kateb, 'Notes on Pluralism,' *Social Research* 61 (1994), 511–37.

[18] For other examples of theorizing about ethnicity, culture, or nationalism that put the avoidance of evils first, see Thomas W. Simon, 'Prevent Harms First: Minority Protections in International Law,' *International Legal Perspectives* 9 (1997), 129–66, and Kiss, 'Five Theses on Nationalism.'

who try to alter or leave their cultural communities. Borrowing from Shklar, I call this theory a multiculturalism of fear.

LEVELS OF GENERALITY

In the arguments that follow, I do not often morally differentiate among the ethnic and cultural groups to which people feel allegiance, although I do draw many empirical distinctions. Treating 'ethnicity,' 'cultural identity,' or 'nationalism' as general phenomena tends to annoy both scholarly specialists in and lay partisans of one group or another. It is sometimes said that American nationalism is different from and morally superior to nationalism in general, or that the demand for loyalty to a minority community cannot be considered on a par with the same demand from a majority community, or that each indigenous people has its own conceptions of law and land, making general theoretical discussions about indigenous law and land rights irresponsible. With the partisans of particular identities and communities I have little sympathy. The claim that *this* community is uniquely valuable and morally superior is itself a general phenomenon of ethnic politics, susceptible to general analysis.[19] Indeed, the ubiquity of such feelings of superiority is part of what makes ethnic politics so dangerous.

The specialists' complaint does contain an element of truth which it is always valuable to keep in mind. There is a useful but real tension between the thick description of particular ethno-cultural communities and conflicts and theorizing about such communities and conflicts in general. The same is true of the study of any phenomenon in human society, and so the tension pervades the social sciences. There may be a kind of normative theory that mirrors the anthropologists' emphasis on individual cases, particularities, and differences. But this book often uses the level of generality more common to comparative political science studies of ethnic politics.[20] It often uses particular cases to illustrate possibilities, limits, causes for worry, or empirical trends; but it is not *about* the cases. In part I use the more general level of abstraction

[19] See e.g. Robert Goodin, 'Conventions and Conversions, or, Why Is Nationalism Sometimes So Nasty?' in *The Morality of Nationalism* (Oxford: Oxford University Press, 1997).

[20] See, *inter alia*, Donald Horowitz, *Ethnic Groups in Conflict* (Berkeley: University of California Press, 1986); Ted Robert Gurr, *Minorities at Risk* (Washington, DC: United States Institute of Peace, 1993); and H. D. Forbes, *Ethnic Conflict* (New Haven: Yale University Press, 1997).

simply because some level must be chosen, the trade-off between detailed nuance and general trend must be made at some point.

But there is another reason as well. The specialist's approach, and especially the anthropologist's approach, emphasizes the importance of understanding a group's self-understanding. It takes what H. L. A. Hart called the internal point of view. But if we wish to say anything about situations of inter-cultural contact or conflict, we need something more than the internal point of view. How members of different groups perceive each other is perhaps as important as how they perceive themselves. The moral equivalent of the anthropologist's approach suggests that we all have an obligation to see others on their own terms, to take each of their internal points of view in turn. Avishai Margalit and Moshe Habertal 'consider the best formulation of the right to culture to be internal to the viewpoint of the members of a particular culture.'[21] In the first place, I doubt that it is possible to understand, much less even provisionally adopt, everyone else's internal point of view. But more important, it is certainly not possible to articulate a general system of rights on the basis of what each group thinks its rights are. The internal point of view does too little to help us understand possible institutions of coexistence, to help us understand how to live with those whom we do not fully understand, or who do not understand us, or who do not even wish to do so.

AMERICAN DEBATES

This book is not, for the most part, about the multiculturalism debate in American politics and education; but there is a sort of critique implicit in this silence. Americans talking about multiculturalism in America seem to have the luxury of a certain lack of gravity. The fact that the American debate can be so focused on school curricula itself demonstrates that luxury. The United States is spared the experience of a national minority threatening to break the state, or the experience of massive state violence directed against such a minority. In peaceful democratic Canada (to say nothing of more-troubled states like Turkey or Israel), the future of Quebec is arguably the most important political and constitutional question. There is little likelihood of Puerto Rican opinion swinging in favor

[21] Avishai Margalit and Moshe Habertal, 'Liberalism and the Right to Culture,' *Social Research* 64 (1994), 491–510, 505. See also James Tully, *Strange Multiplicities* (Cambridge: Cambridge University Press, 1997).

of independence unless the U.S. government actually tries coercively to Anglicize the island. But even if Puerto Rico were to secede, it would have nothing like the same significance for the polity as a whole that Quebecois and Kurdish independence would in Canada and Turkey. By the same token, independence is a far less pressing issue for Puerto Ricans than for, say, Kurds in Turkey (even though the latter are full citizens with democratic rights, as Puerto Ricans are not).

Illegal immigration in the US has nothing like the social consequences of the massive refugee flows characteristic of much of the world; and even illegal immigrants who are cut off from some state services (as in California) do not face the hardship and physical vulnerability of refugees or of outcast minorities like the Roma in much of the world. The attempts of some multiculturalists to characterize the United States as fundamentally unjust toward and oppressive of cultural minorities ring false when we look at the violence and suppression so common in situations of ethnic politics. So do the cries of American civic nationalists who warn of impending balkanization, when we look at—for example—the real Balkans. The US has not always been in this fortunate position, and it would be foolish to assume that it will always remain so; but it is there right now. And in the absence of secessionist threats, destabilizing refugee flows, widespread ethnic violence, and so on, Americans debate the inclusion of non-European authors in 'the canon,' and similar issues—serious as questions of educational policy, but not as grave as the problems faced in much of the world.

The partial exceptions to this generally pacific picture are the indigenous peoples of the continental US, and African Americans. If we sometimes fall into debates about multicultural ephemera because we lack harder questions, we also sometimes do so because it is too hard to confront the American racial problem head-on. Nathan Glazer has argued that the real reason, and sufficient justification, for the multicultural preoccupation of American curricular debates is the continued exclusion of African–Americans from mainstream American life.[22] Showcasing the historical accomplishments of Irish–Americans qua Irish–Americans, Jewish-Americans qua Jewish-Americans, and so on has little educational or social urgency. Showcasing the accomplishments of African–Americans qua African–Americans has both, if only because we have so little idea what will or will not work in overcoming the gaps in educational and economic advancement between African–American and the rest of society.

---

[22] Nathan Glazer, *We Are All Multiculturalists Now* (Cambridge: Harvard University Press, 1997).

More generally, the history of slavery, public violence and discrimination against former slaves and their descendants, and public indifference toward private violence and discrimination has left a legacy that Americans have not overcome and do not know how to overcome. The same is true of the history of warfare against and dispossession and attempted forced assimilation of American Indians. If the standard American debate overstates the ongoing problems of oppression or separatism with regard to most ethnic groups, it also belittles these two cases by tying them in with the rest. I cannot here jump ahead of the argument of the book and describe how these histories matter and what I think ought to be done. I mean only to indicate why the debate to which most American books with 'multiculturalism' in the title contribute is mostly absent from this work.

OUTLINE OF THE BOOK

The book is laid out in three parts, the first two more theoretical, the third more concerned with applying the normative theory to cases. In Part I I describe and defend the multiculturalism of fear. Drawing on Shklar and Montesquieu, I describe a liberalism which is centrally concerned with preventing political violence, cruelty, and institutional humiliation. I argue that such a liberalism must come to terms with the facts of multiculturalism, since ethnic and nationalist conflicts are among the most important sources of those evils. I then argue that such a liberalism of fear is a useful normative theory for thinking about multiculturalism and ethnic conflict, preferable to a multiculturalism of recognition, a multiculturalism of rights, and consociational pluralism. I also defend the use of negative political theory, such as a liberalism of fear, and identify the uses and limitations of such theories. I describe four characteristic dangers arising from cultural pluralism, dangers with which a multiculturalism of fear must concern itself: forcible inclusion of an ethnic minority which wishes to retain its own identity; forcible exclusion from citizenship and the protection of the state of small and stigmatized minorities; internal cruelty, arising from attempts by communal leaders to prevent members from assimilating to or hybridizing with a neighboring culture; and the outcast status of those who leave their ancestral ethnic communities.

Part II examines arguments for the moral value of cultural diversity, pluralism, and membership. These theories, in a variety of ways, make more aggressive claims on behalf of cultural communities than does the multiculturalism of fear. Chapter 3 argues that universal theories of nationalism must fail, that national membership is neither intrinsically good nor intrinsically wicked. A liberal view of nationalist secession is neither celebratory not rejectionist but contingent on the treatment of the national minority in its current state and the likely character of the post-secession state. Chapter 4 examines a number of more general arguments for the moral importance of political action that protects cultural variety. It argues that cultural pluralism is not the instantiation in the world of moral pluralism, that different cultures do not embody different moralities which are incommensurable and incapable of judging one another. Cross-cultural criticism and intervention has characteristic hazards, but is not simply impossible the way it would be if cultural and moral pluralism were as closely linked as is sometimes suggested. The fact of cultural pluralism does and should make us wary of certain kinds of moral judgments; it warns us against elevating all of our own practices and norms into universal moral truths. Cultural diversity should make us especially wary of politically imposing certain kinds of moral judgments on other cultural communities. It should not, however, prevent us from making or acting on such judgments when a cultural community's practices are violent or cruel. And it argues for caution in treating cultural communities as public goods.

Part III of the book begins with 'Classifying Cultural Rights.' There I argue for separating out cultural rights-claims and policies of multicultural accommodation into exemptions from generally applicable laws; special assistance to allow a minority to take part in the same activities as the majority; internal restrictions on what members of a community may do and still remain members; external restrictions on the activity of outsiders who might weaken a community; self-government; the recognition and enforcement of customary law; and claims for symbolic recognition. I describe each of these, suggest what other normative theories of multiculturalism have to say about each, and indicate their uses and dangers by the standards of a multiculturalism of fear.

Chapters 6 and 7 deal with how self-government and the recognition and enforcement of customary law must be constrained within a multiculturalism of fear. While many ethnic conflicts come from granting insufficient space for autonomy or separateness (these might be resolved through federal arrangements or secession) others come from failing to accommodate the brute fact of togetherness. Sometimes two groups must come to terms with each other; they must and will interact. Indigenous and religious minorities often seek or have separate legal systems from the majority society; these legal systems differ from dominant liberal systems on issues of land law, family law, and punishment,

among others. There must, however, be a framework for interactions
and exchanges between those systems. In Chapter 6 I discuss different
ways that the dominant legal system can incorporate the minority one:
treaties and semi-sovereignty, customary law, and common law. I
discuss what is necessary for each to be part of a stable framework for
intercultural interaction, and argue that there must be significant
common law elements for any of them to provide such a framework.

Chapter 7 describes the framework necessary to accommodate
indigenous and/or nationalist conceptions of land within a liberal society. It argues for a political settlement based on the need for peaceful
coexistence of groups with liberal and non-liberal views of the social
role of land, rather than basing liberal law on traditional comprehensive
liberal (e.g. Lockean) views about land. This settlement, this framework, includes provision for both individual and collective ownership;
no provision for permanent inalienability; a separation of ownership
and sovereignty; and adverse possession. I argue that this settlement
meets important liberal concerns about mobility without the unjustifiable suppression of indigenous land claims that comes from the Lockean
view; and that it allows for the stability necessary for inter-ethnic peace.

Chapter 8 examines symbolic ethnic politics: the politics of place-
names, group names, national symbols, official apologies, and other
matters that do not affect the rights or resources of any particular
persons. Such symbolism is important in ethnic politics, and a theory
with nothing to say about it is unsatisfactory. Disputes over symbolic
issues, however, are poorly suited to compromise and easily escalate into
rallying points for wider conflicts, which the multiculturalism of fear
seeks to avoid. In addition, it is often impossible to meet the symbolic
demands of all groups simultaneously. This impossibility means that a
multiculturalism of fear must counsel limits on symbolic claims. I argue
that the chief constraint on symbolic politics should be nonhumiliation,
a standard which *can* be met for all groups simultaneously. Meeting a
standard of nonhumiliation would defuse many disputes over symbolism; insisting that the standard not be higher could restrain the spiral of
symbolic claims and alleged symbolic harms.

1

The Multiculturalism of Fear

MONTESQUIEU'S MULTICULTURALISM

The political and social thought of the eighteenth-century French liberal Baron Charles Secondat de Montesquieu spanned a sometimes dizzying range of subjects and interests; it is notoriously difficult to reduce to a system or doctrine. But a number of themes and methods reoccurred throughout his life. A central normative ideal of his work was moderation, closely linked with the prevention of cruelty. Despotic governments, which ruled by cruelty and fear, were contrasted with moderate governments of whatever form. Immoderate religious passions contributed to the violence and atrocities of the wars of religion. Even immoderation of sexual lusts and jealousy can give rise to monstrous cruelty and tyranny, as demonstrated by Usbek's rule over his harem in Montesquieu's 'sort-of novel,' *The Persian Letters*. Montesquieu's political vision was centrally concerned with diminishing cruelty and violence in social life.

Another frequent theme was the plurality of cultures in the world, the differences among nations and peoples. This is most famously true of his *Spirit of the Laws*, which is in part an attempt to account for both the similarities and the differences among the laws of different nations. It is also in part a compendium of those laws, and in part an argument about what laws—ranging from form of government to regulation of marriage—are best suited to people in a variety of different circumstances. But it is also clearly true of *The Persian Letters*, which satirizes the mores and customs of France by viewing them through the eyes of fictional Persians, while also commenting on (what Montesquieu took to be) the customs of Persia. Cross-cultural comparisons were central to Montesquieu's method. But he also had crucial substantive concerns about coexistence and conflict among different peoples with different ways of life, concerns which were often related to the normative arguments about violence and cruelty.[1]

---

[1] Todorov elaborates some of the links between Montesquian fear of cruelty and support for moderation, on the one hand, and cultural diversity on the other. Todorov observes that Montesquieu's distrust of extremes and extremism issues *both* in a general

Religious wars, the brutal Spanish conquest of South and Central America, and the treatment of peoples subject to the Roman Empire were just a few of the subjects he considered when thinking about the too-often-terrible results of encounters between cultures. While Montesquieu was a comparativist methodologically, he never pretended that the objects of his comparison existed in isolation from one another. Human societies have always interacted and they have often interacted violently. He had much to say both about how conquests happen and about what does or should come after the conquest. In his work on ancient Rome, he observed that 'It is the folly of conquerors to want to give their own laws and customs to all the peoples they conquer. This accomplishes nothing . . .'[2] The idea recurs in *The Spirit of the Laws*: 'In conquest, it is not enough to leave the vanquished nation its laws; it is perhaps more important to leave it its mores, because a people always knows, loves, and defends its mores more than its laws.'[3]

Customs, mores, and manners—the cultural traditions and practices of a people—were, Montesquieu argued, strongly resistant to change. He maintained that states should change these by force only in extreme circumstances. This meant that he was frequently attacked by his contemporaries as what we would now call a cultural relativist. He anticipated the charge and, over and over again, denied it. 'In all of this, I do not justify usages; but I give the reasons for them.'[4] 'I have said none of this in order to lessen at all that infinite distance which separates virtue and vice. God forbid!' But, he continued, he wished to 'make understood that not all political vices are moral vices; and that not all moral vices are political vices; and that this must not be ignored by those who make laws which shock the general spirit of a nation.'[5] He

defense of cultural pluralism (against presumptuous universalism) *and* in the condemnations of such evils as slavery and torture. Tzvetan Todorov, *On Human Diversity* (Cambridge, Mas.: Harvard University Press, 1993), 353–83.

[2] 'C'est la folie des conquérants de vouloir donner à tous les peuples leurs lois et leurs coutumes: cela n'est bon a rien . . .' *Considérations sur les causes de la grandeur des Romains et de leur décadence* (Paris: Garnier-Flammarion, 1968 [1748]), ch. VI, 69.

[3] 'Dans ces conquêtes, il ne suffit pas de laisser à la nation vaincue ses lois; il est peut-être plus nécessaire de lui laisser ses moeurs, parce qu'un peuple connaît, aime et défend toujours plus ses moeurs que ses lois.' *De l'esprit des lois*, ed. Victor Goldschmidt (Paris: Garnier-Flammarion, 1979 [1758]), book X, ch. XI, vol. i, 281. (All subsequent citations are to this edition and will be given as book, chapter, volume, page number.)

[4] 'Dans tout ceci, je ne justifie pas les usages; mais j'en rend les raisons.' Ibid. XVI. IV. i. 412.

[5] 'Je n'ai point dit ceci pour diminuer rien de la distance infinie qu'il y a entre les vices et les vertus: à Dieu ne plaise! J'ai seulement voulu faire comprendre que tous les vices politiques no sont pas des vices moraux, et que tous les vices moraux ne sont pas des vices politiques; et c'est ce que ne doivent point ignorer ceux qui font des lois qui choquent l'esprit general.' Ibid. XIX. XI. i. 465.

acknowledged a wide morally legitimate range in customs, wider perhaps than many Enlightenment Europeans would like. And he argued that 'the laws are the particular and precise institutions of a legislator, and manners and customs the institutions of a nation in general. From this it follows that when manners and customs are to be changed, it must not be done by laws; that would seem too tyrannical; it would be better to change them with other manners and other customs.'[6] And even these qualifications did not apply to the condemnation of massacres or torture; evils such as slavery and the domestic slavery of women might be explained but were not to be accepted.

Today we know that, in his explanations of cultural variety, Montesquieu overstated the causal relationship between physical climate and mores and customs. But he was by no means a simple determinist; his work was filled with proposals for the deliberate reform of customs and laws, proposals that would have made little sense if such things were straightforwardly determined by geography.

But these proposals were shaped by Montesquieu's views about the climactic determinants of manners and mores. He thought that customs were difficult to change, and that they were almost impossible to change radically and suddenly. It is this very moderate reformism that remains of interest. Today, when indigenous and non-indigenous peoples share the various climates of the Americas and Australasia, when Algerians live in the climate of Paris and Pakistanis that of London, it won't do to think that the morals and manners of a people are simply decided by where they live. But it remains true, as D'Alembert put it in his account of the argument of *The Spirit of the Laws*, that 'Laws are a bad method of changing manners and customs; it is by rewards and example that we ought to endeavour to bring that about. It is however true at the same time, that the laws of a people, when they do not grossly and directly affect to shock its manners, must insensibly have an influence upon them, either to confirm or change them.'[7] The effect—the durability of cultural traditions—is in this sense more important than Montesquieu's sometimes-too-simple account about the causes. And the lesson Montesquieu draws from that effect, that governments should be reluctant to change traditions with laws except when the traditions are

---

[6] '[Nous avons dit que] les lois étaint des institutions particulières et précises du législateur, et les moeurs et les manières des institutions de sa nation en général. De là il suit que, lorsque l'on veut changer les moeurs et les manières, il ne faut pas les changer par les lois; cela paraîtrait trop tyrannique: il vaut mieux les changer par d'autres moeurs et d'autres manières.' XIX. XIV. i. 467.

[7] M. D'Alembert, 'The Analysis of the Spirit of the Laws,' in *The Complete Works of M. de Montesquieu*, iv (London: Evans and Davis, 1777), 210. I have taken the liberty of updating archaisms such as ' 'tis' in this 18th-cent. translation.

genuinely cruel, remains an important one for contemporary multicultural states.

The concerns with cruelty and with cultural pluralism interact in a number of ways. Gross atrocities are a real possibility among nations; conquest, slavery, forced religious conversion, and genocide were among the evils that Montesquieu knew had to be avoided. But a nation's own mores and manners, its own internal traditions, might themselves be terrible. And today that fact has a special importance in the politics of multicultural states. Unlike in Montesquieu's 'nations,' in today's multicultural states the traditions which state officials might want to change are often those of a cultural minority. Those who make the laws are often culturally alien to those who live under the cultural rules under debate. Montesquieu reminds us that there is good reason to be slow in legislatively changing deep cultural traditions, even as he denies that cultural difference is any barrier to the moral criticism of genuine cruelty. These issues will be discussed in greater depth in the next chapter.

In one crucial respect Montesquieu fails to instruct us today. In *The Persian Letters* he (or rather the Persian Usbek, but Usbek sounding quite authorial in an extended discourse on population) opines that 'Men ought to stay where they are.'[8] He suggests that migration has been partly responsible for the supposed decline of population since ancient times. This opinion is partly inspired by the wickedness and savagery of the Spanish conquest of the Americas, by their 'extermination' of the Indians; indeed, almost all of the examples cited are examples of the conquest, colonialism, expulsion, or forced transport of enslaved peoples. But 'the climate is filled, as plants are, with particles from the soil of each country. It affects us so much that our constitution is fixed. As soon as we are transported to another country, we become sick.'[9]

We have some reason to be suspicious of this; it is, after all, being written by a Persian character who has taken up long-term residence in Paris. Montesquieu may have intended the irony. But the usual reading has been that Usbek speaks for Montesquieu in the series of letters on population decline. Much of what Usbek says on population is later echoed in *The Spirit of the Laws*, even though this argument is not (at least in not so extreme a form).[10] In any event, this view—strikingly

---

[8] 'Il faut que les hommes restent où ils sont.' *Les Lettres persanes*, ed. Laurent Versini (Paris: Garnier-Flammarion, 1995 [1721]), letter 121, p. 238.

[9] 'L'air se charge, comme les plantes, des particules de la terre de chaque pays. Il agit tellement sur nous que notre tempérament en est fixé. Lorsque nous sommes transportes dans un autre pays, nous devenons malades.' Ibid.

[10] See esp. *De l'esprit des lois* book XXIII; extracts from the English translation reprinted as 'Montesquieu on the Effects of Laws on Population,' *Population and Development Review* 17:4 (1991), 717–29.

similar to opinions expressed by nationalists like Herder and by Gandhi, which will come up in Chapter 7—doesn't help us live in a world in which men have never stayed where they were. The advice was already too late in the eighteenth century; it is far too late now. Certainly the expulsions, forced transportations, and colonial conquests Usbek condemns should still be condemned and prevented. But migrations of some sort are a fact of life.

THE LIBERALISM OF FEAR

Judith Shklar coined the phrase 'Liberalism of Fear' in an influential 1989 essay.[11] The liberalism of fear, strongly inspired by Montesquieu, begins 'with a *summum malum,* which all of us know and would avoid if we could. That evil is cruelty and the fear it inspires, and the very fear of fear itself.'[12] In particular, political cruelty and political terror are to be feared and avoided, not because the state is somehow a morally unique agency, but because it in fact has an unparalleled capacity to act cruelly, to inflict violence and pain, to inspire fear. The liberalism of fear is contrasted, sometimes explicitly, sometimes implicitly, with (among other things) the liberalism of rights and justice, the liberalism of applied Kantian moral philosophy. Shklar insists that liberalism is a political doctrine first, and one which must be sensitive to political realities. In particular, it must be responsive to the realities of where cruelty comes from and what form it takes.

This seems at first glance to be a rephrasing of the liberalism of negative liberties and fundamental human rights, a liberalism which consists of a series of 'thou shalt not' statements directed at governments. Shklar's account is in fact more subtle and more interesting than that, although the protection of those liberties is certainly a part of her project: her liberalism is, for example, psychologically richer and concerns building resistance to the temptations of cruelty and power as

---

[11] Judith Shklar, 'The Liberalism of Fear,' in Nancy L. Rosenblum, ed., *Liberalism and the Moral Life* (Cambridge, Mass.: Harvard University Press, 1989). See also Shklar, *The Faces of Injustice* (New Haven: Yale University Press, 1990), Ordinary Vices (Cambridge: Harvard University Press, 1984), ch. 1, and 'Injustice, Injury, and Inequality: An Introduction,' in Frank S. Lucash, ed., *Justice and Equality Here and Now* (Ithaca: Cornell University Press, 1986). This essay anticipates 'The Liberalism of Fear,' and explains more fully than does the later piece the relationship between fear and rights. The two complement each other in important ways, making it very odd that 'Injustice' was not included in the collection *Political Thought and Political Thinkers.*

[12] Ibid. 29.

well as building institutional barriers; but this is not the difference of most immediate interest here.

In a later book on the citizenship of American women and blacks, Shklar notes the historically intimate links between denial of the vote and denial of the opportunity for an independent income, on the one hand, and the general injustices visited on those groups, on the other.[13] She then articulates an American liberalism in which a right to vote and a right to work have a distinctively prominent place. This is neither a move toward theories of the innate value of political participation, nor a shift toward a Rawlsian account of the general moral status of the distribution of goods. Shklar remains a liberal of fear; but the positive political program of the liberalism of fear depends on the kinds of cruelty and the history of political wrongs being responded to.[14]

Shklar subordinates the evil of 'moral cruelty' or humiliation to the evil of physical cruelty, but acknowledges the reality and the harm of such moral cruelty. 'It is not just a matter of hurting someone's feelings. It is deliberate and persistent humiliation, so that the victim can eventually trust neither himself nor anyone else.'[15] Avishai Margalit has subsequently argued in a more systematic fashion that, while the prevention of cruelty comes first, the prevention of humiliation comes second, still ahead of the promotion of justice and the protection of rights.[16] A state may not be entirely just but may still be decent, where 'decency' is equivalent to 'the avoidance of institutional humiliation' (with the lexically prior condition of avoiding institutional cruelty and violence). It is worth noting that humiliation does not include just anything which happens to give offense. It is not tied to the self-esteem of particular persons or groups. Margalit uses the term to mean 'any sort of behavior or condition that constitutes a sound reason for a person to consider his or her self-respect injured.'[17] Each of the key terms in this definition is analyzed and defended at length; but the 'sound reason' clause indicates that

---

[13] Judith Shklar, *American Citizenship: The Quest for Inclusion* (Cambridge, Mass.: Harvard University Press, 1991).

[14] In the analysis of the relationship between 'The Liberalism of Fear' and *American Citizenship*, I am persuaded by Nancy Rosenblum, 'The Democracy of Everyday Life,' in Bernard Yack (ed.), *Liberalism without Illusions: Essays on Liberal Theory and the Political Vision of Judith N. Shklar* (Chicago: University of Chicago Press, 1996). For a different interpretation of that relationship, one which sees a move from negative liberalism in 'Fear' to a democratic positive liberalism in *American Citizenship*, see Amy Gutmann, 'How Limited is Liberal Government?' in the same volume.

[15] Judith Shklar, *Ordinary Vices* (Cambridge, Mass.: Harvard University Press, 1984), 37.

[16] Avishai Margalit, *The Decent Society* (Cambridge, Mass.: Harvard University Press, 1996).   [17] Ibid. 9.

claims of humiliation are to be morally evaluated, not simply accepted. In any event, the overall thrust brings the meaning much closer to 'degrading' than to 'embarrassing' or 'insulting,' and the work as a whole is closer to 'The Liberalism of Fear' than it is to the counsel to walk on eggshells and avoid giving offense to any person or group.

Deciding what is humiliating is not a matter of *a priori* reasoning. The political program of non-humiliation can no more be wholly derived from general categories and rules than can the political program of non-cruelty. While Margalit's work is more analytic and abstract than Shklar's, it still clearly offers an account which is responsive to particular histories and political realities.

William Hazlitt attributed the following story to the memoirs of Granville Sharp, saying that it was 'an anecdote . . . of the young Prince Naimbanna,' a visitor to England from an area in what is now called Sierra Leone.

Being asked, why he would not extend his forgiveness to those who took away the character of the people of his country [i.e. publicly insulted them, although he could forgive any physical attack], he answered—'If a man should try to kill me, or should sell me and my family for slaves, he would do an injury to as many as he might kill or sell; but if any one takes away the character of Black people, that man injures Black people all over the world; and when he has once taken away their character, there is nothing that he may not do to Black people ever after. That man, for instance, will beat Black men, and say, *Oh, it is only a Black man, why should I not beat him?* That man will make slaves of Black people; for when he has taken away their character, he will say, *Oh, they are only Black people, why should I not make them slaves?* . . . That is the reason why I cannot forgive the man who takes away the character of the people of my country.'[18]

This suggests (though of course it does not prove) part of the affinity between humiliation and cruelty. When we humiliate someone—either individually or as a member of some larger collective—we make subsequent cruelty to that person easier, for ourselves and for others. If a person or group of persons is routinely referred to, thought of, and treated as demons, objects, machines, animals, or otherwise subhuman, physical cruelty is a short leap away.[19] Indeed, physical cruelty is a likely follow-up to thoroughgoing humiliation. If the humiliated persist in being human, in acting human, in *seeming* human, then the humiliator's rage at being denied or refuted may well manifest as physical abuse in

---

[18] William Hazlitt, 'Race and Class,' in *Selected Writings* (New York: Penguin, 1982), 464 (italics in original).

[19] See Margalit, *The Decent Society*, 'Being Beastly to Humans,' 89–90.

an attempt to *make* the humiliated act in a way that accords with the humiliator's vision.

Conversely, deliberate cruelty is scarcely separable from deliberate humiliation. There may be physical torture which is *only* designed to produce staggering physical pain, but it is much more common for the tortured to be degraded and humiliated at the same time. Between torture sessions victims are imprisoned in too-small rooms with their own waste, to be made to feel like animals. From the infliction of cigarette burns to the sodomizing of victims with all manner of objects, the forms of torture themselves are often meant to degrade the victims, to make them feel degraded.

None of this is to elide the distinction between physical cruelty and humiliation. The latter may be a facilitating condition of the former; moral cruelty may be a routine companion of physical cruelty; but this does not mean that the torturer is morally on a par with the insulter. We may say that humiliation is to be avoided because it contributes to or worsens cruelty without thereby saying that it *is* cruelty, or even that it is nearly as grave an evil as cruelty.

Still, the prevention of cruelty and the prevention of humiliation are typically complementary projects (in a way that e.g. the prevention of cruelty and the prevention of hypocrisy are not[20]). I think that the liberal must pursue these projects somewhat differently; humiliation by private actors is less subject to public constraint than is cruelty by private actors. But humiliation by public actors is something that the liberalism of fear should try hard to avoid; and this complements rather than distracts from the avoidance of cruelty. And part of avoiding public humiliation is avoiding ongoing public reminders of past violence and cruelty. Even though the lack of a job does not itself constitute violence or cruelty toward African–Americans, Shklar thought it too much a symbol and reminder of past violence toward them. This, I think brings her close to Margalit's attention to humiliation. I will treat symbols of past violence as a form of humiliation, and humiliation as a lesser evil than cruelty but still near the center of the liberalism of fear's vision.

The liberalism of fear, emphasizing the avoidance of cruelty, humiliation, and political violence, is distinctly well-suited to a discussion of multiculturalism and nationalism. This may cut against the grain of some of the beliefs that Shklar herself held.[21] It might seem that what

---

[20] '[T]o make hypocrisy the worst of all the vices is an invitation to Nietzschean misanthropy and to self-righteous cruelty as well.' Shklar, *Ordinary Vices*, 44.

[21] Sandy Levinson, 'Is Liberal Nationalism an Oxymoron? An Essay for Judith Shklar,' *Ethics* 105 (1995), 626–45, discusses Shklar's beliefs about tribalism and nationalism.

liberals of fear need to do with ethnicity is figure out how to constrain its pernicious influence, nothing more. Nothing in the modern world is more prone to generate political violence and cruelty than the claimed ties of ethnicity and culture. Surely, then, the last thing liberalism should do is encourage persons to see themselves as parts of tribes rather than as individuals.

Such a reaction is too simplistic by far, though it exaggerates a caution that is of critical importance. The violence, cruelty, and humiliation which routinely accompany ethnic politics are not avoided by attacking ethnicity, any more than the violence, cruelty, and humiliation of the wars of religion were ended by convincing people not to be religious. The institutional accommodations and arrangements which make up the separation of church and state and the protection of freedom of religious exercise are the model to be followed (in spirit if not in all particulars). The liberal of fear does not say that the proper way to handle religious pluralism is to govern as if everyone were an atheist, and ought not say that the proper way to handle cultural pluralism is to govern as though everyone were a worldly cosmopolitan.[22]

The presence of large ethnic minorities—say, the Tutsi or the Kurds—in a state should alert the liberalism of fear to the possibility of ethnic civil war. The presence of small ethnic minorities—say, the Roma (Gypsies) in many European countries—should alert us to the danger of less visible but more routine cruelty and humiliations: police beatings, judicial discrimination, children taken from their parents to be raised by majority families, and all the vast array of degradations of names and languages. The liberalism of fear, so attentive to psychological and political realities, cannot respond to these situations with simple calls for neutrality or for civic patriotism transcending ethnic loyalties.

The social facts about nationalism and multiculturalism described in the Introduction generate social situations in which the fears of a liberalism of fear may be realized. They provide the opportunity for political violence and cruelty. But it is also true that a liberalism of fear can allow us to discuss certain matters in ethnic politics which a liberalism of rights would not.

---

[22] Compare Kiss, 'Five Theses on Nationalism,' Thesis 3: 'A commitment to human rights should lead us to regard efforts to elevate nationalism to a principle of political order as morally dangerous and efforts to denationalize politics as morally suspect' (312). 'Attempts to forcefully denationalize political life may disguise the exclusionary nationalist aspirations of a majority,' as in the case of the Bulgarian ban on ethnic, racial, and religious political parties, which 'had the predictable effect of outlawing . . . the major political organization representing the interests of Bulgaria's Turkish minority' (314).

SYMBOLS AND NAMES

For many years the Communist government of Bulgaria required that all personal and family names be in Bulgarian; that is, the sizable Turkish minority could not use Turkish names. What was wrong with this, on a liberal account? One could certainly construct an argument based on freedom of speech, or freedom of expression, or a right not to be forced to identify oneself in a way which one rejects. But such an argument would condemn the government of Bulgaria no more than a government which chose, for administrative convenience, to disallow name changes like that of the artist formerly known as Prince (to a symbol for androgyny which can neither be pronounced nor typed on a standard keyboard). If we have reason to distinguish the Bulgarian government from the one which disallows such changes, then something more subtle than a freedom of speech or freedom of association argument is necessary. Perhaps there is no such reason. Perhaps an American requirement that names be written in Roman letters—rather than in, say, Chinese characters—is every bit as unjust as the ban on Turkish names in Bulgaria, and Prince only offers a silly-seeming example of who might get caught in what is really an unfair rule.

Again: imagine if the United States Census replaced its racial category 'black' with an otherwise identical category 'nigger.' What would be wrong with the adoption of such a Census category? True, it would force many people to identify themselves officially in a way which conflicts with how they would choose to identify themselves; but that is true for any system of racial classification. Before the 2000 US Census, those who were strongly committed to the designation 'African–American' were none the less forced into the identity 'black.' Arabs and persons of biracial or multiracial descent are among the others forced to choose among categories none of which may correspond to their self-identification. All of this counts against adopting any official system of racial classification. But it does not allow us to say why forcing blacks to identify as 'niggers' would be worse than forcing firmly committed African–Americans to identify as 'black.'

Or again: the Hindu nationalist government of Bombay has changed the name of that city to Mumbai, a change which is commonly understood to reassert the city's identity as Hindu and Maharashtri at the expense of its recent history as cosmopolitan and pluralistic. 'Mumbai' is arguably a more accurate rendition of the city's precolonial name than is 'Bombay,' and the change is publicly defended as a rejection of colonialism. Although it is an assertion of Hindu dominance, it is not as overtly religious a name as Providence, Rhode Island; Corpus Christi, Texas; or Los Angeles or San Francisco, California. If there is something wrong in the name change, it cannot simply be that it violates the separationist requirements of a liberal secular constitution.

What, if anything, can a liberal political morality say about such cases? The liberalism of fear is helpful in a way that the analysis of rights and justice is not. The Bulgarian restrictions on Turkish names, the American use of the word 'nigger,' and the name Mumbai are historically and intentionally linked with violence and cruelty toward excluded communities in a way that disallowing Prince's name change, the unavailability of a 'biracial' category, and the name San Francisco are not. One must be careful here; the name San Francisco was part of a missionary impulse which also included a great deal of cruelty and injustice toward the indigenous inhabitants of the Americas. But the goal of the name Mumbai is to make clear that non-Hindus are to be excluded from full membership in Bombay; it is to serve as a constant reminder of the ranking of power. It has been a terribly long time since 'San Francisco' immediately brought to mind 'Catholic monks and missionaries.'

In general, liberalism will have little to tell us about (for example) changing the name of a city. But a liberalism of fear, once aware of a particular society's history of political oppression along communal lines, might have a great deal to say about certain name changes. The name Mumbai is an ongoing taunt in a society in which violence along religious lines has been all too common. The multiculturalism of fear refuses to say to Bombay's non-Hindus that they should be content because, after all, none of their property has been taken, none of their liberties infringed. The government intended to humiliate them, and the multiculturalism of fear is willing to say that they have been wronged thereby.[23]

The rule against Turkish names is to be contrasted with an administrative requirement that names be spelled in Roman characters, not by some fine analysis distinguishing the importance to individuals of the pronunciation of their name from that of their name's written appearance, but by attention to the political context. The rule on names was part of a package which included a ban on all use of the Turkish language and systematic political suppression of the Turkish minority in

---

[23] To say that a liberal theory offers grounds to criticize a policy is not the same as insisting on a particular institutional solution, say, the rejection of the name change by a liberal judiciary. I think that symbolic wrongs and expressive harms are politically and morally important but nonetheless poorly suited to judicial correction. I return to this problem in Chapter 8.

Bulgaria. I take it that names do have to be in Roman characters on United States census forms, tax forms, and voter's rolls; but such an administrative rule (probably not even articulated as a rule) is *not* accompanied by the suppression of all use of non-Latinate languages, much less persecution of all those who read and write such languages. Someone signing a private letter, an article in a minority-language newspaper, or any variety of documents in non-Roman characters has broken no law and will see no punishment. Ballots in some parts of the country are printed in the very characters in which one can presumably not fill out a voter's registration card. The choice of an alphabet for administrative forms isn't tightly linked with any more general attacks and suppression. In the United States, for all of the ethnic and cultural conflicts it has faced, the divide between Latinate and non-Latinate languages has simply not been one of the areas of contention.

On the other hand, there are many states in which the choice of an alphabet might be hopelessly linked with a variety of other issues; think of Israel, or Bosnia, or Estonia, or Malaysia. In such places a rule adopting one set of characters must be seen as an attempt to exclude one or two particular rival alphabets which are used by particular communities. In a state deeply divided between ethnolinguistic communities from different language families, the choice of characters cannot be a simple, neutral, administrative problem. An awareness of ethnic and cultural politics gives the liberal the resources to distinguish two facially identical administrative rules.

WHY LIBERALISM?

It may seem odd to use liberalism's apparent silence about some kinds of cruelty as an argument for a particular kind of liberalism. Mightn't it make more sense to point to the pervasiveness of ethnic and nationalist loyalties, and of calls for ethnic group rights, as an argument *against* liberalism's appropriateness or workability?[24]

In fact, attention to the fact of cultural pluralism and to the manifestations of ethnic conflict provides good reason to move toward liberalism, particularly a liberalism of fear. In too many ethnic conflicts we see

[24] Such arguments have indeed been made. See Frances Svensson, 'Liberal Democracy and Group Rights: The Legacy of Individualism and its Impact on American Indian Tribes,' 27 *Political Studies* (1979), 421–39, and Vernon Van Dyke, 'Collective Entities and Moral Rights: Problems in Liberal-Democratic Thought,' *Journal of Politics* 44 (1982), 21–40.

the greatest fear of liberalism come true: the state as an effective tool of violence and power whose capture becomes all-important. The difference between controlling and not controlling a state becomes the difference between killing and being killed. The greater the power of the state, the greater the stakes for its capture.

When the state was the guardian of the all-important soul, nothing could matter more than capturing it for one's faith; liberalism was a political doctrine concerned to lower those stakes and remove the state's relationship with the soul so as to end the violence of religious wars and allow peaceful pluralism. As religious wars fade into history, such justifications may seem crude; liberalism may come under criticism for its alleged stands on metaphysics or epistemology. Ethnic conflict refocuses attention on *politics*; it underlines the need for a political theory concerned with preventing cruelty and making it possible for members of potentially antagonistic groups to live together peacefully.

MULTICULTURALISMS

Not only is the multiculturalism of fear a distinctive version of the liberalism of fear; it also stands in contrast to other accounts of multiculturalism, for which Herder rather than Montesquieu is often an inspiration. A stark contrast is with the multiculturalism of recognition discussed and partially endorsed by Charles Taylor.[25] On the latter account, cultural groups rightly expect that they will be affirmed, respected, and recognized by the states they inhabit. For example, cultural groups rightly expect that the state will publicly recognize their value and worth. Is this respect just the positive face of non-humiliation? It is not. For one thing, there is the problem of the compossibility of respect and recognition for each group simultaneously. Again, an analogy with religion may help. Without question it is possible to be tolerant of every religion simultaneously. But it is not possible to affirm the positive value of each religion simultaneously. To the non-believer, a great many religions must seem foolish and misguided at best, dangerous at worse. To the deeply committed believer, faiths other than one's own (or perhaps a narrow set close to one's own) are seen as mistaken

---

[25] Charles Taylor, 'Multiculturalism and the "Politics of Recognition," ' in Amy Gutmann (ed.), *Multiculturalism and the 'Politics of Recognition'* (Princeton: Princeton University Press, 1993).

on some of the most important questions of human life. Not all religions make exclusionary claims to the truth, though many do; but no religion can be completely accepting of other faiths and retain any content. We are unaccustomed to thinking in these terms, because in the liberal states tolerance and respect for our fellow citizens as persons are so ingrained that few go around telling others that their religions have no intrinsic value. Indeed, many believe that every religion may have value for its believers, in the comfort or security or strength it brings them. But this is not to affirm what a committed believer thinks is worthwhile in the faith.

The same impossibility is evident for culture. Non-cruelty, non-humiliation, and genuine tolerance are possible if not always easy. Public affirmation of respect and recognition, though, cannot be available to all cultures simultaneously. Ethnocultural groups develop in contrast to others; all too often a particular trait is valued precisely because it makes members seem better than some neighboring group. To recognize what a group values in its own culture is to accept a standard by which some other groups fail to be worthy of respect. To give recognition and respect based on standards external to the culture similarly sets up a measure by which some will fail, and moreover includes the (hardly respectful) assumption that one's pre-existing culture includes the resources for judging all others in the world.[26]

The multiculturalism of fear counsels against spending our time trying to define what it is in cultures that we respect or recognize. The political actors being asked to judge, respect, and recognize belong to cultures of their own, and may be all too ready to take advantage of the paradox of standards in order to reject the cultures of others. But if the finding that a particular person does not command our respect does not license cruelty to that person, how much less does the finding that his or her culture does not command that respect.[27]

Will Kymlicka derives a liberal theory of multiculturalism from what he argues to be the status of membership in a stable and secure culture

---

[26] Taylor recognizes this paradox. 'The standards we have ... are those of North Atlantic civilization. And so the judgments implicitly and unconsciously will cram the others into our categories. For instance, we will think of their "artists" as creating "works," which we then can include in our canon. By implicitly invoking our standards to judge all civilizations and cultures, the politics of difference can end up making everyone the same,' ibid. 71. He resolves it by calling for an initial presumption of the equal worth of all cultures, a presumption which informs the subsequent study of what a particular culture has actually created or contributed.

[27] Margalit gives extensive consideration to the problems involved in deciding when someone is worthy of respect, or at least worthy of non-humiliation. *The Decent Society*, ch. 4–6.

as a Rawlsian primary good.[28] Chandran Kukathas derives an opposing liberal theory from the liberal first principles of toleration and freedom of association.[29] Either sort of a multiculturalism of rights sometimes leaves too little room for flexibility in institutional design, and sometimes gives too much leeway to symbolic insults. Throughout the following chapters I will be returning to specific areas of disagreement with these writers, but for now what is important is the different starting place of a multiculturalism of fear. Kymlicka's theory accords moral significance to cultural membership because it serves as the prerequisite for the exercise of all other liberal freedoms. Kukathas's theory actually accords *no* special significance to cultural membership; cultural communities are just another kind of association that free individuals might form or in which they might acquiesce. The multiculturalism of fear, by contrast, does see ethnic communities as morally important and distinctive, not because of what they provide for individuals, but because of what they risk doing to common social and political life. Those risks come in patterns; in the next chapter I examine the recurring kinds of dangers in ethnic politics.

VARIETIES OF FEAR[30]

'Fear' in the phrase 'liberalism of fear' plays a dual role. Cruelty and the terror it inspires are the greatest of evils; fear makes up a part of the *summum malum*. But Shklar's is also a *fearful liberalism*, a liberalism characterized by its cautions more than by its hopes. What does it mean to base a political theory on fear, or on the avoidance of evils rather than the pursuit of goods? I have already suggested some of the characteristics of a political theory that focuses on the negative. It will certainly not operate in the realm of what is called 'ideal theory,' and it will likely lean toward the realist side of the realist–idealist spectrum, that is, it will take more rather than less of the world as given. It must incorporate psychological, historical, and other empirical information.

[28] Will Kymlicka, *Liberalism, Community, and Culture* (Oxford: Oxford University Press, 1989).

[29] Chandran Kukathas, *The Liberal Archipelago* (Oxford: Oxford University Press, forthcoming).

[30] My understanding of the issues discussed in this section has benefited from many conversations with Jonathan Allen, and from his very useful essay 'Political Theory and Negative Morality,' forthcoming in *Political Theory*, in which he shows that 'although negative morality is not a free-standing justificatory moral theory, it has a degree of independence and distinctiveness as a moral and political disposition.'

Some of this ground has long-since been covered by those utilitarians who emphasize the minimization of pain and suffering. It is worth noting that if fear-based political theories are to be distinctive they will likely be more consequentialist than deontological; their prescriptions will often take the form 'Minimize and prevent cruelty' rather than 'Do not commit cruelty.' But more than this needs to be said. I do not think that a political theory can be built *entirely* on fearful grounds. Contrary to what Hobbes seems to have thought, the identification of a *summum malum* will not suffice to generate particular political rights and duties.

Michael Walzer's gloss on the liberalism of fear is that we cannot be liberals *simpliciter;* 'we can only be something else *in a liberal way,* subject to liberal constraints. *Liberal* in this sense, is properly used as an adjective: liberal monarchist, liberal democrat, liberal socialist, and insofar as the major religions are political in character, liberal Jew, Christian, Muslim, Hindu, and so on. In these formulations, the adjective expresses our fears, the noun, our hopes.'[31] This takes Shklar to mean that the fear of cruelty is *constitutive* of liberalism, and quite rightly tells us that fear of cruelty cannot be exhaustively constitutive of an entire way of life or even an entire polity. In this view what liberalism *is* is negative political morality. But perhaps instead 'liberal' is one, but only one, of the things which we can be in a fearful way. There is more content to liberalism than *only* the fear of cruelty, because the fear of cruelty does not uniquely dictate *liberal* politics. *Liberal* is not merely a modifier of other substantive kinds of politics; but *fear* is. Shklar herself gestures in this direction; the injunction to put cruelty first is joined with liberal social theory about the sources of cruelty and the strategies for its prevention. A different social theory might generate a republicanism of fear, or a conservatism of fear, or a socialism of fear.[32] These might not, for example, accord the primacy to *state* cruelty and

---

[31] Michael Walzer, 'On Negative Politics,' in Bernard Yack (ed.), *Liberalism Without Illusions: Essays on Liberal Theory and the Political Vision of Judith N. Shklar* (Chicago: University of Chicago Press, 1996), 23.

[32] John Kekes argues that really putting cruelty first will *necessarily* result in conservative, not liberal, politics, because 'the only way in which [cruelty can be restrained] is by curtailing the autonomy of cruel people, and that, in turn, depends on reducing their plurality of choices and actions, restricting their rights, diminishing their freedom, not showing equal concern for cruel and decent people, and not providing the goods cruel people need to pursue their pernicious activities' ('Cruelty and Liberalism,' *Ethics* 106 (1996), 834–44, 844). I find this unpersuasive, partly because I see no reason to think that the freedom of cruel persons must be diminished to any greater degree than forbidding them to be cruel, i.e. insisting that they refrain from using or threatening violence against others, a perfectly liberal thing to do; and partly because Kekes does not, as a liberal must, ask whether widespread curtailment of the autonomy of cruel persons can only be attained by giving officials of the state even greater opportunity for cruelty.

political violence that Shklar does.[33] Or one might agree with Shklar that the cruelty and violence of the police, military, and paramilitary sectors of the state pose the greatest of dangers, but think that liberal democracies are prone to the social tumult which provokes violent reactions from these state sectors.

Thus, there could be fearful theories of multiculturalism which are not liberal. These might, for example, be rigidly pluralist. Rigid forms of pluralism attempt to maintain social peace in an ethnically diverse state through more or less rigorous segregation and mutual recognition of cultural autonomy. The millet system of the old Ottoman Empire, its contemporary descendants in states like Israel, and the settlements reached in consociational states from Belgium to Malaysia are all pluralist solutions to the dangers of ethnic conflict.[34] Pluralist settlements include some or all of: restrictions on the speaking or publication of statements which might incite ethnic violence; separate legal systems, whether differentiated by the religious law applied by or by the language spoken in the courts; residential segregation; separate schools; and an emphasis on cooperation across the elites of the various ethnic groups, sometimes including a ruling coalition of ethnic parties.

This pluralist solution is built on recognition of the power of ethnic loyalty but not of the malleability of ethnic identity. It correctly aims to prevent widespread ethnic political conflict and the violence and cruelty which accompany it. It does not, however, worry about the violence or cruelty which can be used against members of cultural communities to make sure that they remain members. Neither does it worry about the conflicts which can erupt out of the failure to create a secure legal framework for interactions or migrations between cultural communities.

Alternatively, a theory might put a vice other than cruelty first, might fear something else more than it fears cruelty and terror. This is not quite done by Margalit, who focuses on the evil of humiliation but (usually) says that the prevention of cruelty morally precedes the

---

[33] Yael Tamir denies that state cruelty should be the central fear even of liberals, who should pay attention to violence and cruelty within the private, cultural, and familial spheres and embrace state intervention to stamp out such evils. Yael Tamir, 'The Land of the Fearful and the Free,' *Constellations* 3:3 (1997), 296–314.

[34] On consociationalism and its requirement for the autonomy of each ethnic 'segment,' see Arend Lijphart, *Democracy in Plural Societies* (New Haven: Yale University Press, 1979). Michael Walzer identifies the commonalities of the imperial and the consociational models of toleration in *On Toleration* (New Haven: Yale University Press, 1997), and notes the links between the millet system and Israel's pluralist legal system on pp. 40–3.

prevention of humiliation.[35] Probably any vice or evil *could* be made the
center of a political or social theory. The fear of violent death (without
a concomitant fear of cruelty) was the foundation of an eminent and
coherent political theory, albeit one that has no claim to being called
liberal. Building a political theory around the need to prevent vanity,
greed, envy, hypocrisy, or snobbery first—ahead of violence, cruelty, or
humiliation—is a recipe for brutality. But, for example, some versions
of socialist thought are more characterized by a desire to understand
and root out exploitation than by a positive vision of equality.

Thus, after the decision has been made to formulate political theory
in a negative light, there remain decisions regarding the choice of evils
to be accorded primacy; the choice of social theory about which social
actors are most likely to commit those evils, or which actors we care
about most; and the choice of assumptions about which aspects of society are relatively mutable and which are not.

After all of those choices have been made, can we say that we are left
with a self-sufficient political theory based exclusively on the avoidance
of certain evils? I do not think so. Many of those choices must themselves be made with an eye toward some positive moral considerations,
and it won't do to then claim that the theory was built without reference to such considerations. Moreover, the injunction to prevent violent
political conflict can often (not always) be invoked against either party
to a conflict; the politics of fear cannot itself guide us on allocating
credit or blame, on saying which party to a conflict should stand down
and relinquish its claims. Such judgments require more positive moral
theory. Shklar sometimes seems to suggest that we can listen to the
victims of injustice first, in advance of developing a positive theory of
justice.[36] But we are often confronted with competing claims of victimhood, and need a rudimentary account of justice to have an idea who
the real victims to whom we should listen are. Finally, there is a great
deal of political space within the constraints of avoiding cruelty,

---

[35] Margalit is sometimes ambivalent on this point. He suggests that 'the psychological
scars left by humiliation heal with greater difficulty than the physical scars of someone
who has suffered only physical pain,' *The Decent Society*, 87, and that we are unsure
how to judge between the colonial regimes that humiliated their subjects and the succeeding local tyrants that were more likely to be physically cruel (148). He decides the issue,
however, in favor of putting cruelty first. As an aside, I am not at all convinced that the
post-independent tyrants were any less humiliating to many of their subjects than the pre-
independence colonial regimes. They may have considered *some* of their subjects 'fellow
nationals or fellow tribe members,' but there were many subjects who were *not* ethnic or
cultural fellows. In this light it is worth remembering that local ethnic minorities often
opposed anti-colonial independence movements.

[36] Shklar, *The Faces of Injustice* (New Haven: Yale University Press, 1990).

violence, and humiliation, and there is no reason to say that we cannot morally reason about what goes on within that space.[37]

It may not even be possible to fully describe the injunctions against political cruelty and humiliation without invoking rights, or some moral concepts taking the place of rights. So Margalit, who explicitly rejects the idea that a concept of rights is necessary for a concept of humiliation, still resorts to formulations like 'Humiliation is the rejection of an encompassing group or the rejection from such a group of a person with a legitimate right to belong to it.'[38]

Fearfulness is thus neither necessary nor sufficient to constitute liberalism. Other political theories may be formulated in a fearful way, either positing a different *summum malum,* or providing a different social theory about the sources of cruelty, or simply offering nonliberal moral reasoning about politics within the constraints of noncruelty. Liberalism may be aspirational or comprehensive rather than fearful and political—think of the liberalism of Joseph Raz.

The multiculturalism of fear, or the liberalism of fear, cannot do everything which needs doing. The liberalism of fear and the liberalism of rights live in a necessarily symbiotic relationship. Persons who suffer or witness or learn about various kinds of political cruelty and humiliation articulate rules and principles and what it is about their victims that these wrongs have violated. Deontological theories of rights and justice are in part responses to the kinds of violence and suffering seen in the world. This is not to say that some such theories might not be true or morally correct; but they are (they must be) grounded in social and political reality. In turn, these concepts of rights become accepted, and something which is experienced as a rights-violation is that much more likely to be experienced as cruel or humiliating.

But the multiculturalisms of fear and of rights are not assimilable to one another. Non-cruelty and non-humiliation are in some ways a less demanding standard than justice, in some ways a more demanding one. Sometimes, perhaps, the liberal of fear looks at a set of social arrangements and says, 'good enough', when not all of the demands of justice have yet been met. On the other hand, no one's rights have exactly been violated by changing the name of Bombay to Mumbai, but the multiculturalism of fear says that we have grounds to condemn the change nevertheless.

In the remainder of this book I often discuss particular policies which

---

[37] Nor would Shklar have said so. See 'What Is the Use of Utopia?' in her *Political Thought and Political Thinkers*, ed. Stanley Hoffman (Chicago: University of Chicago Press, 1998). [38] *The Decent Society*, 141.

might be appropriate for a variety of situations of multiethnic politics. The multiculturalism of fear—like many other theoretical frameworks—probably does not yield unique policy prescriptions; it is less determinate than that. It provides guidance, ruling out many options and directing our attention to particular considerations in trying to decide among the rest. It 'tells us what to think *about*, rather than what to think.'[39] So the solutions I discuss to particular problems are not the only ones compatible with avoiding cruelty, with recognizing the endurance and the flexibility of ethnic identities, and so on. Still, they differ from the policies that would be recommended by a theory which primarily emphasized the recognition of cultural communities, or the transcending of particularistic identities.

CONCLUSIONS

The fact of cultural pluralism provides a moment of application for the liberalism of fear. Violence, cruelty, and humiliation are common attributes of ethnic politics, and often cannot be well-understood outside of that context. Institutional protections against political violence in a society like Rwanda must, in effect, treat ethnic groups as more real, more permanent than some liberals might like. Whether those institutions take the form of power-sharing representation arrangements, self-government arrangements like devolution and federalism, language rights, or what have you, they will politically recognize the fact of ethnicity. This is no more illiberal than the various institutional accommodations reached to allow multireligious societies to avoid religious conflict; although those institutions must be designed in a liberal fashion, with institutional space for individuals who modify or reject their cultural identity.

Political cruelty and humiliation, too, are often ethnically motivated. Sometimes little follows from that fact; the multiculturalism of fear adds little to what the liberalism of fear has to say about torture, for example, other than perhaps some knowledge about the psychology of some torturers. But sometimes the cruelty or humiliation cannot be recognized without reference to cultural pluralism and particular histories of ethnic conflict, as in the cases about naming mentioned earlier (and returned to in Chapter 9).

If multiculturalism adds to and sharpens the liberalism of fear, then

---

[39] Allen, 'Political Theory and Negative Morality.'

the liberalism of fear does the same to multiculturalism. Whether or not minority cultures ought to be helped in sustaining themselves, whether assimilation or diversity is desirable, whether and how to forge common identities—the multiculturalism of fear insists that these are secondary questions. Neither identities nor groups are the center of attention. Rather, the danger of bloody ethnic violence, the reality that states treat members of minority cultures in humiliating ways, the intentional cruelty of language restrictions and police beatings and subtler measures which remind members of a minority that they are not full citizens or whole persons, these are the focus of attention. The treatment that persons are given because of their group membership, or that they are accorded when they try to belong to their groups, takes priority.

2

Cruelty and Conflict in Multiethnic Politics

The dangers of life in a multiethnic world come in patterns. The fluidity of ethnic identity at the margins and the perceived urgency of protecting communal boundaries, political imperatives toward uniformity and the constant disruption of uniformity on the ground, the institutional and the moral–psychological dimensions of culture interact in complicated but foreseeable ways. These give rise to recurring kinds of problems; and these problems, in turn, may have recurring kinds of solutions.

A variety of explanations, not necessarily incompatible, have been offered for the tendency of modern states to seek uniformity, in particular cultural and linguistic uniformity. States, in short, seek to become *national* states. They try to appear as natural, enduring, and unified communities. Those that succeed may have the advantage of an additional source of political resilience and solidarity, a sense of shared history and destiny that can survive even changes in government.[1] They may more easily gain the advantages of a large modern economy, by having a literate and linguistically homogenous labor pool, members of which can take on any of the different positions required by a division of labor.[2] They may lack the social rancor created by a constant sense of *us* being subservient to *them,* because (for example) civil servants and managers are drawn from the same cultural group as citizens and workers.[3] They may have higher levels of social trust, and accordingly smoother social interactions in a number of ways, not least improved prospects for democracy.[4] All of these are probably at least true in part;

[1] Margaret Canovan, *Nationhood and Political Theory* (Cheltenham: Edward Elgar, 1996).
[2] Ernest Gellner, *Nations and Nationalism* (Ithaca, NY: Cornell University Press, 1983).
[3] Ernest Gellner, 'Reply to Critics,' in J. A. Hall and I. C. Jarvie (eds.), *The Social Philosophy of Ernest Gellner* (Amsterdam: Rodopi Publishers, 1996); Charles Taylor, 'Nationalism and Modernity,' in Robert McKim and Jeff McMahan (eds.), *The Morality of Nationalism* (Oxford: Oxford University Press, 1997); Isaiah Berlin, 'Nationalism,' in *Against the Current* (New York: Viking Press, 1980).
[4] Canovan, *Nationhood and Political Theory*; David Miller, *On Nationality* (Oxford: Oxford University Press, 1995).

and they add up to a strong institutional imperative for states to be what Rogers Brubaker calls *nationalizing* states, states seeking to become nations.[5] (They also create a strong incentive for cultural groups that wish to maintain their own language and community to begin to understand themselves as *nations* and then to seek states of their own.)

But states have to *seek* such uniformity precisely because it is not already present. For countless reasons—migration, conquest, the constant willingness of some people to alter their cultures and identities over time, and more—units of territory are culturally heterogeneous over most of the world, no matter how borders are drawn. Nationalizing states often respond either by trying to forcibly include minority groups whose identity is not that of the majority culture—to assimilate them—or by forcibly excluding them, by denial of citizenship, expulsion, or extermination. The same state may alternate between one strategy and the other in its treatment of a given minority; this has certainly been true of the United States' treatment of American Indians and Australia's treatment of Aborigines. At the extreme, this alternation may begin to seem like a single policy, with the directive 'Assimilate or be killed.' We have no right to be surprised if the offer of inclusion does not seem benign to a group that has, in living memory, been forcibly excluded.

But the drive to uniformity exists at the level of the cultural community as well as at that of the state (and so is probably not driven solely by institutional imperatives). Internal minorities, dissenters, and those who seem likely to leave the community may be subject to terrible mistreatment at the hands of those trying to keep community and traditions intact. The potential ability to leave polarizes the beliefs and actions of those who want to stay.[6] Moreover, some cultural practices and traditions are themselves violent and cruel. Internal cruelty flows from both of these sources.

Even when cultural communities accept the need to coexist without either assimilating or exterminating one another, intercommunal relations will not automatically be pacific. Whether through the evolved rules or explicit agreement, they must develop a framework for interaction—the interactions of their members, as well as the interactions of their traditions and norms and rules. And some such frameworks are more successful, more stable, more able to defuse more conflicts, than others.

[5] Rogers Brubaker, *Nationalism Reframed* (Cambridge: Cambridge University Press, 1996).
[6] H. D. Forbes analyzes this dynamic in *Ethnic Conflict: Commerce, Culture, and the Contact Hypothesis* (New Haven: Yale University Press, 1997).

Forced incorporation, forced exclusion, internal cruelty, and the lack of a framework for interaction—this is certainly not an exhaustive list of the dangers of ethnic politics, and there are other ways of dividing up what it does cover. The categories moreover aren't mutually exclusive. The relationship between any given ethnic group and the state might include elements of each; and sometimes even a single issue will high-light more than one kind of danger. For example, state attempts to elim-inate cruel practices within a minority group often raise difficulties in arranging the framework of interaction between state law and minority customary law. But these four dangers cover rather a lot that is both empirically important and theoretically interesting; it is worth examin-ing each of these kinds of dangers in some depth.

FORCED INCORPORATION AND SECESSION

One kind of danger is that of forced incorporation. Kurds are told that they are really Mountain Turks, Turks are told that in order to be good citizens of Bulgaria they must be Bulgarian, Basques and Catalans are forbidden and attacked in order to establish the unity of all of Spain. Long before Brubaker coined the phrase 'nationalizing states,' a gener-ation of social scientists referred to 'nation-building states.' Walker Connor argued that this rested on a false assumption that it was the destiny of the state to become national. Connor insisted that the ethnic groups rather than the states were the real nations, so the states should be referred to as 'nation-destroying.'[7]

The large minorities which are forcibly included typically react with outbreaks of nationalist sentiment and activity. The liberalism of fear ought to take a contingent, context-dependent view of such activity. It should not engage in the search for conceptual affinities or compatibil-ities between liberalism and nationalism; but neither should it take a straightforwardly hostile view toward nationalism. In the Introduction, I made reference to the Mill–Acton debate over whether and how nationalism could support liberty. Mill thought that a pluralistic state would lack fellow-feeling and political sympathy among its people and

---

[7] I dispute Connor on this point in Ch. 3. Brubaker captures what the minorities and the states have in common with his contrast between nationalizing states and national minorities. Rogers Brubaker, *Nationalism Reframed*. See also Walker Connor, 'Nation-Building or Nation-Destroying?' and 'A Nation Is a Nation, Is a State, Is an Ethnic Group, Is a . . .' in *Ethnonationalism: the Quest for Understanding* (Princeton: Princeton University Press, 1994).

between its people and its army, and that the state could manipulate societal cleavages to its own advantage. Acton thought it desirable if people had national loyalties which were not identical to the loyalties to the state, so that they would be properly skeptical of the state. Each view seems to be right sometimes, and Mill and Acton's successors should be willing to engage with these questions of contingency and circumstance.

When evaluating a particular manifestation of nationalism, the liberal of fear might begin with a presumption against it, but the presumption must be refutable. If the nationalism is secessionist, what is the character of the current, larger state? How does it treat the national minority? Do we have reason to think that the would-be new state will be better or worse to its new local minorities? Perhaps every secessionist nationalism carries the potential for civil war, certainly an occasion for political violence and cruelty to be greatly feared. But, for example, Kurdish nationalism is in part a response to the slaughters and violence visited upon Kurds by (primarily) three states. Even if the liberal resolutely and rightly insists that the status of Kurd has no special moral claim on an individual's loyalty, it is *as Kurds* that a great many people have been killed, tortured, or imprisoned. Something similar might be said of the Tibetan and the (now-successful) East Timorese secessionist movements; it strains credulity to think that there would be *more* political cruelty and violence in the world were Tibet an independent state, and it seems very likely that there would be much less. The violence that accompanied East Timor's separation from Indonesia was terrible, but so was the violence that was a constant condition of its presence inside that state; and the violence of separation was comparatively brief.

Of course, the fact that the old regime was violent does not *necessarily* mean that the new one will be an improvement; the remains of Yugoslavia stand as a stark reminder of what there is to fear both in nationalism and in secession. But, especially when the current regime is politically cruel to a national minority on the basis of the national division, sometimes secessionist nationalism can result in more freedom and peace. When the majority behaves tribalistically and equates the state with its own culture, counseling the minority to be patriotic rather than nationalistic is a blind application of inappropriate categories, not a move toward cosmopolitan individualism.

So the multiculturalism of fear can occasionally be a nationalism of fear, recognizing that some group has been so badly treated by the state that it lives in, because the state views them as members of that group, that it makes sense for the group to compete with the state for its members' loyalty. In an important sense this is not really *nationalism* at all. Ultimately nationalism is a claim for loyalty, a demand that persons put the welfare of their state or their linguistic community or their ethnic group or what have you above the welfare of the other groups and ultimately above the person's own welfare. Liberalism is properly skeptical of any demand to put loyalty to a group ahead of particular persons or universal moral duties. But when faced with a choice between loyalty to a state and loyalty to a nation, it is a mistake for liberalism to mechanically prefer ostensibly patriotic loyalty to the state. Both can be dangerous, and which poses the greater danger is an empirical question.

In the wake of the disaster of the Balkans in the 1990s, some self-described realists have begun advocating ethnic partition as a general strategy for peace. The partition of Cyprus has led to a tense, decades-long armed peace—perhaps 'cease-fire' would be more apt—surely an improvement on war. Similarly, it seems that each of the three (so far) Yugoslav wars—the war of Croatian secession, the Bosnian war, and the Kosovo war—has ended only when populations were uprooted and political units were made ethnically homogenous. 'Ethnic cleansing' has sometimes been a euphemism for mass murder, mass rape, and other horrors; but (so this theory goes) the mere 'cleansing' of a territory by forced population transfer is ultimately necessary for peace in deeply divided societies. The liberal multiethnic state imagined by some western leaders is nothing more than a foolish and dangerous illusion. When people come to hate their neighbors on ethnic grounds, populations should be unmixed, separated.

   If the empirical claim here were true, then according to a multiculturalism of fear the normative argument would have something to it as well. The partition view obviously requires abandoning anyone whose identity is mixed between the two warring groups, but that is not the worst to be said of it. In the first place, forced population transfers are themselves horrible, bloody affairs. The partition of the Indian subcontinent provides only the most vivid example of the century. The realist might accept this but—again remembering Cyprus—respond that partitions at least hold out an endpoint, a time at which the bloodshed could stop; this is an improvement over endless war.

   This seems plausible when territorial questions are well-settled, when we know *where* each of the populations is to go and where the boundary between them will be. But there is no reason to expect this to be the usual state of affairs. The logic of partition-as-peace-plan provides no solution to the Kashmir problem. The violence surrounding the partition of Palestine was not one-time transitional violence; it has lasted, in various ways, for half a century. Indeed, a rule of separate-and-partition creates an incentive to go to war over land, to ethnically cleanse pieces of territory in order to determine where the line of division will finally be drawn. From the partition of India to the Bosnian war, this has been a constant trait of political situations in which division is foreseen.

FORCED EXCLUSION

The presence of a small and disfavored minority in a state should alert us to dangers somewhat different from those of a conflict between two or more large and entrenched groups. Ethnic civil war isn't the chief danger posed by the coexistence of Roma and a dominant group, for example. Groups like Roma or Jews, the remnants of imperial peoples like Russians or Hungarians, numerically small indigenous populations, and more are often treated as outcasts from the polity, marginally citizens when they are citizens at all. They are subject to the physical dangers that accompany outcast status, including not only police brutality but also the lack of police protection against private attacks; and hand in hand with that they are subject to the ongoing stigmatization as enemies, aliens, or worse. The dangers are of ongoing stigmatization, violence by the officers of the state, being cast out from the protection of the state, and at the extremes being enslaved, expelled, or killed.

Expulsion and what we have come to call 'ethnic cleansing' may be slightly more benign forms of forced exclusion than slavery or genocide, but that's not saying very much. If we fear violence and cruelty then we must greatly fear expulsions and the creation of refugees. The stateless are outside of anyone's official protection and are almost necessarily subject to rule by simple force, perhaps the armed forces of a neighboring state. This is true for refugees of all types, but many—in today's world perhaps most—refugees are expelled or forced to flee because they belong to a disfavoured ethnic group.

When excluded minorities remain physically within the boundaries of the state, there is often a thin and blurred line between state and private violence against them. Urban ethnic riots against Muslims and Sikhs in India, or against Chinese in Indonesia, village riots against Roma in Romania, *Kristallnacht* in Germany, and lynch mobs in the American South were or are all ostensibly private acts of violence. But often the police make it quite clear that they will not intervene to protect the outcast minority, sometimes they cut off escape routes for those fleeing such violence, and sometimes they simply join in. Indeed, for all the talk about ethnic violence being a kind of uncontrollable passion, it seems that police protection of the minority can keep the passion in control quite nicely. Lynchings in the south increased and decreased, not in response to the waxing and waning of racial animus, but in response to the *de facto* position of the law on whether killing a black was a punishable offense. Donald Horowitz's research into ethnic riots has found that most take place when rioters feel they have tacit official approval, or at least that the police will not act and so they can commit violence with impunity. A clear early demonstration by the police that they will try to check rather than encourage a riot does a great deal to discourage would-be rioters.[8] The mob that destroyed the Babri Mosque in Ayodhya in 1992—a critical event in the last decade's polarization of Hindu–Muslim relations in India and in the rise of the Bharatiya Janata Party (BJP) to power—did so with security officers standing by and watching.

Mobile and nomadic minorities confronted with the apparatus of a modern state are at particular risk, for reasons James Scott has highlighted.[9] Transient populations are not 'legible' to state officials; they cannot easily be taxed, counted, monitored, conscripted, or administered. States have often attempted—violently and coercively if necessary—to push such groups into permanent settlements, at the cost of massive disruption to their livelihood and culture. (This has often been accompanied by the seizure of the large areas of land that most such groups previously occupied.) And we have sometimes seen much worse than that, as states decide that the wandering populations are more trouble than they are worth. Indigenous peoples in settler states, the Roma throughout Europe, the Bedouin throughout the Middle East, and Berbers in the Maghreb have all been subjected to violent treatment and/or come into conflict with states trying to force them into more modern, more easily-administered, and less land-intensive ways of life. Nomadic indigenous groups in India, Indochina, and sub-Saharan Africa have clashed with both colonial states and their modernizing post-independence successors. Neither the attempt to render such minorities more administratively legible nor the desire to seize their lands, nor both combined, completely accounts for the often brutal mistreatment of nomadic peoples by the states they inhabit; but both play a part.

---

[8] Donald Horowitz, *The Deadly Ethnic Riot* (forthcoming).
[9] James C. Scott, *Seeing Like A State* (New Haven: Yale University Press, 1997).

Moreover, we can expect conflicts between mobile minorities and states even in the absence of any malice or ill-will on the part of state officials (though malice and ill-will are often present). Settled, stable populations are far easier to integrate into a democratic voting system, a system of free state education, and so on. Peoples whose travels regularly take them across state boundaries are difficult to integrate into the modern understanding of citizenship. So even a modern state that sought to provide its characteristic benefits to such minorities—rather than inflicting costs like taxation and conscription on them—could be expected to try to change the minorities' way of life. Hunting-gathering or nomadic herding are likely to leave their practitioners at a subsistence level economically. Even states that want to provide material benefits to these minorities rather than simply imagining more profitable uses of their land may well try to force them into settled agricultural or urban ways of life. Doing so often devastates rather than improves the level of material well-being; but of course no state ever thinks that its plans for economic development will go disastrously wrong.

The existence of nomadic and other mobile minority groups in a world of modern and modernizing states is thus yet another of the circumstances of danger, another of the situations that requires us to expect state violence against ethnic minorities. The danger in such cases is a combination of forced inclusion and forced exclusion. Members of these groups that do not accede to the forced inclusion in the state via resettlement may be forcibly excluded as non-citizens and, their persons and their lands outside the protection of the law. The Roma have often been subjected to forced exclusion and forced inclusion simultaneously. The state resettles them, and then their new neighbors and the local officials from the dominant group treat them as outcasts and second-class citizens or non-citizens.

FRAMEWORKS FOR INTERCULTURAL INTERACTION

In a world of cultural pluralism, cultural communities are always interacting with one another in a variety of ways. Two cultural communities living side by side or intermingled in the same territory may aspire to separation and purity, but they can never quite have it. Their members fall in love with one another, trade with one another, and commit crimes against one another's laws. All of these require conventions or laws about them, and those laws cannot simply be of the sort which prohibit interaction. If forced incorporation is the failure to adequately recognize the degree of separateness of two communities, the lack of a framework is insufficient recognition of the fact of togetherness.

A British Islamic court has issued a sentence of death against the playwright Terrence McNally, on the grounds that his play *Corpus Christi* portrays Jesus (an honored prophet in Islam, though not the Messiah) as homosexual.[10] It happens that, unlike the decade-long *fatwa* against *Satanic Verses* author Salman Rushdie, this sentence is explicitly not to be carried out by individual Muslims, but only by any Islamic State McNally enters. But the more interesting difference, from our current perspective, is that McNally has never been Muslim. Unlike in the Rushdie case, there is not even a pretense of a community judging one of its own.[11] Leaving the community alone to manage its own affairs is not an option; a conflict has arisen between the laws of the state and the (presumably authoritatively-interpreted) legal tradition of a minority culture. The customs, rules, and legal traditions of neighboring communities interact and conflict in all sorts of ways. The communities must have some framework for managing those interactions, and some frameworks are better than others. In this case, a framework that allowed British Muslims to attack McNally (if such had been the terms of the *fatwa*) would be much worse than the existing one, in which the state insists that the protections of the criminal law against violence take absolute priority over the rules of any minority community.

Jeremy Waldron has suggested that we see *Romeo and Juliet* in this light, and as exemplary of a real social danger, saying that it can be read

as a deeper text about the dangers that beset a new and unforeseen initiative—in this case a romantic initiative—in circumstances where the only available structures for social action are those embedded in the affections and disaffections of the existing community . . . What this indicates is the importance of a structure of rights that people can count on for organizing their lives, a structure which stands somewhat apart from communal or affective attachment . . . some basis on which individuals and groups can reconstitute their relations to take new initiatives in social life without having to count on the affective support of the communities to which they have hitherto belonged.[12]

---

[10] James Lyons, 'Islamic Court Condemns Author Who Depicts Jesus as a Homosexual,' *The Independent*, Saturday 30 Oct. 1999, 3.

[11] In the Rushdie case, of course, pretense is all that it was, especially as regards the actions of the state of Iran.

[12] Jeremy Waldron, 'When Justice Replaces Affection: The Need for Rights,' in *Liberal Rights* (Cambridge: Cambridge University Press, 1993), 377, 379. This has been a recurring theme in Waldron's work; see also 'Kant's Legal Positivism,' *Harvard Law Review* 109 (1996), 1535–66, and 'Citizenship and Identity,' in Will Kymlicka and Wayne Norman (eds.), *Citizenship in Diverse Societies* (Oxford: Oxford University Press, 2000).

In a number of articles, Waldron has continued this theme and made what seems to me a compelling case for he refers to as cosmopolitan right. Cosmopolitan right does not refer to a cosmopolitan lifestyle, or to the transcendence of particularistic attachments.[13] Rather, it is an argument for the need for conventions and law to govern interactions among groups, an argument premised on the fact that we live 'unavoidably side-by-side' in a crowded world and so can never rest simply on our own communal laws, rules, and social understandings. Because our claims and our demands and our beliefs about what is right collide with one another, no one group's demands or identity or beliefs about justice can, by themselves, provide sufficient reason for decisions of law and public policy in favor of the group. We must always think about the problems of compossibility—whether one group's demands, desires, identities, or beliefs can coexist with those of the other groups that live side-by-side with them.

Waldron has applied this argument to a number of areas of multicultural coexistence. In democratic discussion, an identity-claim is no substitute for an argument; identity-claims by themselves don't come to terms with the fact of our cohabitation and coexistence. There can't be any right to be protected against offensive descriptions of my religion; such a right cannot coexist with even a basic right of others to freely practice and profess their own religions. The justice of indigenous land rights cannot be decided without reference to the needs and rights of other persons, and the other uses to which that land might be put. Money, alienability, and prices, and so on force each of us to confront the value others place on the resources we're holding onto. They not only allow but require us to come to terms with all the various other individual and social understandings others place on our goods, or on the goods we're trying to acquire.[14] Our social understanding can no more be the end of the story than can our identity; others have their competing claims. Money is an institution of cosmopolitan right, a way of getting us to come to terms with one another's competing claims without coming to blows over them.

This example reminds us that Kantian cosmopolitanism was also of concern to F. A. Hayek. In an 'extended order' we can never live only by the codes of kith and kin, blood and tribe. We have to have institutions

---

[13] Thus Waldron's 'Minority Cultures and the Cosmopolitan Alternative,' which does argue for a cosmopolitan lifestyle, is only partly in the same stream of argument as his various articles on cosmpolitan right (*University of Michigan Journal of Law Reform* 25 (1992), 751–93).

[14] Waldron, 'Money and Complex Equality,' in David Miller and Michael Walzer (eds.), *Pluralism, Justice, and Equality* (Oxford: Oxford University Press, 1995).

and rules of just conduct that transcend all of those codes and claims—
not because groups are ontologically unreal and individuals are ontologically real, not because individuals need to be free to leave their
groups, but because the extended order of our coexistence is incompatible with full-blooded endorsement of the morality of the thick community. We have, and need to have, impersonal institutions (like money, but
also like the common law) that mediate among our various local
demands and urges. There are differences between Waldron's formulations of the problem and Hayek's, but they have in common a recognition of the underlying problem, and the idea that there's a link between
cosmopolitanism and these impersonal mediating institutions.[15]

To put these points in more general terms: conventions regarding
intercultural exchanges and transactions cannot simply codify the traditional internal morality of one group or the other; and they cannot
simply pretend that such exchanges will not exist. Interactions will take
place, as will changes in cultural identity and migrations across communal lines. In order both to mitigate the danger to individuals of their exile
from their cultural communities and to forestall the danger of more
widespread conflict arising from such interactions, there must be social
and legal structures to accommodate the relevant changes.[16]

James Tully has argued that under such circumstances the requirements are simply that each group recognizes the equal status of the
other, and that they proceed to negotiate or deliberate about the terms
of their coexistence. But, at least for some cultural communities at some
times, what the *leaders* of the communities will do in formal negoti-
ations is agree to remain separate and pure. We have little reason to
think that they will make arrangements for intermarriage, for example.
Yet, inevitably, *members* of the two communities will fall in love, have
children, trade, commit crimes against each other, hybridize their
languages or settle on a *lingua franca,* prosletyze and convert and apostasize, and so on. If there are not legal arrangements that can accommodate these interactions, if the law rests on an assumption of integral
and discrete communities, then there are risks of intercommunal conflict
and of intracommunal oppression of those who are seen to jeopardize
communal purity.

[15] Hayek, *The Fatal Conceit* Chicago: University of Chicago Press, 1988), chs. 1–7.

[16] Forbes makes a persuasive case that one source of ethnic conflict is precisely such
interactions and migrations. As contact between cultural groups increases, as some
become more and more willing to cross the cultural boundary and assimilate into the
other culture or hybridize it with their own, other members of the culture feel driven to
further differentiate it from its neighbor, to pull away, to increase hostility. As I discuss
below, a pluralist solution would be to try and maintain the boundaries all the more
rigidly, while (as Waldron suggests) the liberal solution is something quite different.

Those who blur the boundaries or bring about changes may find themselves as outcasts from both communities. Some of liberalism's critics suppose that liberals would welcome this, seeing those cast out as better off because able to reclaim their Robinson Crusoe-like asocial liberty. In fact, liberals recognize the perilousness of the status of outlaw, the stateless, and the refugee. Of course, not *only* liberals recognize the dangers associated with statelessness; thinkers as different as Judith Shklar, Michael Walzer, and Hannah Arendt all see that (in Shklar's words) 'to be a stateless individual is one of the most dreadful fates that can befall anyone in the modern world.'[17] The more cultural communities come to resemble states—with mutually exclusive boundaries and considerable control over their members' lives—the more being cast out comes to resemble such statelessness. The legal institutions which mediate between cultural communities must also protect those who are cast out or who leave.

Intercommunal interactions will always take place, as will changes in cultural identity and migrations across communal lines. In order both to forestall the danger of intercommunal conflict and to protect those individuals who cross communal lines, there must be social and legal structures to accommodate the relevant changes. Chapter 6, on the legal incorporation of indigenous and religious law, and Chapter 7, on land claims, address such problems of frameworks.

INTERNAL CRUELTY

The potential for cruelty and conflict also exist within cultural communities. Traditional cultural norms are coercively enforced, or the norms themselves sanction coercion or violence. If multiculturalism is properly grounded in the avoidance of these evils rather than in any distinctive moral status of cultural groups, then there isn't any particular moral difficulty (whatever practical difficulties there may be) in restraining such practices. In Britain some South Asian Muslim families have actually hired contract killers to track down their daughters who rejected arranged marriages and fled. While states cannot and should not forbid parents to try to arrange marriages, they can and should forbid

---

[17] Judith Shklar, *American Citizenship: The Quest for Inclusion* (Cambridge: Harvard University Press, 1991), 4. Compare Michael Walzer, *Spheres of Justice* (New York: Basic Books, 1983), 32: 'Statelessness is a condition of infinite danger'; and Hannah Arendt, *The Origins of Totalitarianism* (New York: Harcourt Brace and Co., 1973 [1950]), 276–90.

marriages that are actually forced, marriages against the will of one or both spouses. And there's certainly no legitimate cultural defense for murder. But it's worth pausing to discuss the difference between preventing internal cruelty and simply remaking internal cultural practices that we don't like.

Many of the most heated disputes about multiculturalism in western societies involve marriage and family law, or, to put it another way, the treatment of women within minority cultures. In Nebraska, an Iraqi immigrant arranged marriages for his two young teenaged daughters; after they ran away, the father and both husbands were charged with criminal offenses. Hmong men in California have faced criminal rape charges for what they insist is a longstanding cultural practice of betrothal by 'capture.' A Somali immigrant in Georgia was charged with child abuse after she botched an attempt to cut the genitals of her niece; she was acquitted. Less gruesome but at least as publicly controversial were *l'affaire des foulards*, the French controversy over whether to allow Muslim schoolgirls to attend state schools while wearing their headscarves, and *Santa Clara Pueblo v Martinez,* a Supreme Court case that held that the federal courts had no jurisdiction to review a Pueblo tribe's sexually discriminatory membership rules.

Surveying all of this, Susan Moller Okin concludes that women in sexist minority cultures 'may be much better off if the culture into which they were born were either to become extinct (so that its members would become integrated into the less sexist surrounding culture).'[18] But cultural extinction is rarely an option; aiming at it tends to produce inter-ethnic violence and cruelty without much diminishing internal cruelty.

A multiculturalism justified in terms of preventing violence and cruelty offers no cultural shield to protect violent and cruel internal practices. Accommodating the law to multicultural social realities in some way, however, is often in the interests of women in the minority culture. This means that a legal system which refuses to acknowledge cultural difference will not effectively protect the interests of women in minority cultures. Sometimes this accommodation of law to multicultural realities will be directed at change of minority cultural practices, but when it is, proscription of those practices should be used only in fairly extreme cases—cases of real cruelty—and often partial or constrained recognition of cultural practices will be more conducive to cultural reform and the protection of women's interests than will proscription or nonrecognition.

[18] Susan Moller Okin, 'Is Multiculturalism Bad For Women?' *The Boston Review* 22:5 (Oct./Nov. 1997).

Moreover, just as the range of cultural practices that are subject to legitimate reform is wider than the range that is subject to proscription, so is the range that is subject to legitimate criticism wider than that subject to reforming state action. To put it another way, not every cultural practice that is worthy of criticism as sexist is a legitimate target for state attempts to change it, and not every cultural practice that is a legitimate target for such external pressures for reform is a legitimate object of prohibition. This, by the way, is applicable to the criticism, reform, and proscription of cultural practices generally, and not only those whose problem is that they are sexually discriminatory. Recall D'Alembert's summary of Montesquieu's argument on this point: 'Laws are a bad method of changing manners and customs; it is by rewards and example that we ought to endeavour to bring that about. It is however true at the same time, that the laws of a people, when they do not grossly and directly affect to shock its manners, must insensibly have an influence upon them, either to confirm or change them.'[19] There can be legal institutions that encourage internal reform and liberalization (by 'rewards and example'); but the blunt tool of proscription—so likely to shock the culture's manners—is best used sparingly.

Feminist worries about multiculturalism have real force and weight. In modern multicultural, multiethnic, and multireligious societies, there is constant pressure on minority cultures. It is difficult to maintain and transmit a culture when surrounded by alien influences. If schools, television, politics, and business are all conducted in an alien culture, then the home becomes the primary location for culture to be transmitted and carried on. This makes mothers especially central to the nationalism or cultural traditions of minority groups, and raises the pressure on them to maintain the purity of old ways.

More than that, family practices are one of the few remaining areas in which a wholly privatized culture can continue at all. Traditional ways of making a living are undermined by the modern economy, but at least a minority can hold onto its traditions of family life. Nondiscrimination law means that in many commercial and political contexts no distinction can be made between insider and outsider, but at least nondiscrimination law doesn't apply to the choice of a marriage partner. As one sphere after another is subject to modernizing influences, the stakes for maintaining cultural traditions and purity in the domestic or family sphere become that much higher. And the traditions

---

[19] M. D'Alembert, 'The Analysis of the Spirit of the Laws,' in *The Complete Works of M. de Montesquieu*, iv (London: Evans and Davis, 1777), 210.

regarding family life were typically sexist to begin with, even before they were subject to these aggravating influences.[20] Women may also be more vulnerable to internal cruelty than other so-called internal minorities (women are usually a numerical majority) because they typically lack an option for collective exit. Members of a religious minority subset of a linguistic minority, or vice-versa, might schism and set out on its own if they are subject to abuse; it is much harder to imagine a minority group splitting all at once along sex lines.

The greater Seattle area is home to some several thousand Somali immigrants as well as immigrant populations from Ethiopia, Eritrea, Sudan, and Kenya, all countries where female genital cutting is common. Mothers from these communities asked doctors at the Harborview Medical Center whether they would 'circumcise' their daughters. After more than a year of such requests, as well as indications from parents that if they could not have the operation performed in the United States they would return to their home countries for it, the Medical Center convened a committee chaired by pediatrician Abraham Bergman to examine the issue.

The committee recommended that the hospital begin performing a procedure it referred to as 'sunna circumcision,' a small incision on the clitoral hood. 'Sunna circumcision' can also refer to the complete removal of the clitoral hood, but the Harborview committee and subsequent debate only mentioned the possibility of the incision; the doctors insisted they would remove no tissue. This is the most mild form of female genital cutting. By contrast, the East African countries from which the immigrants came are typically those that practice the most extreme form of genital mutilation, infibulation. If anything constitutes internal cruelty then infibulation does. Typically performed with neither sterile instruments nor anesthesia, girls' genitals are scraped and cut off entirely. Those who do not die of blood loss or infection face a life of great pain during sexual intercourse and great danger during childbirth. Although the cutting is ostensibly a coming of age ritual, the age at which infibulation is performed varies widely; 6-year old victims are common and infants not unheard of.

Unlike infibulation, sunna circumcision does not complicate childbirth or sexual intercourse; unlike clitoral excision (the intermediate

---

[20] Okin emphasizes the degree to which the cultural traditions were sexist to begin with. Ayelet Shachar usefully draws additional attention to the special centrality that rules governing family law—that is to say, in large part, rules governing women—acquire in a multicultural state, as means of preserving group identity and demarcating insiders from outsiders. 'Group Identity and Women's Rights in Family Law: The Perils of Multicultural Accommodation,' *Journal of Political Philosophy* 6:3 (1998), 285–305.

form of genital cutting), it does not impair sexual pleasure. The committee said that the procedure should be performed under a local anesthetic, with the consent of both the parents and the girl, and only on girls aged 12 or older. Dr Leslie Miller, an obstetrician-gynecologist at Harborview, argued that the sunna circumcision was really analogous to, or even less drastic than, male circumcision.[21] At least some of immigrants agreed that a symbolic sunna circumcision could meet the cultural and religious obligation to circumcise their daughters.

The hospital passed the committee's recommendation on to the Washington attorney general for legal review, and promised that it would not begin performing the procedure before a community-wide discussion had been held. Even while making such qualifications, though, medical director James LoGerfo suggested that performing the operation might be the only way to prevent the mutilation of girls 'short of throwing the kids and the mother in jail for twenty years to make sure nothing happens to them.' Refusing to perform the operation in a hospital, some advocates argued, might only mean that more extreme versions of cutting were done in less sanitary conditions and without anesthesia.

News of the proposal created a bitter public dispute. The hospital received hundreds of letters, postcards, and phone calls protesting the idea. Some immigrants insisted that genital cutting of some sort was necessary to maintain girls' dignity and purity, that their daughters would be shamed and unmarriageable without some circumcision. Those engaged in the campaign to end female genital mutilation, however, were outraged. Meserak Ramsey, an Ethiopian immigrant and activist on the issue, said to the *Seattle Times,* 'How dare it even cross their mind. What the Somalis, what the immigrants like me need is an education, not sensitivity to culture.' The cut might have only been symbolic, but it was symbolic of a tradition that insisted on controlling girls, symbolic of a particularly brutal kind of repression. The cultural need that the hospital was seeking to fill was seen as an illegitimate one, the need to have at least the symbols of control over the sexuality of girls and women.

The hospital and some Seattle-area immigrant leaders, however, defended the proposal as a way to ease the transition to a complete end to genital cutting. 'We are trying to provide a relatively safe procedure to a population of young women who traditionally have had some horrendous things done to them,' said hospital spokeswoman Tina

---

[21] Carol Ostrom, 'Harborview Debates Issue of Circumcision of Muslim Girls,' *The Seattle Times,* Friday 13 Sept. 1996, p. A1

Mankowski. Even some Somalis opposed to all genital cutting thought the proposal could save some girls from being brought back to Somalia and having more radical procedures performed under the control of their more traditional grandmothers.[22] There are no reliable statistics on the prevalence of genital cutting of girls who live in the United States, but the Center for Disease Control estimates that as many as 150,000 may be at risk, and there has been at least one high-profile case in which a woman whose visa had expired applied for asylum on the grounds that if she returned to her homeland her daughters would be subject to genital mutilation at the hands of her older female relatives.

After passage of the federal statute criminalizing female genital mutilation, Colorado Democratic representative Patricia Schroeder, one of its primary sponsors, wrote to the hospital and expressed her view that performing this operation would violate the law. It is not clear to me that this was true; the statute bans circumcising, excising, or infibulating 'the whole or any part of the labia majora or labia minora or clitoris' of girls under 18; arguably, the sunna circumcision does none of these. But I'm willing to bracket that question and assume that Schroeder was right about a law she drafted. The hospital ceded to the pressure and backed down, apparently without ever having performed the procedure. A news release from the hospital stated that 'Harborview's role in considering the need for a culturally sensitive, safe alternative to the practices of female circumcision or female genital mutilation has now been concluded.'[23]

The law in a multicultural state has to accommodate itself to cultural and religious realities, to the situation as it exists on the ground. There are many cultural practices which, if a liberal democrat were remaking the world *de novo* he or she would leave out but which cannot therefore be ignored or proscribed in the real world. Female genital cutting of all variants is certainly one such practice. But we do not make the world *de novo*, and passing a law does not simply remake the world according to the law's intent. If their families carried out their original intentions, if they brought their daughters back to east Africa and had them mutilated, then the girls clearly were not made better off by the ban. This is true even if we suppose that a federal ban means that the practices of female genital mutilation will die out in America in another generation or two; we are still sacrificing the well-being of some real,

---

[22] See Tom Brune, 'Refugees' Beliefs Don't Travel Well; Compromise Plan on Circumcision of Girls Gets Little Support,' *The Chicago Tribune*, Monday 28 Oct. 1996, p. 1.
[23] Celia Dugger, 'Tug of Taboos: African Genital Rite vs. U.S. Law,' *The New York Times*, Saturday 28 Dec. 1996, A1

living girls. If the federal ban does not eradicate norms in its favor, if the law doesn't alter the underlying cultural facts, then girls in the next generation like girls in this one will be subjected to brutal practices elsewhere in the world because this society has banned even symbolic proxies for those practices. In that case we don't even have a tradeoff between the interests of living women and the interests of their future descendants but simply a sacrifice of the real interests of real girls to the call of symbolic disapproval. In any event the Harborview Medical Center was willing to consider the path of reforming a cultural practice rather than prohibiting it, but it didn't have the chance.

When the liberal state tries to reform patriarchal cultural practices, it still declines the culturally relativist path. Harborview was expressing a strong if tacit judgement that excision and infibulation are morally unacceptable; it identified constraints on what is tolerable. Excision and infibulation are violent and cruel practices, and the state shouldn't be multiculturally squeamish about prosecuting their practitioners for child abuse. But the interests of women and girls may be better-served by drawing a distinction between that which is cruel and intolerable and that which is wrong but tolerable.

Take polygamy, and particularly polygyny.[24] We may agree that polygyny as it has traditionally been practiced has been oppressive of women, has been in part an instrument of male power within plural marriages. There is dispute over whether this *must* be so; there are Mormon feminists who insist that plural marriages can have significant advantages for women who want a career as well as a family. But it probably *has* been so, for the most part.

What follows from the recognition of this? A natural response may be to criminalize polygamy, or at least to refuse to recognize plural marriages as marriages. But the appropriateness of that kind of response depends on the relationship between law and social practice. If polygyny is a continuing reality, if it continues to exist on the ground, then nonrecognition or criminalization may harm the women they are designed to protect. A woman who is publicly recognized as a wife gains legal rights—rights of inheritance, rights to have a child supported by her husband within marriage or after it, rights to some kinds of material settlements in the event of divorce. If the state does not recognize a woman as a wife, because the man in question already has a wife, or (worse) if polygyny is actively hidden from a state that seeks to imprison its practitioners, then the women involved gain no such rights.

---

[24] Polygyny refers to by far the most common species of polygamy—one man marrying multiple women.

And I think we have strong reason to doubt that polygamy vanishes as a result of the actions of the state. Criminalization has never succeeded in stamping it out among some Mormon sects in the United States, and that's even after the Church of Jesus Christ of Latter-day Saints officially reversed position and condemned it. Criminalization also creates all kinds of moral paradoxes in a modern liberal state. How, exactly, can we justify a state in which any number of adults are free to live together, in any sexual combination they wish, but in which if they attach the name of 'marriage' to their relationship they are liable to be thrown in prison? I doubt that we can. The United States Supreme Court decision that upheld the ban on polygamy a century ago was based in significant part on what is intolerable to Christian folk; it could not be decided that way today.

Another option is nonrecognition, not acknowledging polygynous marriages as legally valid. But nonrecognition is very unlikely to change the underlying norms. Many gays and lesbians in the United States consider themselves to be married, live as married couples, and hold wedding ceremonies despite official nonrecognition. They then rightly complain about the denial of the legal rights that accompany marriage. Nonrecognition of polygynous marriages, if it doesn't change the under-lying cultural norm, leaves participants in the same legal limbo as gay and lesbian couples are today, and that's very unlikely to be to the advantage of the women in the couple. The more we believe that the relation-ships are themselves unequal, the more do the women within them at least need access to the rights associated with the status of legal spouse.

Within a regime that recognizes polygamous marriages, there is room for legal encouragement of reform, or even for changes dictated by law. Indeed, the law has more leverage in a state that recognizes some poly-gamous marriages than in a state that recognizes none of them. The United States has little ability to reform polygamy since it cannot offi-cially acknowledge that the relationships exist. But a state that does recognize some polygamous marriages—South Africa, for example—can make the recognition conditional. The new government in South Africa has in fact imposed an extremely important and valuable condi-tion: universal consent. All prior spouses, not only the husband, must agree to the marriage of a new spouse. The common rule in most poly-gynous traditions is that husbands have the option of unilaterally decid-ing to take additional wives. A requirement of general consent is compatible with at least Muslim edicts on polygyny, which insist that a man must treat all of his wives justly and equally and that if he cannot do so he may not take more than one wife. It also undermines the use of polygyny as a threat within marriage.

The concept of consent is a powerful tool for reform in other marriage practices as well, such as arranged marriages. Actually to prohibit the arrangement of marriages poses all the difficulties characteristic of proscription. There is an almost impossible line to draw between the putatively illiberal practices of the minority group—arrangement—and the ordinary practices of some members of the majority culture: parental pressure about choice of spouse, families introducing potential partners, even the arranged blind date. There is an almost insurmountable problem of detection and enforcement. And there is, in my view, grave moral doubt about whether any such proscription is compatible with the rights of everyone involved.

But in many traditions arranged marriages are *only* agreements between families or between the bride's family and the groom-to-be. A liberal state can and indeed must draw a bright line between marriages to which both spouses consent and those in which they do not. The latter cannot be recognized as marriages at all. The standard of consent can also be used, by the way, to justify a minimum age requirement for all forms of marriage, plural, arranged, or otherwise. Child marriage is, as Montesquieu called it, 'domestic slavery,' and cannot be finessed into compatibility with liberal principles.[25]

One immediate response to an invocation of consent is to doubt the legitimacy or authenticity of consent given in conditions of unequal power. Shall we really view a marriage as consensual when it has been arranged by parents in a culture with strong norms of both patriarchy and obedience? Shall we really take seriously the consent of prior wives to the addition of a new wife, when the husband holds all the economic and religious authority?

I think that these are powerful worries—but they are worries to be invoked at the level of criticism, not at the level of law. Here we face grave dangers of cross-cultural hypocrisy. The law does not interrogate the consent to marriage of women in the majority culture, regardless of any inequalities that exist between bride and groom or within families. But more than that, we have some evidence of the power of a consent criterion. At the beginning of this section I mentioned the young Pakistani women who have refused arranged marriages in Britain, and

---

[25] Though he uses the term, Montesquieu does not openly condemn child marriage. Indeed, he seems to justify it in the context of the hot countries of the south, though he insists that 'in all this, I only give their reasons, but do not justify their customs.' ('Dans tout ceci, je ne justifie pas les usages; mais j'en rend les raisons.') See *De l'esprit des lois*, i, ed. Victor Goldschmidt (Paris: Garnier-Flammarion 1979 [1758]), 412, and generally book XVI chs. III–IV. He does insist that in conditions of 'domestic slavery' it is particularly important that women have the right to unilaterally divorce their husbands.

have subsequently had to flee their communities because their families are actually seeking to kill them. A consent criterion allows the British government unambiguously to take the side of these women; it will not be involved in delivering up disobedient daughters to their parents or would-be husbands. This, by the way, is what happened in the Nebraska case—the two Iraqi girls ran away from their ostensible husbands, and the husbands and fathers went to the police to get help in tracking them down. The police responded, quite rightly, that these nonconsensual marriages amounted to kidnapping and statutory rape, and that the state was on the girls' side, not theirs. Even if the cultural defense the men invoked to try to avoid criminal penalties were legitimate—and it is not—at least the consent criterion means that the state will stand with those fleeing forced marriages rather than with their husbands and fathers. And the fact that the girls fled suggests that there was nothing like successful indoctrination going on, that if consent had actually been demanded at the outset that the girls would have been able to refuse.

A man from Mali who emigrated to France told *The New York Times* 'one wife on her own is trouble. When there are several, they are forced to be polite and well behaved. If they misbehave, you threaten that you'll take another wife.' But that source of power is undercut if their consent is necessary before another wife can be 'taken.' The same article reported on women from Mali, Mauritius, and Senegal complaining about husbands leaving for holidays in Africa and returning to France with unannounced additional wives, or even taking the money the women had earned to pay the brideprice for an additional wife in Africa. But common to all of the accounts was that they were not consulted, that they did not wish for there to be another wife. They were willing to say this, for attribution, in a major newspaper; these were not women cowed into silence. It seems likely that they would be willing to refuse to sign a consent form, refuse to participate in a civil service confirming the new marriage. That's not to say that all of the affected women would be in a position to withhold consent; but there's no question that giving them the option of withholding consent would significantly increase their power within the relationships. It would be strengthened still further if nonconsensual polygamous marriages were not only denied recognition but were actually penalized in the same way that fraudulent bigamy is—but, as in those cases, punishing only one person, not all the 'practitioners' of polygamy. Again, casting the net of intolerable cultural practices too widely can hurt those the state is trying to protect, while conditional recognition can encourage reform.

How should a liberal state, and a liberal society, try to liberalize illiberal or patriarchal minority cultures? Often, I think, the answer must involve policies of multicultural recognition and rights as well as policies that tend to create internal pressure for reform. States ought to recognize those marriages which in fact take place in a cultural community. Sometimes these are polygynous. Sometimes they are arranged. Often they are patriarchal in one way or another. But nonrecognition is rarely in the interests of the women the liberal state means to protect, women who are cut off from any legal rights as wives, ex-wives, widows, and sometimes mothers. Recognition, on the other hand, can grant access to those legal rights, which often exceed the rights women traditionally culturally had. A common civil law of, for example, divorce and inheritance should be accessible to all in publicly recognized marriages. This gives the women in conservative cultural communities options and rights which they might not have had traditionally and which they certainly would not have had if the state had refused to recognize their marriage.[26] Similarly, allowing headscarf-wearing Muslim schoolgirls into the public schools is surely a better long-term strategy for liberalization than is excluding them. This argument requires a prudential calculus, even if one isn't convinced by any moral argument that children in public schools have a right to wear religious garments. Would a ban mostly have the effect of getting Muslim girls in public school to leave their scarves behind, or would it mostly have the effect of keeping them out of the public schools, perhaps encouraging the growth of private schools in which they gain less exposure to a world outside their own community?

Direct state intervention is called for when the rights of women in minority cultures are violated; but for changes in patriarchal norms, a different approach is necessary. That approach commonly requires some policies of multicultural accommodation in order to allow women access to the rights of citizenship and while remaining members of their cultural communities. A rejection of multicultural policies might sometimes hasten the 'extinction' of illiberal cultures. Often, though, it means leaving women (and other victims of the culture's illiberalism) stranded, cutting them off from the rights and resources which might allow them to liberalize their culture from within.

---

[26] Compare Montesquieu's strong defense of the right of women to divorce, and his insistence that this right is more necessary the more unequal a nation's actual marriage customs are. 'In climates where women live in domestic slavery, one would think that the law ought to favor women with the right of repudiation [unilateral divorce], and husbands only with that of [mutually agreed-upon] divorce.' ('Dans les climats où les femmes vivent sous un esclavage domestique, il semble que la loi doive permettre aux femmes la répudiation, et aux maris seulement le divorce.') *De l'espris des lois* XVI. XV. i. 420.

Internal cruelty is a real danger. Many cultural traditions and customary practices are violent; others are so unjust that only violence can enforce them. There is no 'cultural defense,' in morality or in decent law, for such violence and cruelty. But there is an easy tendency to see everyone else's cultures as repressive and intolerant, whereas the socializations and norms of our own culture are invisible to us. We should be very wary of seeing intolerable unfreedom everywhere that people live in a culture which socializes them and holds them to certain norms. We should be careful because it's right to be careful. We should also be careful because carelessness here can easily result in the stigmatization of this or that culture as intolerable and so subject its members to attacks by the wider society. A large community will lash back, creating the danger of widespread violence; a small community may have to suffer in silence but it can still suffer.[27]

Cultural difference should not prevent a state from both criticizing and taking action against violence and cruelty against women. It should, however, remind members of a majority culture to look inward as well as outward for abuses. It's easier to notice someone else's patriarchal or illiberal actions than it is to notice our own; and that ease makes hypocrisy too tempting. Moreover, we should be wary of criticizing cultural norms, values, and traditions as quickly as we do acts of violence and abuse. We are, all of us, born into cultures and socialized into norms. Living in a cultural community—as with belonging to a family, holding a job, joining a voluntary association, or participating any of the other intermediate groupings in which we lead our lives—means, in part, living under rules which would be violations of liberty if imposed as laws by the state. That fact in itself is not a restriction of our freedom or rights; but it is easy and tempting to see the norms and socializations of other cultures as such restrictions. Again, that tempting hypocrisy should be resisted.

NEGATIVE MORALITY AND MORAL BLACKMAIL

The four dangers described above are dangers of life in a multiethnic world and in multicultural polities as such. What follows is a discussion

---

[27] I think that such prudence is not shown, for example, by Andrew Kernohan, *Liberalism, Equality, and Cultural Oppression* (Cambridge: Cambridge University Press, 1998). Kernohan's view that 'the liberal state must take an active role in reforming culture' (p. 25) is usefully contrasted with Joseph Raz's position. In *The Morality of Freedom* (Oxford: Oxford University Press, 1983), Raz endorses a position like Kernohan's as a matter of perfectionist principle, but substantially hedges in that principle with a number of prudential considerations, especially when the state's project of cultural reform would cross cultural boundaries.

of a different sort of danger—a problem in the application of a theory. Negative consequentialism—which makes up a part of negative political morality, like the multiculturalism of fear—can generate a kind of perverse incentive. If the moral standard to which a government holds is preventing some specified evil, then the government can be morally blackmailed by those who threaten to create or inflict that evil unless they get what they want. The rule of preventing an evil creates an incentive to threaten or create that evil to gain an advantage. The best-known example of this kind of problem is hostage-taking and terrorism. If a government puts saving the lives of its citizens first, then those who are willing to take hostages or threaten acts of terrorism can extort any concessions they want from that government.

Similarly, if one criterion of the legitimacy of a secessionist movement is the likelihood and intensity of ethnic conflict if the state remains unified, then by threatening violence a secessionist movement seems to *increase* its own legitimacy. If the state responds with force to secessionist violence, then that fact itself seems to add greater moral force to the secessionists' demands. Either threatening war or provoking a violent response from the other side thus seem perversely attractive.

A history of violence and injustice against a group plays an important part in justifying contemporary cultural rights-claims. Here we seem to face perverse incentive of a different kind, an incentive for exaggerated and competitive claims of victimhood. If a history of oppression legitimates secession or special cultural protections, if it makes us understand a state symbol as humiliating because it celebrates that history, then every cultural group seeking advantage may cry 'victim.' In fact many people do use a history of oppression in this way; and in fact we do see such exaggerated and competitive claims about such histories.

The negative consequentialism of a multiculturalism of fear thus appears to create two kinds of perverse incentives—an incentive to commit, provoke, or threaten violence and injustice in the present and future (moral blackmail), and an incentive to overstate wrongs against one's own group in the past (exaggerated victimhood). Neither kind of behavior should be encouraged, and if the multiculturalism of fear requires us to encourage them then it is self-defeating. To a certain degree these problems might be alleviated by applying the negative consequentialism with a long time horizon. It is already known that a credible policy of never negotiating with hostage-takers, kidnappers, and terrorists is, in the long term, a better way to implement the moral standard of saving lives than is granting every demand such people make. Perhaps an equivalent rule related to multiculturalism would be to insist that neither sovereignty over nor ownership of land could ever be changed by violence, that borders established by force would never be recognized. In the discussion that follows I suggest a different way of solving the problem of perverse incentives. It rests on the recognition that the political implementation of a moral standard for judgment often requires something other than just asking political leaders to judge.

Problems of institutional and legal design come at more than one level; so do the standards of evaluation of institutions and laws. The best standard for evaluating laws and policies about multiculturalism and nationalism is their tendency to prevent the dangers outlined above, but it does not follow that the best decision rule for state officials is to, in each case, take the action that best appears to prevent them. Moreover, knowing what legal rules and institutional frameworks that might make possible a decent and peaceful coexistence of members of different ethnic and cultural groups, while protecting individuals within those groups, differs from knowing what decision-making institutions would be likely to design laws in such ways. There is a possible problem of infinite regress here. We want to be able to make normative statements about laws and policies without having to figure out, all the way down, how to produce the kind of people who would choose the kinds of institutions which would produce the kind of people who would choose the kinds of institutions ... which would make the morally best decisions. And in this book I mostly stay at the first level of that process, not discussing (for example) whether guaranteed minority representation in legislatures would tend to generate better policies from the perspective of a multiculturalism of fear. But we must move at least half a level further into the process, in order to say that officials shouldn't simply use negative consequentialism as a decision rule.

If such a decision rule were used, states and minority groups alike might threaten violence in the future and overstate the wrongs of the past in order to bend the criteria of the multiculturalism of fear to their own advantage. Even if everyone involved has only good faith and good will, there are predictable problems of bias. It is strange to expect the same state that commits injustice against a minority to recognize minority cultural rights as a legitimate response to that injustice. If those who govern do not recognize the initial treatment as unjust, they will certainly not recognize as legitimate any special compensation for it or protection against it.

Allen Buchanan argues, as I do in Chapter 3, that the moral justification for secession is primarily remedial.[28] There is no right of nations to political independence, only a right to protection against certain kinds of wrongs. Nevertheless, he argues for general, neutral procedures that would allow secession after, say, a supermajority referendum vote, or a stable majority across multiple referenda separated by a pre-determined amount of time. This is in significant part because the states most likely to be guilty of the wrongs which justify secession are the least likely to admit to them, the least likely to allow secession.

Similarly, although there is no general moral right of cultural preservation or autonomy, there may still be a good argument for certain general legal and institutional cultural rights, rights that do not require for their exercise convincing the state that there is a present danger of cruelty or a past of state injustice. Rules like adverse possession and the presumptive legitimacy of present state boundaries are justified partly by the need for present and future stability;[29] but if all the past wrongs could be undone at once, borders and ownership could still be stable in the future. Such rules are justified in part because we cannot expect ordinary mortals to have all the information necessary to undo all past dispossessions, *and* because we cannot expect ordinary partial political leaders to have the necessary purely disinterested view of history. Similarly, as Buchanan notes, sometimes it is unreasonable to expect a majority or the state it dominates to pass disinterested judgment on itself, to declare that it has so mistreated a minority that remedial measures are necessary. We may need institutional rules that will allow for the protection of minorities without insisting that a majority pass such judgment on itself. Such rules, such procedures, should also mitigate the problems of perverse incentives that would arise if we simply expected the parties to a conflict to judge themselves and each other.

Beyond that, what can be said is both very simple and very complicated. Restraint has to be exercised—by minority groups, by states, and by third parties exercising their judgment. The temptation, for example, to make exaggerated claims of victimhood is probably always present, and institutional design has only a limited ability to discourage it. Of course, it is not claimed victimhood that justifies rectification or remedial treatment but real victimhood. But, as always, we lack direct access to the underlying moral truth; claims of injustice are all we can hear in political and legal life. That does *not* mean that we should accept such claims uncritically. But examining them, seeking the moral truth

---

[28] Allen Buchanan, *Secession: The Morality of Political Divorce From Fort Sumter to Lithuania and Quebec* (Boulder, Colo: Westview Press, 1991).
[29] See Ch. 7.

beneath the political claims of the day, requires effort. We—whoever we are in this context, whether state officials, members of the minority group, fellow citizens from the majority, or outsiders seeking to know the right and wrong of a situation—have to be willing to evaluate claims of injustice that are made (as well as being willing to make point out cases of genuine injustice that have not yet been recognized). Similarly, when faced with the possibility of violence we have to be willing to evaluate who is at fault rather than simply caving in to threats.

I have no simple answers about how these virtues can be called forth, how to cultivate the requisite moral psychology. But it should be understood that moral theories are not self-enforcing. Even if there are institutions that can reliably produce the morally desired results, people (officials, citizens, group members, or whoever) must be willing to choose those institutions. This may not be any more of a difficulty for the multiculturalism of fear than for other normative arguments in politics—there are always dangers of misapplication and lazy application, always the risk that officials and citizens will be unwilling to do the work of moral evaluation—but it's not any less of one, either. And the possibilities of moral blackmail and of exaggerated claims of victimhood are how those difficulties manifest in this case. They represent the multiculturalism of fear's characteristic form of misapplication, and they must be resisted.

PART II

The Moral Importance of Cultural Membership?

3

The Impossibility of Universal Nationalism

UNIVERSAL NATIONALISM

Humane nationalists from Herder and Mazzini onward—liberal, republican, or otherwise—have shared a vision of universal nationalism, of a world of nationalist nations peacefully coexisting. They have shared, in Yael Tamir's provocative phrase, a nationalism of all nations. They have often been nationalists of their own nations first and foremost, as Mazzini was; but they have thought of themselves as friends to nationalisms everywhere. Those who share this vision have often spoken of a universal right of national self-determination. If nationalism is generalizable, then each nation can determine its own fate without posing any necessary danger to other nations. Nationalisms are not inherently in conflict; perhaps nationalisms-rightly-understood never are. Indeed, those who see nationalism as the enemy of imperialism and not its ally have thought that universal nationalism was necessary for peace; Woodrow Wilson seems to have thought something like this at the time of the Fourteen Points (though he was later disillusioned).[1]

The vision is not attainable. Nationalism cannot be universalized. One can be a nationalist of one's own nation and friendly to the nationalisms of some or many other particular nations. But even if every nation and every nationalism is liberal and humane, a nationalism of all nations is not possible. The argument to this effect takes up much of this chapter, but in essence it is this: It is well-established that there is no single criterion that marks out a human grouping as a nation. And the most plausible descriptive accounts of nationalism include a large element of self-definition and self-identification. The question of which nation, say,

---

[1] The differences in understandings of the relationship between imperialism and nationalism sometimes rest on different uses of terms, but don't have to. When 'nation' and 'state' are elided, then 'nationalism' is simply the (sometimes aggressive and imperialistic) advancement of one state's interests. But even when the concepts of nation and state are kept separate, some states, some empires, are more national and more nationalistic than others. The Hapsburg configuration of empire against nations is not the only possibility; Prussian–German nationalism was closely related to Wilhelmine imperialism.

the Alsatians belong to is answered in part with reference to their own self-understandings. (Remember Renan and his 'daily plebiscite.')

But the nationalist—the person who holds the nationalism of one nation as a normative position—must be committed to the view that these self-understandings can be wrong. Nationalist projects are dedicated to *convincing* some people that they belong to this nation rather than to that one—that they are French rather than German, Turkish rather than Kurdish, Quebecois rather than Canadian (or, in each case, vice versa). The nationalist, in other words, thinks that there is an underlying right answer to the question 'What nation does this person belong to?' Recent political theorists of nationalism have apparently incorporated this element of nationhood into their theories; they all accept that nations are in part 'imagined communities' and much is made of the rejection of primordialism. But these theorists have not quite come to grips with the implications of this subjective element in the definition of the nation. It undermines the possibility of a normative nationalism in any given case, of saying to a person that he or she ought to be loyal to this community rather than to that one.

Moreover—returning to the fact that no single criterion marks out nations even setting aside self-identification—a world in which some nations are defined ethnically, others linguistically, others on the basis of a shared political history, and so on, is a world in which some groups will be claimed by more than one nation and others will be left out of all nations. The Alsatian problem—the problem of a group (and its territory) being claimed by one nation on political grounds and another on ethnic/cultural grounds—will confront us over and over again. So will the Roma problem, the problem of the group that is outside almost every nation's self-definition.

Apparently successful attempts to construct a universal nationalism typically actually justify a position that I call moderate and generalized communitarianism [MGC]. This is the position that we are morally permitted (or perhaps morally obligated) to be at least moderately morally partial to fellow members of all of the affective and cultural communities to which we belong. We may be partial to them as against the rest of humanity, and perhaps we ought to be partial to them and to the group as against our own personal interests. In short, MGC holds that all of our cultural memberships and communal affiliations are morally relevant.[2]

---

[2] MGC does not necessarily equate with communitarianism on any of the issues that divide communitarians from liberals; at least some communitarians would find MGC too pluralistic to offer the kind of shared unifying experiences they think necessary. Allen

This general moral relevance of cultural communities is not the same as, indeed it is contrary to, the kind of special moral relevance for one community, one cultural membership, that all arguments for nationalism and some arguments for minority cultural rights require. So some such arguments gain their plausibility because they show that we owe loyalty, or are allowed partiality, to communities larger than the self or the family and smaller than humanity as a whole; they then leap to the conclusion that special political provision for this or that cultural community is morally justified.

In Chapter 1 I argued for the moral and political significance of cultural pluralism, of the social fact of multiple cultures and ethnicities coexisting in the same state, and of the characteristic dangers of violence and cruelty that arise from that social fact. Here, however, I argue mostly against ascribing ethical significance in politics to cultural membership, preservation, or loyalty *per se*. Arguments for political recognition of cultural attachments rely on claims about the relationship between persons and their communities; for most persons, there exist several cultural communities with which he or she has this kind of relationship. However, the proposed political institutions or policies—national self-determination is the one I discuss at greatest length but the point is applicable to many less drastic forms of cultural protection—give one such cultural community priority, and do not recognize the comparable ties members of that community have with larger, smaller, or crosscutting communities. Nationalism and policies of minority cultural preservation gain the most plausibility when the alternative to some particular national or cultural community is imagined to be either undifferentiated humanity or alienated individualism. In fact, however, the alternative is often some other community to which persons also have some attachment. If all those attachments are morally relevant, then none can be given the kind of political priority which excludes the others.

I thus argue against duties of participation in or belonging to one particular level of cultural community; I also suggest that some kinds of arguments for cultural or national rights stand or fall with the arguments for such duties. First I argue that *national* identity and loyalty cannot have even the moral significance ascribed to them by theorists of moderate, liberal, or universalistic nationalism. In Part II I offer a more general critique of theories of cultures as public goods. In both sections I argue that universal, non-remedial arguments for some kinds of

Buchanan has argued that a position very like MGC yields liberal political principles in 'Assessing the Communitarian Critique of Liberalism,' *Ethics* 99, (1989), 852–82.

cultural rights depend on the moral status of cultural membership which I am disputing.

Nationalism as a normative political view addresses two kinds of normative claims to members of the nation.[3]

1.   *This* unit (Quebec, or Canada, or Croatia, or Yugoslavia, or Turkey, or Kurdistan) is and rightfully ought to be considered your nation.
2.   You should be loyal to your nation.
2a. You ought to be willing to place the needs of your nation and of your co-nationals *above the needs of outsiders*, ultimately including a willingness to kill outsiders for the nation. You ought to support your nation's struggle to attain or preserve self-determination against the attempts by outsiders to make the nation a subordinate part of some state or empire.
2b. You ought to be willing to place the needs of your nation and of your co-nationals *above the needs of subsets of the nation*, including ethnic, religious, economic, or political subgroups. You as an individual are also a subset of the nation and so ought to be willing to put its interests ahead of your own; ultimately, this includes a willingness to die for the nation.[4] You ought to support your nation's struggle to preserve its unity against factions that seek to break it up; you ought to oppose attempts to secede from the nation.

Portions of (2a) and (2b) may be combined in a familiar way:

2c. You ought to support your nation in its attempts to make, or to keep, the political and the national unit congruent.[5] You ought to

---

[3] It also addresses a normative claim to outsiders, which is something like 'You ought to recognize this unit as the a nation,' This may entail, *inter alia*, granting the nation political independence if it is not currently independent and respecting it as an appropriate unit of self-determination and an appropriate object of its members' loyalty. Our attention here is on the internal normative claims; I take it that they are prior to the external ones logically and morally if not always chronologically.

[4] On the duty to kill and to die for the nation, see Yael Tamir, 'Pro Patria Mori!' in Robert McKim and Jeff McMahan (eds.), *The Morality of Nationalism* (Oxford: Oxford University Press, 1997). On its face it may seem that only very extreme nationalists would make such demands; but many moderate normative nationalisms would accept that (*a*) nationhood is a criterion of legitimacy for statehood and (*b*) citizens of legitimate states have at least a moral duty to defend those states by force of arms during wartime. As noted below, the duties to kill and to die may be sharply constrained by other moral obligations; but I think Tamir is right that nations—unlike many other collectivities, like classes, professions, or even religions—are widely thought to have a moral claim over life and death *in extremis*.

[5] Cf. Ernest Gellner, *Nations and Nationalism* (Ithaca, NY: Cornell University Press, 1983), 1: Nationalism is the claim that 'the political and the national unit should be congruent.' Nothing in what follows is affected if we accept Paul Gilbert's formulation of a nation as 'a group of a kind that has, other things being equal, the *right* to independent

support the nation's political independence from larger units while opposing the attempts of any subsets of the nation to secede or, if already separate, to remain so.

Normative nationalisms come in a very wide range of intensities, and most elements of these claims can be significantly moderated leaving a recognizably nationalist view. The moral partiality shown to members may be only *prima facie*. The duty of loyalty to the nation may be subordinated to other moral obligations; the acts members are called on to perform may be constrained by basic universal principles. Sovereign statehood may be replaced by self-government within a larger state. But for a normative view to be nationalist, it must at least identify which community constitutes a nation, and hold that members ought to be loyal to their nation above and against larger, smaller, and crosscutting human communities.

What I will argue in this section is that these claims cannot be defended simultaneously in a way that is simultaneously universalizable and plausible.[6] Arguments for generalized or universal nationalism either justify MGC and then simply skip argumentative steps to reach nationalistic conclusions; depend on a tacit assumption that we already know which units in the world are nations and which are not, that the general form of claim (1) is empirical rather than normative; or correctly treat claim (1) as normative but in so doing undermine any argument for claim (2).

These normative claims are ordinarily made simultaneously. One can imagine conceptually, but never hears in reality, 'This unit is your *nation,* but you really ought to be loyal to your *state* instead.' The word *nation* is so normatively loaded that who invokes it typically invokes

statehood,' which as he notes is more moderate than Gellner's formulation, since there might be good reasons not to exercise the right. Not every nation can simultaneously have such a right. Paul Gilbert, *The Philosophy of Nationalism* (Boulder, Colo.: Westview Press, 1998).

[6] I exclude at least one kind of claim which nationalists also make, claims about land and territory. I discuss these in Chapter 7. It of course tends to be true that nationalists make expansionist claims about land which cannot be generalized, but here I am concerned to establish that even in principle nationalistic claims cannot be universal. *If* nations were clearly and uncontroversially identifiable, their claims to territory in principle might be compatible or at least amenable to general compromise. Similarly, I do not mean to exclude critiques of nationalism like that offered by Jamie Mayerfeld, namely that 'nationalism is dangerous in any form because it cannot be dissociated from certain attitudes which . . . make violence more likely'; I offer a more benign account of nationalism only for the sake of showing the limits that even it encounters. Mayerfeld, 'The Myth of Benign Group Identity: A Critique of Liberal Nationalism,' *Polity* 30:4 1998, 555–78.

loyalty to it. It was not always so; Lord Acton was perfectly capable of identifying one level of community as the nation and another level as the appropriate state. Nor is it universally so; those cosmopolitans who care little for loyalty to state or for loyalty to nation can certainly call a unit a nation without demanding loyalty to it. But, for example, states that are trying to command loyalty, and to undermine nationalist movements, do not deny claim (2). Instead, they change the proper noun in claim (1). Of course you ought to be loyal to your nation; but your nation is Turkey, or Canada, or China; Kurdish is only an ethnicity, French only a language, Tibetan a nonentity. These are, in Rogers Brubaker's useful terminology, nationalizing states, seeking to shift loyalty away from state-seeking national minorities.[7]

Rupert Emerson was, I think, nearly correct when he defined the nation as 'the largest community, which when the chips are down, effectively commands men's loyalty, overriding the claims both of lesser communities within it and those which cut across it or potentially enfold it within a still greater society'—but only nearly.[8] The nation is typically the unit for which the speaker thinks one *ought* to have that loyalty. Some analysts have been misled in looking for some universal empirical marker for that unit; Walker Connor thought he had found it in the largest unit for which people are willing to imagine a common blood ancestry. I submit that there is *no* such universal empirical trait, not even a universal trait on which the national imagination centers. The questions of whether Turkey or Kurdistan, France or Brittany really *is* a nation do not admit of empirical answers. One cannot go into the world accepting claim (2) and then engage in a dispassionate empirical analysis into which proper noun belongs in claim (1). One cannot do this because there's no true answer lurking out there; and one probably cannot as a matter of moral psychology, either. It is difficult to imagine someone who believed that he or she owed *some* group the kind of loyalty demanded by claim (2), but who did not know *which* group that was. The feelings of obligation and loyalty which persons feel to nations are intimately tied up with their feelings about particular groups and places, that is, with the particular unit they identify as their nation. In any event, what would the inquiry of the nationalist who did not know to which nation he or she belonged look like?

I do not mean to suggest that there are no *wrong* answers. There are

---

[7] Rogers Brubaker, *Nationalism Reframed* (Cambridge: Cambridge University Press, 1996).

[8] Rupert Emerson, *From Empire to Nation* (Boston, 1960), 95–6, quoted in Walker Connor, *Ethnonationalism: The Quest for Understanding* (Princeton: Princeton University Press), 1993, 156.

human communities with which a given individual has no plausible claim to membership, with which he or she does not share a language or a territory or a history or a religion or ... (If I declare that I am Japanese, then on its face I am mistaken.) But this isn't the sort of situation we typically confront in the world. The circumstances in which nationalism has normative political work to do are usually precisely those circumstances in which there are competing communities each of which can make a plausible claim to being a nation.

It is important to note that nationalism does not *only* claim that one ought to be partial to some subset of humanity and that one ought to be loyal to something larger than one's family. One might be so partial and loyal to many communities simultaneously. There could be some obligations one owes to one's co-religionists, some to one's fellow citizens of a state, some to the other speakers of one's language, and so on. This kind of morality, moderate and generalized communitarianism is utterly incompatible with nationalism. MGC says that the Kurdish Turk or the Quebecois Canadian owes something to both groups, to both identities. State and ethnic group alike should be placed ahead of self, on the one hand, and the whole of humanity, on the other. Nationalism, however, makes a claim of *priority*. One ought to choose one's nation over one's current state, over the claims of religion, and so on. The nationalist does not ask me to choose between (Kurdistan or Turkey) and (the rest of the world) but between Kurdistan and Turkey, not between (Quebec or Canada) and (the rest of the world) but between Quebec and Canada. In each case the so-called 'civic' nationalist will tell me that the latter unit is truly my nation, the 'ethnic' nationalist the former; but both make the same kind of claim of priority. I return to the civic–ethnic distinction below. For now, the important point is that nationalism, as distinct from MGC, claims that the nation takes priority not only over self and over humanity but also over rival identities, loyalties, and group affiliations.

Isaiah Berlin characterized the four key recurrent elements in nationalist thought as

the belief (1) in the overriding need to belong to a nation; (2) in the organic relationships of all the elements that constitute a nation; (3) in the value of our own simply because it is ours; (4) and finally, faced by rival contenders for authority and loyalty, in the supremacy of their [the nation's] claims.[9]

The third of these claims is fundamental for MGC; Yael Tamir paraphrases it as 'the magic pronoun "my." '[10] The first claim is a

---

[9] Isaiah Berlin, 'Nationalism: Past Neglect and Present Power,' in *Against the Current* (New York: Penguin, 1979), 345, numeration added.

[10] Yael Tamir, *Liberal Nationalism* (Princeton: Princeton University Press, 1993), ch. 5.

moral-psychological one rather than a directly normative one. The second claim, to which I give little attention because of its speciousness, is sociological, and an attempt to explain both the moral importance of nations and how we pick them out.[11] It is the fourth claim, 'faced by rival contenders for authority and loyalty, in the supremacy of [nations'] claims,' that I am seeking to elaborate here, the normative demand which is distinctive to nationalism and which sets it apart from MGC. In this spirit Anthony Smith characterizes one of the 'central propositions of the ideology' of nationalism as 'The nation is the source of all political and social power, and *loyalty to the nation overrides all other allegiances.*'[12]

Arguments for universalized nationalism often defend a nationalism of a moderated kind, so that the loyalty demanded is *prima facie* and constrained by other moral principles. The usual strategy in such arguments is to identify some characteristic of nations which would allow them to make moral claims which are both particularistic (that is, allowing for less than universal application, allowing for preferences for fellow nationals as against outsiders) and collective (that is, allowing for moral demands to be made on individual members, justifying giving priority to the nation over individual claims). Thus, Thomas Hurka argues for national partiality and loyalty on grounds of sharing a history of common enterprises in the collective production of valuable social goods. Jeff McMahan claims that fair play and gratitude can justify general nationalism. Kai Nielsen relies on a sense of common history and shared attachment to particular territory.[13]

Assume for the moment that some such moral arguments are correct, that fair play, or gratitude, or a need for a context of choice, or a need for recognition, justify moderate moral partiality to a group larger than oneself but smaller than humanity. The difficulty is that such arguments do not uniquely pick out the nation as the sole or primary object of that partiality and loyalty. They give no grounds for believing in the supremacy of the nation's claims. Instead, they justify MGC—loyalty to and partiality to all those groups to which one belongs that cooperatively produce valuable goods, that warrant gratitude, or that have a shared sense of history and shared attachment to a piece of land.

[11] By 'speciousness' I do not mean that Berlin is wrong to attribute the claim to nationalism, only that the claim itself is wrong.

[12] Anthony Smith, *National Identity* (Reno: University of Nevada Press, 1991), 74, emphasis added.

[13] Thomas Hurka, 'The Justification of National Partiality,' in Robert McKim and Jeff McMahan (eds.), *The Morality of Nationalism* (Oxford: Oxford University Press, 1997); Jeff McMahan, 'The Limits of National Partiality,' in ibid.; Kai Nielsen, 'Liberal Nationalism, Liberal Democracies, and Secession,' *University of Toronto Law Journal* 48 (1998), 253–95.

Yael Tamir's argument, which draws support for group attachments and loyalties from moderately individualistic premises, similarly justifies those attachments without marking out the nation as special. The groups to which such attachment is justified are those groups in which one finds oneself, those groups one can imagine joining, those in which one's loved ones find themselves, and those which one can imagine one's loved one's joining. Nothing in that argument distinguishes nation from ethnic group from language community from religion. So, if the moral argument is successful, it justifies moral consideration for all of those groups. It entirely fails to justify giving priority to one of them—even a moderate and conditional priority.

But this in turn means that Tamir's argument cannot support (2c). She has justified only a variant of MGC, a moderate moral concern for our constitutive identities and the groups that help define them. But an argument that nations should have political self-government depends on some differentiation of the nation from the other kinds of group that do that kind of thing.

Of all the claims set out above, (2c) most obviously requires that the nation be differentiated from and set above all other groups which might be the object of loyalty; it is in the demand for self-determination that the alleged priority of the nation over rival communities is made most explicit. (2c) claims that sovereignty and self-government ought to inhere in the nation, and as sovereignty is an exclusive concept, that means it cannot inhere in rival collectivities. (2a) and (2b) also require such differentiation, but in a more subtle way. After all, one might acknowledge a duty to die for one's nation (in appropriate circumstances) without forswearing a duty to die for one's faith (in appropriate circumstances). One might be partial to fellow nationals as compared with aliens, and also be partial to coreligionists as compared with nonbelievers. Perhaps the more such identities one shares with another, the more partial one ought to be toward that person. This is a coherent (and, to many, intuitively appealing) idea about the nature of our obligations.

So far, however, it is again nothing more than MGC; it is not nationalism. MGC says that one has obligations of various kinds to communities which are larger than oneself but smaller than the world. One ought to give preference to the needs of fellow members against the needs of generalized humanity, and against one's own individual needs. But nationalism does not only claim priority for the nation against the world and against the individual; it also claims priority against all other collectivities. The nation's needs have priority not only over the individual's, but also over the ethnic group's or the church's. Fellow nationals have priority not only over strangers, but also over co-religionists, co-linguists, or fellow citizens of an existing multinational state who are not co-nationals.

For it to be generally morally true that national communities have this kind of priority over all other communities, that national identities have priority over other kinds of identity, there must be something morally distinctive about nations as such. Here we run into the problem of trying to generalize normative claim (1). For nations as such to have a distinctive moral character, nations as such must presumably share some trait or traits with each other which they do not share with other collectivities. That is, an argument for claim (2) as a universal claim must identify something which all nations and only nations have in common, something besides that they are the proper objects of the loyalty described in claim (2) itself. But if there is no general empirical attribute which marks out real nations as distinct from other communities, if 'X is your nation' is always a normative rather than an empirical statement, then how can *every* person's obligation to his or her nation be grounded?

But that is exactly what one needs to be able to do if claim (2) is to be coherent as a generalizable moral claim. And the generalizability of claim (2) is crucial for universalistic nationalism, the position that we *all* ought to be nationalists, that every nation and every state ought to be a nation-state, that everyone ought to be loyal to his or her nation and partial to his or her fellow nationals.

Claim (1) must in a sense be empirical rather than normative for claim (2) to be generalizable. For claim (2) to be generalizable, every person must be able to give a unique and determinate answer to the question 'What is my nation?' I cannot owe the kind of loyalty demanded by claim (2) to multiple communities simultaneously.

If the question 'What collectivity is my nation?' admitted of a unique, determinate, empirical answer for each of us, if 'nation' were an *is* word rather than an *ought* word, then universalistic nationalism could be credible. If, say, nations were defined exclusively by language, then one could (at least in principle, leaving aside the complications of multilingual communities) simply find out the native languages of persons or communities and know their national identities. But if some nations can be constituted linguistically, some politically, some ethnically, and so on, then claim (2) legitimizes incompatible demands of supreme loyalty. I might have a supreme political duty to Quebec *and* to Canada, to Kurdistan *and* to Turkey. As noted above, such a situation is particularly absurd since the choices being faced in conflicts over national identity and obligation are precisely *between* Canada and Quebec, Kurdistan and Turkey.

Rogers Brubaker has persuasively argued that even the social reality of nationalism should not lead us to treat the 'analytically dubious notion of "nations" as substantial, enduring collectivities.'[14] Nationness, Brubaker says, is something that *happens* in discrete ways at identifiable times, 'something that suddenly crystallizes rather than gradually develops.'[15] The Serbian republic turns into a nationalizing state and generates Serbian nationness. There is nothing to be gained and much to be confused by supposing that there was always, really, an underlying Serb nation waiting to express itself. This is perhaps the most promising way of dealing with what social scientists of nationalism have long known: the category 'nation' used by nationalists does not reliably correspond with any empirical criterion or set of criteria in the world. Nations are defined by statehood, or by language, or by religion, or by ethnicity, or by whichever other line of demarcation was locally important in helping a group to feel like a politicized 'us' and not part of 'them.' But if this is true, then claim (1) cannot be empirical; and as a normative claim it cannot be generalized. For claim (1) to be generalizable, it has to be able to tell each person what his or her nation is, without conflicts or inconsistencies.

If one is willing to say that *all* nations should be marked off in the same way that *this* nation is marked off—e.g. that all nations should be linguistically defined—then the position does appear universalizable at the cost of empirical plausibility. Universalized linguistic nationalism requires thinking that all Spanish-speaking countries should be viewed as one nation, as should all English-speaking countries and all Arabic-speaking countries, but that India should be thought of as dozens of nations. Religion marks some nations and nationalisms apart from their neighbors, as in the former Yugoslavia, but is obviously ineligible as a general criterion.

Of course, there are often good reasons for ethnic advocates not to suggest generalizing the criterion they use to demarcate their own group. Defenders of the position that there ought to be an ethnically defined Kurdish state, or a religiously/ethnically defined Jewish state, should still be nervous about saying that the rump Turkish state, or the world's Christian and Muslim states, ought to abandon whatever civic orientation they might have and define membership along the relevant ethnic or religious–ethnic lines. There are and would remain Kurdish and Jewish minorities in those states, minorities that could only stand to lose from the ethnicization of citizenship. Similarly, if Quebec secedes from Canada on the theory that nations are defined by language, that

---

[14] Brubaker, *Nationalism Reframed*, 21.   [15] *Ibid.* 19.

bodes ill for the Francophone minorities in the rest of Canada (now reunderstood as *Anglophone* Canada).

If, by contrast, the claim is made that *we* ought to have an ethnic nation state but *you* should retain or increase the civic orientation of *your* nation, then the position is no longer a universalistic one. In recognition of this, nationalists often argue that existing nations are really already defined along the relevant ethnic divide, even if under civic coloration—and they are sometimes right. Thus Zionists argued that Jews were not genuinely accepted by any of the nations of Europe, that those nations already defined Jews out of membership; and Kurdish nationalists say that the Anatolian state is in reality as well as in name already a *Turkish* state. Still, this is some distance from a generalizable rule about how nations ought to be demarcated.

One possible solution to this problem, one reminiscent of Renan's 'daily plebiscite,' is to posit that a nation just is a social collectivity whose members feel themselves to be a nation. Language, religion, shared statehood, and the rest are neither necessary nor sufficient; it is the sentiment of a nation's members that marks off a nation, and that sentiment can be sparked by any or all of these traits, or by something else entirely. Thus Tamir suggests that 'Only one factor is necessary, although not sufficient, for a group to be defined as a nation—the existence of national consciousness.'[16] This is the most analytically and empirically plausible kind of answer to the question 'What is a nation?'

However, it vitiates the possibility of a coherent argument about claim (1) in any particular case. When the nationalist says to me, 'You ought to view X as your nation' and I reply 'But I view Y as my nation,' the discussion must stop. By virtue of the fact that I think Y is my nation, it is. No room remains for the nationalist to say, 'But you are mistaken; X really *is* your nation.' I cannot be mistaken about which unit it is that I owe ultimate loyalty to, if the only defining characteristic of such a unit is that it is the one to which people think they owe ultimate loyalty. It won't do to make the nation actually plebiscitary, to say that whatever unit a majority of the people consider to be their nation *is* their nation, and that members of the minority are mistaken about their identity. Even if one holds with such Rousseaunian thinking in other contexts, 'majority' and 'minority' cannot be specified in advance of identifying the nation. (A majority of what or whom? Canadians or Quebecois, Turks or Kurds?)

The plebiscitary model jeopardizes moral arguments for claim (2) in the same way. It is difficult to ground moral duties on a unit the distinctive

---

[16] Tamir, *Liberal Nationalism*, 65.

character of which is that its members feel that it is the unit to which obligations are due. The plebiscitary nationalist must simultaneously say that what sets a nation apart from other communities is that its members feel themselves to owe duties to it and not to the others, *and* that those who feel themselves to owe loyalty to some other unit instead are mistaken.

The problem described with defining nations with reference to the feelings of their members applies even if such feeling is only one of several criteria. For David Miller the fact that a community is 'constituted by shared belief and mutual commitment' is only the first of five criteria; but that is enough to make his account vulnerable to the criticism described here. The other four criteria, such as connection to a particular territory, are all applicable to most or all of the rival claimants to the title of nation; Canada and Quebec both have distinct public cultures, connections to particular territory, and so on. All that can separate the valid from the invalid demand for national partiality and obligation is the shared beliefs criterion; and then persons' obligations are defined with reference by the feelings that they or their putative compatriots have about their loyalties.[17] Hence, as Paul Gilbert puts it, 'attempts to combine subjectivist with nonsubjectivist accounts seem bound to lead to disaster, for either it is, say, their belief that they share certain characteristics which constitutes people as a nation, or it is the shared characteristics themselves which do so; it cannot be both.'[18]

Here, then, is the knot which cannot be unraveled. Arguments for (2) gain their plausibility from the assumption that the problem of identifying the nation has already been solved, and sometimes from contrasting the nation only with the self and with humanity rather than with rival collectivities. Empirically plausible general arguments about (1) leave no room for the justification of (2).

Any argument for universalistic nationalism, as opposed to MGC, must make reference to some characteristic which nations share which other communities do not. Nations cannot be defined by a plurality of characteristics, since that would put some in the position of owing ultimate loyalty to two units simultaneously. Any credible candidate for the single characteristic which all nations and only nations share must be something like 'nations are those units which their members believe to be nations' or 'nations are those units to which their members believe

---

[17] David Miller, *On Nationality* (Oxford: Oxford University Press, 1995), 27.
[18] Gilbert, *The Philosophy of Nationalism*, 171.

they owe ultimate loyalty.' But if that is what nations are, then claim (1) becomes incoherent as a normative claim and, more importantly, there is no non-circular moral argument for claim (2).

It might be objected that this argument only has force when national identity is contested rather than clear, and that these are marginal cases. Perhaps it is true that the majority of persons in the world have neither doubt nor dispute about which nation they belong to. David Miller writes that

very often we find groups who are living side-by-side, who are largely descended from the same ancestors, who speak the same language, who share many of the same practices, and whose members think of themselves as having a common identity. Groups like that often acquire a shared national identity, and demand political autonomy, and when they do several kinds of considerations will converge to reinforce their claim. Now hypothetically we could imagine a world in which these features did not overlap, in which physical proximity and language, or language and culture, and so forth, were not connected, and in that hypothetical world we would have to ask ourselves why, for instance, the bare fact that a group of people speak the same language should give them any kind of right to their own state. But although it is contingent , it is not just accidental that in the real world group characteristics like those listed above tend to overlap, and the plausibility of nationalism, I suggest, depends in large measure on that fact.'[19]

No doubt. But precisely what these group characteristics do is *overlap;* they do not *coincide*. Geography, political history, language, religion, and so on all influence one another down through the ages. But in the here and now they leave us with overlapping, competitive claimants to the title 'nation,' and to the moral and political primacy over other communities that goes with that title. And the cases in which doubt or dispute exist are hardly marginal; they are both widespread and central to much theorizing and argument about nationalism. They are the cases in which we are most likely to find nationalist movements and sentiments. These movements and sentiments are not usually directed against the rival 'humanity' the rival 'individualism;' they are directed against some other community which also shares some of the group traits Miller mentions. If those traits stacked neatly on top of each other, nationalism would be easy—and also largely pointless, or at least invisible. But human communities migrate and intermingle, coming to live side-by-side with those with different ancestors; they share a history which then diverges because of a partial

---

[19] David Miller, review of Gilbert, *The Philosophy of Nationalism, Journal of Applied Philosophy* 16:2 (1999), 191–2.

conquest; they share a language but then divide on religious grounds; and so on. This is all contingent, perhaps, but it is none the less very commonly true. And so our understanding of the moral psychology of nationalism doesn't take us any closer to thinking it is a plausible normative principle. Those cases in which a particular nationalism would have normative work to do are precisely those in which there are overlapping but not coinciding communities each of which *might* be a nation—that is, those in which nationalism as a general principle can have nothing to say.

One reader has suggested that it is implausible to put much weight on the potential conflict of loyalties since the world is today characterized by all too many people with fanatical devotion to one and only one group identity.[20] It might seem that the most fanatical forms of nationalism are the least vulnerable to my argument, because for their adherents the problem of identity choice and conflicting loyalties does not arise. But even in situations of intense nationalistic conflict, there are many people struggling to choose between the rival communities. Many Quebecois have struggled between loyalty to Quebec and loyalty to Canada for a generation. David Laitin has documented and modeled the process of identity choice which Russian-speakers in newly independent Soviet republics experienced beginning in 1991.[21] In Yugoslavia, there was a time when, in standard nationalist consciousness-raising fashion, nationalist leaders like Tudjman were exhorting Yugoslavs to become (in this case) Croats. Certainly some always considered Serb or Croat to be their true national identity, but—especially in Bosnia-Herzegovina and among intermarried families—there also seems to have been considerable attachment to a Yugoslav identity, attachment which had to be overcome by Tudjman and his counterparts.[22] There are fanatics who are far too sure of their national identities, but they have to persuade, cajole, or coerce their putative fellow nationals to feel the same way. In any event, the normative theory of generalized nationalism can hardly be shored up by pointing to the fanatics.

---

[20] Jeff Spinner-Halev, in comments at the 1998 Annual Meeting of the American Political Science Association.

[21] David Laitin, *Identity in Formation: the Russian-Speaking Populations in the Near Abroad* (Ithaca, NY: Cornell University Press, 1998). Laitin's work is helpfully supplemented by Timur Kuran, 'Ethnic norms and their transformation through reputational cascades,' *Journal of Legal Studies* 27:2 (1998), 623–59.

[22] Bogdan Denitch, *Ethnic Nationalism : The Tragic Death of Yugoslavia* (Minneapolis: University of Minnesota Press, 1994); Russell Hardin, *One for All* (Princeton: Princeton University Press, 1995), ch. 6.

CIVIC AND ETHNIC NATIONALISM

It is often claimed that there is a significant moral distinction to be drawn between 'ethnic' and 'civic' nationalism, and that the latter is morally benign while the former is not. But the basic moral and normative claims of nationalism, and the puzzles those claims raise, do not differ between its ethnic and civic variants. What differs is the unit specified in (1). Claim (2) and its subclaims can be made more or less moderately, but there is no necessary correspondence between that moderation and the kind of unit specified in (1).

Civic nationalism could take one of two forms: morally laden civic nationalism, which makes national loyalty conditional on the justice of the state's political principles and practices, and state-nationalism, which stipulates that states are nations, and that the loyalty owed to nations is owed to states. These are sometimes confused but are quite different; it is, to simplify, the difference between, on the one hand, consent or adherence to common political principles as the principle of membership or citizenship and, on the other, and *jus soli*.

The former urges people to love their country only because, and to the degree that, it is just—liberal democratic, republican, social-democratic, or whatever the preferred conception of justice may be. Loyalty to one's fellow nationals is said to come from their shared adherence to political principles. This can have only a very dubious attachment to liberalism, for it has the necessary implication that dissent is a form of treason. The McCarthyist appellation 'un-American' relies on a purely civic idea of nationalism; to be an American is to hold a certain set of beliefs that are incompatible with (*inter alia*) Soviet Communism. As Bernard Yack puts it, 'Were Americans, for example, to make citizenship contingent upon commitment to political principles instead of the mere accident of birth (to citizen parents or on American territory), they might become considerably more suspicious of their fellow citizens' declarations of political loyalty. Birthright citizenship can promote toleration precisely by removing the question of communal membership from the realm of choice and contention about political principles.'[23]

In any event this variant of civic nationalism entirely fails to solve the problem of specifying the proper noun in claim (1). It must either assume the pre-existence of a nation of some kind ('Be loyal to America because and to the degree that it is just') or give advice of the form 'Be

[23] Bernard Yack, 'The Myth of the Civic Nation,' *Critical Review* 10:2 (1996), 193–211.

loyal to the nation that is the most just' or 'Be loyal to the nation that most accords with your conception of justice'—regardless of its distance or difference from the land of one's birth or current residence. This is a position which is never actually stated or advocated; no one suggests that borders be endlessly redrawn or that persons endlessly migrate around the world in response to changes in the relative justness of states or changes in which particular conception of justice is shared by which persons. When civic nationalism is invoked in order to justify nationalism of a particular unit on any grounds other than that it is the most just, the argument must rest on a tacit assumption that the problem of claim (1) has already been resolved. When, for example, civic nationalism is used as an argument against Quebecois secession, it begs the question. Granted that one only ought to be loyal to a just state and that one ought to share a concept of justice with one's fellow citizens, how do we know that *Canada* is the right unit in which to do those things, as opposed to either Quebec or North America? Civic nationalism on this understanding is really nothing but a set of constraints on claim (2), and much confusion results when it is thought of as a rival to more complete accounts of nationalism which include normative claims (1) and (2).

Maurizio Viroli takes Machiavelli to have been a prototypical republican patriot or civic nationalist;[24] but this leaves unexplained where Machiavelli discovered the idea of *Italy* to call for its unification. The pure civic nationalist should not have been a patriot of Italy until after the *Riorgimentiso* had already succeeded; he should only have been a patriot of (e.g.) the Florentine Republic. This is typical; civic nationalism is never *only* civic. Civic nationalism usually assumes some pre- or extra-political cultural nation to which people have an emotional attachment, and then puts a political gloss on it. 'Italy' or 'France' is presumed to exist; the civic nationalist then attributes some shared political doctrines, history, or destiny to that nation.

The move to shared political doctrines cannot, however, define the nation in the first place. What I have in common with my fellow nationals and not with the rest of the world can hardly ever be a set of political principles (unless political indoctrination in my nation has reached some terrifying new height). Any political principles which are broad enough and vague enough to command universal loyalty within a modern state are also so broad and vague as to cut across boundaries. Neither liberal democracy, the free market, social democracy, nor republicanism, nor even any particular conception of these concepts is

[24] Maurizio Viroli, *For Love of Country: An Essay on Patriotism and Nationalism* (Oxford: Oxford University Press, 1995).

the unique inheritance of any one state. If civic nationalism requires a culturally-defined pre-existing nation in order to make sense, then it cannot pose as a solution to the problems of such cultural nationalism.

The Gandhi–Nehru Indian National Congress tradition of Indian nationalism is sometimes taken to be exemplify civic nationalism in contrast with Hindu chauvinist nationalism of various kinds, today represented by the Bharatiya Janata Party (BJP). But, just as with Machiavelli's patriotism, Indian civic nationalism must depend on some previous identification of India. An India which is tolerant of internal diversity must still be an *India*. Nehru's *Discovery of India*, a reconstruction of a putatively always-Indian history, is thus of a piece with his nationalism; it is not a deviation from his views. 'The continuity of Indian culture' is a necessary premise; he argues that '[w]hatever the word we use, Indian or Hindi or Hindustai, for our cultural tradition, we see in the past that some inner urge towards synthesis, derived essentially from the Indian philosophic outlook, was the dominant feature of Indian cultural, even racial development.' Despite millennia of linguistic, religious, and political fragmentation, 'I think that at almost any time in recorded history an Indian would have felt more or less at home in any part of India, and would have felt as a stranger in any other country.'[25] If the BJP and its apologists stress the central roles of Hinduism and Hindi in that synthetic unity, so did Nehru. The difference lay in the latter's more liberal understanding of Hinduism, and in his belief that Islam did not disrupt the unity of India. But Nehru and Gandhi faced a project of political unification as well as of separation from the British Empire. Like Machiavelli and Mazzini, they insisted that there was some real underlying nation—defined in cultural terms—which ought to be unified in a single state.

Civic nationalism's other form goes to the opposite extreme, recommending to every person that he or she have nationalistic loyalty to the state in which he or she is a citizen. This nationalism abandons the object of claim (1) to the vagaries of history. The pure civic nationalist in 1988 Vilnius was a patriot of the Soviet Union; in 1992 she was a patriot of Lithuania. The civic nationalist in Charleston was a patriot of the United States in 1858, of the Confederacy in 1862, and of the United States again in 1866. The proper object of loyalty of Alsatians simply changed every time France or Germany regained control from the other. The moral justification for national obligation blurs into the moral justifications for obeying the law and for duties to the state. I share with

---

[25] Jawaharlal Nehru, *The Discovery of India* (New Delhi: Oxford University Press, 1985[1946]), 87, 76, 62.

my fellow citizens, as such and regardless of the boundaries of the state, a set of political, legal, and social institutions and structures. We therefore share a duty to make them work peacefully and efficiently.

One apparent virtue of this civic nationalism, or state-nationalism, is that it *does* seem to be universalizable. If state-nationalism offers a general rule for correctly identifying nations—that they are to be identified with currently existing states—then several of the problems I have noted seem to dissolve. The rule that everyone ought to be a nationalist for his or her own nation is universalizable, since every person (in principle though not in practice) is a citizen of some state, and no person need be a citizen of more than one state. Moreover, civic nationalism might be thought to have the added virtue of bolstering stability. Civic nationalism calls on citizens to increase their allegiances to their states as currently constituted, whereas ethnic nationalism typically demands border changes. Changing borders is, of course, a dangerous process to begin, one that does not necessarily end easily.

The first difficulty, however, is that universal state-nationalism does *not* put an end to demands for border changes. At best, it might an end to demands for secession. Civic nations can, however, be expansionist, irredentist, or militaristic. The second difficulty is that *pure* universal civic nationalism is utterly implausible, and that anything less only contributes to the problem noted above of a world with multiple criteria for identifying nations, i.e. the lack of a unique specification for which units are nations and which persons belong to them.

Universal state-nationalism is not in fact a position with many explicit defenders or advocates. This kind of civic nationalism is invoked mainly as a putative contrast to disapproved-of ethnic nationalism, not as a coherent stand-alone theory; and it often gains plausibility only by smuggling in morally laden civic nationalism. Sometimes years of living together in the same state can generate feelings of commonality sufficient to give rise to feelings of nationalism. Benedict Anderson points to the nationalism that arose among members of creole elites in Latin American colonies with help from the shared experiences of aspiring to a common local capital and being bound by common administrative boundaries. Renan argued that the shared political history surrounding and following the Revolution helped create a sentiment that bound Alsatians, Bretons, and Basques together with Parisians. Shared state schools and shared experiences in common armed services have sometimes been powerful forces for creating national sentiment.

But it is the common sentiment and sense of shared experience, not the common statehood, that mark off the nation. As Kai Nielsen puts it,

'All nationalisms are cultural nationalisms of one kind or another. There is no purely political conception of the nation, liberal or otherwise.'[26] When a shared political history has created the relevant common sentiments, state-nationalism may manifest and makes sense. Indeed, those shared sentiments might be expected to survive a change in sovereignty. At least some Alsatians under German rule did not transfer national loyalty to Germany but felt themselves to be conquered Frenchmen. It could hardly be otherwise; if the sentiments were so shallowly grounded that they could switch objects immediately upon a change in sovereignty, then they provide poor support for the demands of either nation. Conversely, when shared statehood has not generated any fellow-feeling, or enough to overcome the fellow-feeling generated by some smaller or crosscutting community, it makes little sense to think of the state as a nation.

State-nationalism tries to make use of the moral psychology and emotions of nationalism. It seeks to generate emotional attachments to *this* state, attachments that would make the state worth fighting for (and not merely worth obeying or paying taxes to), attachments that would give its citizens an identity as members of a shared society. But moving from the state as a convenient legal fiction, like a corporation, to the state as an imagined community, requires us to admit the possibility of rival imaginings. If we owe loyalty to the state not simply because it exists and provides certain services but because it is in some sense distinctly *ours*, then there might be other communities which are even more *ours*.

To invoke state-nationalism against the ethnic or cultural nationalism of a subset of the state, for example against a secessionist movement, thus gives rise to a paradox. Attachment to Canada or Turkey which is based on shared history, culture, traditions, and experiences (such as— that most powerful of shared state-national experiences—having fought wars) can be undermined by attachment to Quebec or Kurdistan based on other, possibly more intense or important, shared history, cultural, traditions, and experiences. The loyalty generated by the former attachments cannot be used as an argument against the latter. Abandoning the idea of such emotional attachments and grounding loyalty to existing states simply on prudential concerns (as Hobbes did) is to abandon

---

[26] Kai Nielsen, 'Cultural Nationalism, Neither Ethnic Nor Civic,' *The Philosophical Forum* 28 (1996–97), 42–52 at 50. To oversimplify the difference in our conclusions, Nielsen infers from this that incorrectly named ethnic nationalism is really no more baleful than we have traditionally thought civic nationalism to be. I infer rather that civic nationalism is no less baleful than we have traditionally thought nationalism in general to be.

nationalism, not to modify it into a 'civic' variant—and prudential calculations can go either way. The perfectly true prudential argument against secession—that state breakup is a messy and dangerous business, prone to turn violent—can sometimes be overridden by pointing to violence of the existing state against a minority, or the likelihood of interethnic violence later if the state is not divided now.

Civic nationalism at best can give an account of claim (1) or of claim (2), but not both. Any morally laden variant of civic nationalism, any theory that suggests that one ought to be loyal to one's nation because and to the extent that it is just, fails entirely to aid in the specification of nations. Such theories are indeed dependent on the prior identification of 'nations.' In turn, no theory that identifies nations with existing states can ground the kind of loyalty nationalism demands. We may owe to our extant states or to our fellow citizens of those states some duties regardless of the justness or the borders of those states; but we surely do not owe supreme loyalty to extant states as such. Any attempt to ground such loyalty turns state-nationalism into a cultural nationalism of some kind which, in turn, admits the possibility of rival cultural nationalisms.

In fairness, one contribution which civic nationalism perhaps *can* make—though it does nothing to solve the problem at hand—is to provide a morally preferable account of the nation's needs and interests which the loyal national is supposed to protect and advance. Recall:

2*a*. You ought to be willing to place the needs of your nation and of your co-nationals *above the needs of outsiders* . . .
2*b*. You ought to be willing to place the needs of your nation and of your co-nationals *above the needs of subsets of the nation* . . .

It is no doubt far better for members of a nation to understand their nation's needs as including the need to be virtuous, the need to be right, and the need to protect internal freedom than for them to understand it simply as the need to advance its own material and power interests. Viroli, describing the views of Richard Price, says that 'love of country means not only to give ourselves to her, but also to give her the best that human life can offer; that is, truth, virtue, and liberty.'[27] Yet Yack's criticism is still telling; we have grounds to worry that those whose love of country and love of moral rightness are too tightly wound together will treat moral disagreements as treason. And in any event, this virtuous civic nationalism still requires prior identification of the nation (or, as Viroli would have it, 'country'). It is a moral attitude toward a

---

[27] Viroli, *For Love of Country*, 98.

homeland that we already have, not an answer to the question of which community we should think of as our homeland.

David Miller has offered a compelling account of the ways in which shared statehood can sometimes generate a shared culture and sense of fellow-feeling in a way that makes plausible the claim of nationhood. In his description of the history of Scotland and England within Britain, he notes that even before the union of the kingdoms there were parallel histories and political arguments concerning the Reformation, the relationship of church and state, the idea of ancient and lost liberties, and a hostility toward Catholic foreign powers. After the union, Scots played central roles in the intellectual and political life of the United Kingdom, so that 'interwoven history . . . is not just a matter of the two peoples being locked together in the same state for several centuries, nor is it simply a question of the two peoples having impacted on one another's development . . . What I am pointing to is the active collaboration between members of both nations in determining the course of political change, and so in defining the historic identity of the whole.'[28]

Stories similar in kind can be told about Alsace and France, Catalonia and Castilian Spain, Quebec and Canada, possibly even post-Ottoman Kurdistan and Turkey. (Turkish nationalists, at any rate, make much of the common cause Kurds and Turks made against Armenians, against Ottoman rule, and against European domination of Anatolia.) Sometimes a common political history can generate a shared culture or identity in a way that creates a civic-cultural community which can make a plausible claim on its members' loyalty. But a common political history is not the *only* thing that can generate such loyalty; and as borders shift communities share parts of their political history with different fellow subjects or citizens. So the civic-cultural community is rarely the only community that can make a plausible claim to nationhood and final loyalty, and we return to the problem of having to choose between competing possible nations.

Miller thinks that in such cases the underlying true answer is that *both* communities are nations, that Scotland and Britain are 'nested nationalities.' And he argues that the proper political response is something like the settlement Scotland and Britain have reached—a self-governing Scotland within Britain. Secession wouldn't do justice to British nationhood, and assimilation wouldn't do justice to Scottish. This, Miller argues, allows us to maintain that there is a universalizable principle that nationhood carries with it a moral claim to self-government, a principle

---

[28] David Miller, 'Nationality in Divided Societies,' in *Citizenship and National Identity* (Cambridge: Polity Press, 2000).

which sometimes has to meet the legitimate demands of nested nation-alities. Moreover, it allows us to do so without thinking that there's a single objective marker of nationality and without falling into a completely subjectivist plebiscitary viewpoint.

There is no doubt much to be said for that sort of settlement, where it is available. Unfortunately, not all the communities which make plaus-ible claims to being nations are neatly nested. Scotland is wholly within Britain and Quebec is wholly within Canada, but the Basque country straddles the French–Spanish border and Kurdistan cuts across the borders of four states.[29]

UNIFYING AND DIVISIVE NATIONALISM

Many have tried to differentiate divisive nationalism from unifying nationalism (or, sometimes, unifying 'nationality'), a distinction that often corresponds to but is not identical with that between ethnic and civic nationalism. The Italian and German nationalisms of the nine-teenth century were certainly not civic—they demanded the abandon-ment of actually existing states in favor of ethno-linguistically defined nations—but they are the standardly-given cases of unifying rather than divisive nationalism.

In fact, no such distinction can hold up under scrutiny. When Bosnian Serbs seek to unify politically with the Serbian-Yugoslav state, they are divisive from the perspective of Bosnia but unifying from the perspective of Serbia. Whether this looks 'unifying' or 'divisive' depends on one's perspective, on the unit that's already assumed to be the genuine nation. Proponents of unifying nationalism often speak of the need to emphasize 'what we have in common rather than our differences;' this is parasitic on a pre-existing definition of the relevant 'we,' that is, on assuming claim (1) to be a settled empirical matter rather than a disputed norm-ative one. If we have already defined the Bosnian state as a nation, if we have defined the nationality of the Bosnian Serbs as 'Bosnian,' then the they are emphasizing their differences from their co-nationals and are

[29] While Turkish and Kurdish-Turkish might be nested nationalities, I don't think the same is true for Iranian and Kurdish or Iraqi and Kurdish. The Iraqi and Iranian states have no plausible claim to Kurdish national loyalty. But still, Turkish and Kurdish are not nested identities, since Turkey has no plausible claim on Iraqi, Iranian, or Syrian Kurds. A Scottish solution—a self-governing Kurdish region in Turkey—would leave the putative nation Kurdistan split between different states, a problem not faced by Scotland, Quebec, or Catalonia.

trying to divide their nation. If we have already defined Bosnian Serbs' nationality as 'Serbian,' on the other hand, then they are seeking to overcome the petty political division which separates them from their fellow nationals; they are seeking national unity just as much as the nineteenth-century Italians and Germans did. If I am right that (2*a*) and (2*b*) are both constitutive of nationalism, then this dualism is inevitable. Nationalism seeks to unify the nation and to divide it from other nations, from other communities.

'[N]ationalism was originally a force for unification in Europe,' writes Benjamin Barber, 'bringing together rival clans and tribes under the figment of a larger territorial nation bound together by language and culture if not blood and kinship. But having won its victories of integration, nationalism changed its strategy, becoming a divisive force in the territories it once helped tie together.'[30] Even leaving aside the curious anthropomorphizing of nationalism ('changed its strategy'?) this comment falls into precisely the error I am describing. Nationalism was never simply a unifying force, and it is not simply a divisive force today. Even in its most republican moment, in 1848, the movement to unify Germany distinguished Germans from Poles in a way that the Prussian monarchy felt little need to. French nationalism divided French Basques from their Spanish fellows, and unifying Italian nationalism ultimately succeeded in dividing South from North Tyrolians. Croatian and Serbian nationalism in the 1990s, standard examples of divisive nationalism, sought to unite all the Croats and all the Serbs, respectively, in whatever republics they lived—just what nineteenth-century Italian and German nationalism had sought.

To put the point in terms which are closer to home: making an appeal to Americans to emphasize their commonalities rather than their differences—as is done by the nationalist critics of multiculturalism such as Michael Lind and Arthur Schlesinger[31]—necessarily emphasizes both what differentiates Americans from, say, Canadians as well as what divides e.g. American Catholics or Jews from their coreligionists around the world. Set aside for the moment the danger of overriding morally legitimate identification with groups smaller than and contained within the state. That is, after all, exactly what the anti-multiculturalist nationalist intends to do and he will scarcely count it as a criticism that he does

---

[30] Benjamin Barber, 'Muticulturalism Between Individuality and Community: Chasm or Bridge?' in D. Villa and A. Sarat (eds.), *Liberal Modernism and Democratic Individuality: George Kateb and the Practices of Politics* (Princeton: Princeton University Press, 1996), 138.

[31] Michael Lind, *The Next American Nation* (New York: Free Press, 1995); Arthur Schlesinger, Jr., *The Disuniting of America* (New York: W.W. Norton, 1990).

it. Uniting American to American is inextricably tied to dividing (or at least differentiating) American from Canadian and American Jew from Israeli Jew.

It so happens that right now there is little enough danger in either of these sets of divisions. There is no likelihood of war between the United States and Canada, and the gaps between American Catholics or Jews and their brethren elsewhere are large regardless of American multiculturalism or nationalism. But the United States simply happens to be fortunate in those regards. In many places at many times, emphasizing the supposed unity of one group, and thereby its differences with neighboring or overlapping groups, is dangerously inflammatory. But this is not to say that American nationalism is not divisive and these others are; American nationalism, like all nationalism, seeks or emphasizes the unity of the nation and its differentiation from the rest of humanity.

Craig Calhoun nicely summarizes the relationship between unifying and divisive nationalism. 'If segmentary kinship urges—in the words of an Arab proverb . . .—'I against my brothers, I and my brothers against my cousins, I, my brothers, and my cousins against the world,' the point of nationalism is largely to say: 'never you against your brothers, nor you and your brothers against your cousins; only members of our national family against the world.'[32] *We* are now united, but we are united because of the absolute priority given to the distinction between *us* and all others.

Something which *is* true of the unifying face of nationalism is that it is characteristically democratic and in some sense egalitarian, however illiberal it may be in the suppression of smaller communities which might compete for the loyalty of members. All nationals are equal members of the nation, and all jointly rule it (or it is ruled in their name and on their behalf). Claim (2*b*), which demands the unity of the nation and its priority over smaller communities, is tied up with a nationalist hostility to ranks and distinctions among nationals which might set the latter against each other. As Mazzini put it, 'There is no true Country without a uniform right. There is no true Country where the uniformity of that right is violated by the existence of caste, privilege, and inequality.'[33] This is something which many democrats have long found appealing in nationalism.

The dualism between egalitarian unity among members and division from the rest of humanity is characteristic of nationalism but not unique

---

[32] Craig Calhoun, *Nationalism* (Minneapolis: The Open University Press, 1998), 39.

[33] Giuseppe Mazzini, 'The Duties of Man,' in Omar Dahbour and Micheline Ishay, *The Nationalist Reader* (Atlantic Highlands, NJ: Humanities Press International, 1995), 95.

to it. Christian thinkers have long emphasized the unity of brotherhood in Christ and the equality before God of all believers. Believers might live in different states or speak different languages, but what unites them is said to have priority over such divisions. By no means have all Christians drawn democratic or egalitarian inferences for life in this world, but many have. Much the same is true for Islam.

Yet this attractive egalitarian unity always comes at the cost of divisiveness of another kind. A renewed emphasis on the unity and priority of Christianity (or Islam) would be a divisive influence in Lebanon or Bosnia—or, for that matter, in the United States. It would stand in direct competition with other identities and loyalties, most prominently that of the state. The priority of a religious community is precisely the kind of claim that makes civic nationalists like Lind fear for the splintering and collapse of a civic nation. The egalitarian unity of one group, if combined with any kind of claim of priority, is divisive from the perspective of all other groups and loyalties.

THE NATIONAL RIGHT OF SELF-DETERMINATION

Even if there can be no general duty of national loyalty, can there be a general right of national self-determination? A version of (2c) might stand alone, and without reference to duties of members of the nation:

2c. Nations have the right to self-government and self-determination, to unity and independence, and if a nation chooses to exercise this right, outsiders have a duty to respect that exercise.

Here members of a nation are under no obligation to place loyalty to it above loyalty to all other groups, and indeed they are under no obligation to seek national self-determination at all. The only duties involved are the duties involved in any exercise of rights, namely, non-interference and, under some conditions, assistance in repelling the interference of others.

Dispensing with (2a) and (2b), however, does not dispense with the need for (1), the need for identifying the nation. For (2c) to stand alone, 'nation' and 'outsiders' must already be specified. But it is no easier for outsiders to decide which rival unit claiming the right of self-determination is a nation and which is not than it is for putative members. Indeed, whenever there are two or more communities both claiming the title of nation and the right of self-determination, there are some who cannot know whether they are members or outsiders until the question of national identity is resolved. Are non-Quebecois outsiders to the nation of Quebec who must respect whatever decision Quebec reaches, or members of the nation of Canada (which includes Quebec) who can take full part in any decision on its future? Even more pointedly, are Anglophone and indigenous residents of the province of Quebec members of the Quebecois nation or outsiders who must respect the nation's decision?

Arguments for (2c), for self-determination without nationalist obligations, vary but are similar in kind. People are better off if their states are national, either directly—e.g. because the state institutions will be more comprehensible to them, they will be better able to take part in democratic processes, etc.—or indirectly, because their respective national cultures will be more secure, or will be lived and expressed in the public sphere.[34]

Such arguments seem plausible in cases in which there is a clear disjuncture between *our* national culture and *their* alien state. Tamir invokes Dutch rule over Indonesia, which (she says, quoting Clifford Geertz) made the institutions of law and state opaque to their subjects. Colonial situations, including the situations of indigenous peoples in settler states like the United States and Australia, offer this sort of stark contrast. But often we are not faced with such stark contrasts. Was the Czechoslovak state inaccessible to Slovaks? Is British law opaque to the Scots or the Welsh? There are overlapping and crosscutting communities to which people belong, but political self-determination can only be the right of one of them at a time. Croatian culture was not imperiled in the state of the South Slavs. If Breton culture is not much lived and expressed in the public sphere, then French culture is, to which today's Bretons also belong. The standard arguments for a universal right of national self-determination all suppose that the choice is between national states and states which are hopelessly alien to the national minorities. But real nationalist conflict, at least after the age of colonialism, is often between neighbors who share much culture and history

---

[34] See Tamir, *Liberal Nationalism*, ch. 3; Joseph Raz and Avishai Margalit, 'National Self-Determination,' in Raz, *Ethics in the Public Domain* (Oxford: Oxford University Press, 1994); Nielsen, 'Liberal Nationalism, Liberal Democracies, and Secession,' 253–95; Miller, *On Nationality*, ch. 4; Simon Caney, 'Self-Government and Secession: The Case of Nations,' *Journal of Political Philosophy* 5 (1997), 351–72. Caney's essay is admirable in its clarity on this point. '(P1) Political institutions that further people's well-being are pro tanto valuable. (P2) An individual's membership of a nation furthers his or her well-being. (P3) A nation-state can best further a nation's culture. Therefore: (C) National self-determination is, ceteris paribus, valuable' (361). My argument disputes both (P2) and (P3)—or, rather, it suggests that they both take for granted the existence of a unique and uncontroversial nation.

but differ in religion, or in speaking mutually intelligible but distinct languages or dialects, or in ancestral but not currently spoken language. In short, disputes about self-determination are often not between a clearly defined nation and a clearly non-national state, but between a state and a non-state community, both of which have some of the characteristics of nationhood. In these cases at least, secession cannot be justified with a general argument about the goods that can only be attained when states are national. Neither can resistance to secession be justified with simple reference to national unity; arguments must proceed either in instrumental terms or with specific reference to the attachments members have to the rival communities in the case at hand.[35]

Nothing I have said here affects arguments for self-determination or secession as *remedial* rights, or indeed on arguments for the morality of secession in general. There are perfectly generalizable instrumental arguments for secession, such as that secession is justifiable when and only when the existing state treats the seceding minority unjustly in certain specified ways and the seceding group offers suitable guarantees that it will not do the same to the local minorities on its territory.[36] My critique only touches on arguments that nations as such have an intrinsic right of self-determination, that all nations and only nations have an inherent right to self-government. Moreover, nothing I have said here tells against nationalist secession any more than it counts against the suppression of secession in the name of national unity. My criticism is of the idea that nationhood *per se* can provide the moral grounding for much by way of political obligations or rights.

Indeed, I think that everything I say here is compatible with Margaret Canovan's view that, for all the philosophical and conceptual chaos associated with the idea of the nation, a shared belief in nationhood and in states being national is critically important, maybe necessary, for decent and stable polities.[37] Her argument goes farther than the more common (and, I think, correct) one that social democracy and advanced welfare states need the sort of fellow-feeling generated by nationalism in order to be politically stable. She suggests that the same sense of nationhood is

---

[35] I think this is similar in spirit to Douglas Lackey's conclusion that *even if* nations have a right to self-determination, neither national secession nor opposition to secession in the name of national unity justifies the use of force, in the absence of other considerations. Lackey, 'Self-Determination and Just War,' *The Philosophical Forum* 28 (1996–7), 100–10.

[36] See Allen Buchanan, *Secession: The Morality of Political Divorce from Fort Sumpter to Lithuania and Quebec* (Boulder, Colo.: Westview Press, 1991).

[37] Margaret Canovan, *Nationhood and Political Theory* (Cheltenham: Edward Elgar, 1996).

necessary even for the classical liberal rule of law, or for basic political stability and non-violent democratic politics. But she recognizes that such belief is itself politically generated and has a mythic component to it; she denies that it's based on any pre-existing truth about nationhood; and she explicitly acknowledges that this political good—nationhood— is probably not available to all simultaneously. Those not fortunate enough already to have a shared history and consensus about which unit is appropriately considered the nation may not be able to join the stable nationhood club. Shared belief contributes to shared history, and vice versa, but when two or more communities are competing to be thought of as a nation, there's no way to get the virtuous cycle started. This may not be an anti-nationalist view, but it is a long way from the vision of Mazzini and Wilson. Canovan is openly grim about what she thinks follows from her account, and my argument here suggests that she's right to be. Since those cases in which a shared sense of nationhood would be the most helpful are those in which it is least available, and since neither side in a dispute over which community is rightly under- stood as a nation has the right answer (there is no underlying right answer), nationhood's sometime usefulness offers no grounds for opti- mism.

4

Pluralism, Diversity, and Preserving
Cultural Communities

CULTURAL PLURALISM AND MORAL PLURALISM

It is this condition, in which society intimates a diversity of possibly incommensurable values and worldviews, which is often characterized as cultural pluralism, which I believe ought to be at the top of the agenda of modern states.[1]

In the last chapter I argued that a political theory regarding multiculturalism and nationalism should be centrally concerned with the political evils that go with a world of ethnic pluralism. In this chapter and the next, I engage with arguments that our moral and political thought should be more focused on the cultural communities themselves. In this chapter I examine the idea that different cultures embody rival and incommensurable moral views, making cultural pluralism the embodiment of moral pluralism. In the next chapter I turn to generalized arguments for loyalty to and the preservation of nations or cultural communities as such.

Some of the most prominent contemporary philosophers who analyze issues of nationalism and multiculturalism, those who are most sympathetic to the cultural variety in the world, have also been advocates of the position in moral philosophy known as moral or value pluralism. Isaiah Berlin is the most prominent of these, but thinkers as different from Berlin as Joseph Raz, Michael Walzer, and Charles Taylor have all suggested that the phenomenon of cultural pluralism is closely related to this plurality in the realm of ideals and morality.[2] Others who

---

[1] John Gray, 'The Politics of Cultural Diversity,' in *Post-Liberalism: Studies in Political Thought*, London: Routledge, 1993.

[2] For Joseph Raz, see *The Morality of Freedom* (Oxford: Oxford University Press, 1986), chs. 13–15; 'Liberalism, Scepticism, and Democracy,' 'Facing Diversity,' 'National Self-Determination,' and 'Multiculturalism: A Liberal Perspective,' in *Ethics in the Public Domain* (Oxford: Oxford University Press, 1994); 'Moral Change and Social Relativism,' in Paul, Miller, and Paul (eds.), *Cultural Pluralism and Moral Knowledge*

have endorsed or elaborated this linkage include Avishai Margalit, Moshe Habertal, James Tully, and, perhaps most explicitly and insistently, John Gray.[3] While policymakers and political scientists do not use quite the same language as moral philosophers, I think that Samuel Huntington's 'Clash of Civilizations' thesis as well as the 'Asian values' argument put forward but some leaders of East and Southeast Asian countries also identify moral and cultural pluralism.[4]

There is something tempting about this linkage; but it is too tempting. Whatever the truth of moral pluralism, cultural diversity is not its march through the world; and viewing the various social and moral conflicts to which cultural pluralism gives through the lens of moral pluralism confuses rather than clarifying. The identification of moral and cultural pluralism misunderstands both; the identification of moral and political conflict does so to an even greater degree.

(Cambridge: Cambridge University Press, 1994); and 'Value Incommensurability: Some Preliminaries,' *Proceedings of the Aristotelian Society* 166 (1985–6), 117–34. For Charles Taylor see *Reconciling the Solitudes: Essays on Canadian Federalism and Nationalism*, ed. Guy Laforest (Montreal: McGill-Queens University Press, 1993); 'Multiculturalism' and 'The Importance of Herder' in *Philosophical Arguments* (Cambridge, Mass.: Harvard University Press, 1997); 'Leading a Life' in Ruth Chang (ed.), *Incommensurability, Incomparability, and Practical Reason* (Cambridge, Mass.: Harvard University Press, 1997); 'Nationalism and Modernity,' in Robert McKim and Jeff McMahan (eds.), *The Morality of Nationalism* (Oxford: Oxford University Press, 1997); and 'The Diversity of Social Goods' in *Philosophy and the Human Sciences* (Cambridge: Cambridge University Press, 1985). For Michael Walzer, see *Spheres of Justice* (New York: Basic Books, 1983); *Thick and Thin* (Notre Dame: University of Notre Dame Press, 1993); and *On Toleration* (New Haven: Yale University Press, 1997). For Isaiah Berlin, see 'The Pursuit of the Ideal,' 'The Decline of Utopian Ideas in the West,' 'Alleged Relativism in Eighteenth-Century European Thought,' 'European Unity and its Vicisssitudes,' 'The Apotheosis of the Romantic Will,' and 'The Bent Twig' in *The Crooked Timber of Humanity* (New York: Vintage Books, 1992); 'Montesquieu' and 'Nationalism: Past Neglect and Present Power,' in *Against The Current* (New York: Viking Press, 1980); 'Rabindranath Tagore and the Consciousness of Nationality,' in *The Sense of Reality* (New York: Farrar, Straus and Giroux, 1996); 'My Intellectual Path,' *The New York Review of Books* 14 May, 1998, 53–60; *Vico and Herder* (London: Hogarth Press, 1976); and *The Magus of the North* (New York: Farrar, Straus, and Giroux, 1993).

[3] See Auishai Margalit, *The Decent Society* (Cambridge, Mass.: Harvard University Press, 1996), and 'The Moral Psychology of Nationalism,' in Robert McKim and Jeff McMahan (eds.), *The Morality of Nationalism* (Oxford: Oxford University Press, 1997); Margalit and Moshe Habertal, 'Liberalism and the Right to Culture,' *Social Research* 61:3 (1994), 491–510; James Tully, *Strange Multiplicities: Constitutionalism in an Age of Diversity* (Cambridge: Cambridge University Press, 1996); and John Gray, *Isaiah Berlin* (Princeton: Princeton University Press, 1996), 'From Post-Liberalism to Pluralism' in Russell Hardin and Ian Shapiro (eds.), *NOMOS XXXLVIII: Political Order* (New York: New York University Press, 1996); and 'After the New Liberalism,' *Social Research* 61:3 (1994), 719–35.

[4] See Samuel Huntingon, *The Clash of Civilizations and the Remaking of World Order* (New York: Simon & Shuster, 1996).

Moral pluralism is the claim that the fundamental goods of human life, the great moral values, are plural, unrankable, incommensurable, and often incompatible. We are often forced to make tragic, agonistic choices among them, not only because of flawed or unjust circumstances but in the very nature of things, in the nature of the goods, values, and ideals themselves.

This is not a form of moral relativism; for the pluralist thesis to be coherent, it must rest on moral realism. (Some have argued that it is not coherent and that it ultimately collapses into relativism, but that is a separate claim.) The incommensurability of the great goods does not disparage the difference between good and evil (or between goods and evils). We may not be able to rationally decide between liberty and equality, but trading off liberty without any gain in equality is simply a moral loss. Liberty and equality may be incommensurable, but liberty and slavery are not.

The incommensurability of (some) values, the lack of any single metric by which we can measure them, is arguably the most distinctive part of the value pluralism thesis, and is sometimes used as shorthand for the whole. But incommensurability, unrankability, and mutual exclusivity are all important parts of the picture of the moral world painted by the pluralists. Incompatibility, the idea that the great goods collide with one another, is what gives incommensurability its bite. If moral values didn't come into conflict, if there were never a need to choose among them, then the lack of a common scale, the inability to rationally compare them, would be a curiosity at most.

Michael Walzer's *Spheres of Justice*, for instance, rests on a plurality of standards of justice but does not suggest the need for irresolvable conflict or agonistic choice among them. Walzer offers us principles of adjudication, methods of morally sorting out which principle of distribution to live by when. In Walzer's work as a whole I think there are two such principles, complex equality and shared understandings, and it is an interesting question which of them has priority. Perhaps complex equality is the just formal relationship among spheres and principles of distribution, which must be given content in each specific cultural context; or perhaps justice consists of what each people thinks it consists of, and we, here and now, think that it consists of complex equality. Sometimes Walzer seems to think both of these things, and indeed there's no necessary conflict between them if each culture has a complex-equality story underlying its local conception of justice.

In any event, these two principles are meant to tell us how to handle the plurality of principles of distribution. Merit, need, equality, and market are incompatible (and, perhaps, incommensurable) moral criteria for distribution, but they do not come into agonistic conflict because complex equality and shared understandings in principle tell us the just way to incorporate each in its place. This does not, of course, mean that the shared understandings are easy to identify or that complex equality is easy to define; but our moral problems are at least in principle soluble in a way that they are often not in pluralistic theories, because for Walzer the pluralism does not take place at the foundational level.

This illustrates the need to specify the level of morality at which pluralism operates. Discussions of value pluralism often suffer from over-generality. Pluralism might describe only a portion of the moral universe. It might describe the relationship among virtues (philosophic introspection, martial valor, devotion to family), among political ideals (liberty, equality, community), or among moral systems (utilitarianism, Kantian deontology, perfectionist virtue-promotion). A persuasive argument that pluralism describes one such cluster does not show that it describes another, much less that it describes the whole of morality.

Pluralism would not mean quite the same thing at all these levels. Sometimes we are faced with trade-offs of a rather mundane kind rather than wholesale incompatibility. Trade-offs allow the possibility of having some of each good. They are sensitive to diminishing marginal returns, and accept that it is better to have some of both than all of one and none of the other. The political ideals seem to be of this sort. There are not mutually exclusive unitary bundles of 'liberty,' 'equality,' and 'community;' there are trade-offs and balances struck in different ways at different times and by different political systems. Even if these three goods are somehow equally fundamental and final, we—as individuals, cultures, or states—simply do not face the need for an agonistic and radical choice among them. If the list lengthens—to include, say, peace, order, and material well-being—then the trade-offs may get more complicated, but the underlying logic does not change.

At this step we have already disposed of crude but common versions of the Asian values thesis, which maintain that western countries have opted for liberty while east Asian countries have chosen community and order. None of the western democracies is in a state of anarchy; and outside of North Korea, the east Asian states are at least partly free. Switzerland is not only more orderly than the United States; it is also more orderly than the Philippines. Belgium is not only more orderly than China; it is also freer.

It was arguably Herder who first linked ethnic and moral pluralism, and he was concerned with the nations of Europe, especially France and Germany. Today it would be difficult to suggest that French and German culture embody rival moral principles. The moral gap between

Nazi Germany and today's Federal Republic, or between the Vichy regime and the Fifth Republic, is far greater than that between the Federal and Fifth Republics. The moral diversity within cultures far exceeds the moral gaps between them.

Indeed, the thesis of the importance of culture to individual identity is in tension with the notion that cultures are the units that make the radical moral choices whose necessity is posited by value pluralism. Cultures, traditions, and civilizations are complex, and contain within themselves enough resources to present themselves as the universes within which persons can live their lives. That very complexity is what allows us (each of us living within a culture) to appreciate the difficulty of choosing between, say, liberty and equality, to recognize what seems to be tragic about the choice, for it to be comprehensible to talk about there *being* a choice.

The level of value pluralism concerned with excellences seems better-suited to a link with cultural pluralism than does that concerned with political ideals. It might be that excellence in poetry, in philosophy, in political leadership, and in family life are all great goods but that trade-offs are an inappropriate way to make decisions among them, because virtues in one of these fields (a philosopher's determination to wait and deliberate for a true answer) are vices in another (a political leader's inability to act decisively because he or she is 'still thinking'). Most people believe that there are conflicts like this (even if they believe that they are rationally resolvable, e.g. they think that it is right for everyone to put family ahead of poetry).

In his essay on Berlin's understanding of nationalism, Margalit writes 'The idea is that people make use of different styles to express their humanity. The styles are generally determined by the forms of life to which they belong. There are people who express themselves "Frenchly," while others have forms of life that are expressed "Koreanly" or "Syrianly" or "Icelandicly." ' He then analogizes leading a life to painting, an activity that can be done in any one of a number of styles or schools, or eclectically, drawing on all schools but belonging to none.[5]

But even if whole cultures face these kinds of choices—rather than just individuals—this does not seem to rise to the level of great moral conflict. Often it would lead to ethnic divisions of labor due to special-izations and comparative advantage—that is, assuming that one group's members wants to read some poetry even though they rarely write it, and the other group's members want to watch professional sports even

---

[5] Margalit, 'The Moral Psychology of Nationalism,' 84.

though they do not play them. Even if not, there seems to be little reason why different groups valuing different values and customs cannot tolerate one another and peacefully coexist.

For cultural pluralism to be importantly related to moral pluralism and moral conflict, these incompatible excellences would have to be deeply tied up with moral systems. Alasdair MacIntyre suggests that this is true—that, for example, the ancient Greek philosophical system was tied up with martial virtue, and is now incomprehensible to those of us who do not understand ancient heroism. There are rival moral universes, made up of practices and habits, values and virtues, which only make sense as wholes.[6] This, to say the least, is something far removed from what Berlin had in mind.

Contrast this view with that of Yael Tamir. For all of Berlin's influence on her, Tamir actually doesn't endorse this marriage of moral and cultural pluralism. Her value pluralism operates at a different level: liberalism and nationalism are equally fundamental principles, both of which must be satisfied in a just world, neither of which has priority over the other. But even nationalism is a universal principle, the needs it satisfies are universal needs. The nations of the world do not embody different moralities.[7]

The equation of moral and cultural pluralism, of moral and ethnic conflict, also misunderstands a great deal about ethnic diversity. Professing to describe the views of Berlin and Raz, Gray argues that 'when rivalrous values are embodied in mutually exclusive cultures, their incompatibility cannot be other than agonistic. The relations of cultures constituted by uncombinable values will be competitive, even when their formal relationship is one of peaceful coexistence. When they share, or overlap, the same territory, their relations will often be ones of enmity.'[8]

But such deep moral differences are by no means necessary for ethnic enmity. Just as conflict over material goods can easily arise—indeed, may arise most easily—between people with similar motivations, so can ethnic conflict arise among groups with similarly motivated but incompatible aspirations. Speakers of different languages, for instance, may all want to be able to live, work, socialize, and educate their children in their own respective languages, but it may not be possible for all of them

[6] See Alasdair MacIntyre, *After Virtue* (Notre Dame: University of Notre Dame Press, 1984).

[7] In Ch. 3 I will argue that Tamir's universalistic nationalism does not succeed, that she is forced into a moderate generalized communitarianism without room for any special status for nations. But that criticism is independent of the current point.

[8] Gray, *Isaiah Berlin*, 113.

to do so, especially not if they live intermixed with one another. Common attempts to link languages with underlying values notwithstanding (one language is emotional and passionate, another practical and commercial, a third subtle and philosophical), such linguistic competitions do not require a plurality of values or motivations. They require only diversity, and widespread but incompatible desires to be able to live in one's native language. As has been widely noted, the conflict between Quebec and Anglophone Canada has intensified precisely as the cultures have become more similar, as Quebec has liberalized, industrialized, and urbanized.

It is little surprise that an immigrant community within a larger society will show solidaristic behavior, will seem more community-oriented than the majority. As I suggested in the last chapter, it is even unsurprising that the minority culture might begin to put special duties of cultural preservation on its women. This does not require that the minority be defined by values which are more conservative, more communal, or more patriarchal than the majority. It just requires that members of the minority want to preserve their culture and community and that they understand the pressure which being surrounded by a much larger cultural community places on those goals. In other words, if Americans or English were embattled minority communities in Pakistan or Korea, they would likely begin to act more solidaristically, and so on.

Sometimes, perhaps, we do seem to face gulfs as great as those between MacIntyre's ancients and moderns. Settler–indigenous relationships in places like Australia and the Americas have certainly been hampered by the much larger than usual gap between the kinds of moral reasoning used by the two sides. In Chapter 7 I argue that there is a genuine and enduring gap over the problem of how to understand land, for example. But even this gap is not one in which *each culture* has a moral understanding incomparable with those of its neighbors. Rather, there is a recurring moral understanding of land common to many indigenous cultures, and present in milder form in many forms of nationalism (in the west and elsewhere).

And most cross-cultural encounters do not resemble moral pluralism that closely. The Hutu–Tutsi conflicts in Rwanda, Burundi, and Congo are straightforward power struggles. The combatants in Bosnia may have been separated by religion, but it is striking how little of the conflict there has been over, say, the competing moral demands of Islam and Orthodox Christianity. In more peaceful places, Catalonia and Castilian Spain, Scotland and England, and the Swiss language and religion groups are all divided over much more ordinary problems than the incommensurability of values they might embody. Imputing deep moral conflict to these political contests makes them harder than they need to be.

One consequence of a disjuncture between moral and cultural pluralism is that we should be reluctant to characterize any culture as intrinsically liberal, illiberal, patriarchal, traditionalistic, hierarchical, and so on. Even when one cultural community happens to be clearly (e.g.) more sexist and patriarchal than another, we should not leap to the conclusion that the members of the more feminist culture ought to try to stamp out the other in order to liberate the women who live in it. The possibility of internal reform and change of cultural values should always be recognized. Sometimes members of one cultural community will be in a position to encourage such reform, as when the more patriarchal culture is a minority in a state dominated by a more feminist culture. By contrast, if Gray is right that 'when rivalrous values are embodied in mutually exclusive cultures, their incompatibility cannot be other than agonistic,' if we must simply make radical choices between two cultural communities and the values they embody, there is little reason to expect such reform. The larger liberal culture must probably simply outlaw the sexist practices of the minority culture and try to force rapid assimilation, giving rise to, as Gray puts it, 'relations . . . of enmity.'

The agonistic view also renders much cross-cultural moral criticism impossible or nonsensical. Only relativism actually claims that *all* such criticism is meaningless; if pluralism is really to be distinguished from relativism, it must leave space for some moral criticism. If the fundamental moral principles are plural but finite in number, and one culture sacrifices one principle without a corresponding gain in any other (or if it fails to satisfy *any* of the fundamental human ends, fails to abide by *any* of the fundamental moral principles) then so far it may be condemned. At least Raz, Berlin, and Taylor regard this as unlikely. They think that every enduring human culture probably satisfies some of the fundamental needs and embodies some of the fundamental moral truths.[9]

Raz, Taylor, and Walzer all defend both multiculturalism (of a sort) and nationalism (of a sort). Berlin thought that the two differed in important ways, and he was dubious about multiculturalism. He suggested that assimilation within a state or separation into different are required, that

---

[9] I think that Walzer's view differs from that of Raz, Berlin, and Taylor on this point; Gray's opinion is not clear to me.

pluralism can only safely manifest at the national level.[10] In the context of certain philosophical debates, multiculturalism and nationalism seem to line up on the same side, against individualism, or materialism, or any other mindset that discounts the importance of cultural memberships. But in practice—in the practice of individuals trying to resolve difficult questions of identity and loyalty, and in the practice of states adopting policies designed to promote cultural diversity or cultural unity—the two are in sharp conflict. Sometimes multiculturalism and nationalism are formally identical, differing only, as it were, the proper noun, the particular cultural community which an advocate claims is owed loyalty by members and respect by outsiders. This difference may be minor in a moral sense but is, of course, tremendously important in the political sense.

There is, however, this much formal difference between multiculturalism and nationalism, captured by Berlin's comments about Arabs and Jews:[11] nationalism marries culture to geography, seeing the world as divided up into different physical spaces in which the various ways of life can be led or practiced. Normative multiculturalism is less concerned with geographic separation (though not all normative theories of multiculturalism actually embrace intermixture). If people are deeply committed to living Icelandicly, can they peacefully live dispersed among others committed to living Koreanly? Or can peace only follow segregation? This question is complicated further by the tight relationship of nationalist theories to land and particular places, the subject of Chapter 7. The Israeli–Palestinian conflict is not really about the incompatibility of ways of life. Israel grants substantial autonomy to its religious minorities, and the conflicts between ultra-Orthodox and secular Jews about how to live with one another are much more dramatic than those between Jews and Muslims. Put another way, there is little that would prevent the peaceful coexistence of Arabs and Israelis in another place, say an imperial capital of old like Istanbul. Unlike ultra-Orthodox and secular Jews, Jews and Arabs do not face a particularly deep conflict over values or ways of life. The problem is simply that each group makes an exclusive claim over the land both groups share.

CULTURAL DIVERSITY

Gray has interpreted Berlin's life work as being governed by the 'master idea' of pluralism. But another recurrent theme in Berlin's work was

[10] See Berlin, 'In Conversation with Steven Lukes,' *Salmagundi* 120 (1988), 52–134 at 119–21.   [11] Ibid. 109–10.

what might be referred to as anti-Procrusteanism.[12] Many time he examined the moral psychology of those who would enforce uniformity, as well as criticizing the intellectual underpinnings of moral monism. In his criticisms of totalitarianism as well as of many forms of nationalism, Berlin railed against those who forcibly, violently, try to reshape a messy and complex world to accord with an ideological plan or a vision of uniformity. Anti-Procrusteanism thus certainly overlaps with pluralism. But there is a difference between affirmatively valuing the sheer diversity of tall and short people in the world, and being acutely aware that nothing humane and decent can be *done* about the range of heights. Anti-Procrusteanism is akin to the liberalism of fear, but specially emphasizes one source of cruelty: the desire to make the world fit a preconceived idea or regularity, order, progress. Humanity cannot be made uniform, made to fit a plan of history or social order, and the attempt to make it do so routinely turns bloody.

Anti-Procrusteanism may provide us with reason to proceed as if pluralism and diversity were intrinsically valuable. According moral weight to diversity as such might help to counterbalance the imperialist temptation in moral universalism. That temptation isn't a morally or conceptually necessary part of universalist moral thought, but there does seem to be a psychological affinity. Once we've discovered or decided what the moral truth is, we're going to go tell everyone else— and if they don't listen, we'll do considerably more than just *tell* them. If they remain attached to some benighted foolishness that distracts them from the truth, then we'll stamp out that benighted foolishness. There was something like this in the imperialism of the nineteenth-century liberals, in the attitudes of enlightened Europeans toward American Indians, Australian Aborigines, India proper, in the French Jacobin attitude toward regional and immigrant minorities.[13]

Thinking diversity itself to be morally important may help us to be chastened and cautious when passing cross-cultural moral judgments. None of that is to say that we have moral reason for making diversity paramount, for abandoning moral universalism, or for giving up on cross-cultural judgments. But there are important reasons to be cautious

---

[12] I owe this way of putting it to Jonathan Allen, in his review of Isaiah Berlin, *The Sense of Reality*, *South African Journal of Philosophy* 17:2 (1998), 173–7, at 176. This theme is certainly most apparent in *Four Essays on Liberty*, but even in *Against the Current* and *The Crooked Timber of Humanity*, Berlin spends strikingly more time discussing the errors and the psychology of monism than he does actually celebrating the diversity that the Procrustean monists would destroy.

[13] See Bhikhu Parekh, 'Superior People: The Narrowness of Liberalism From Mill to Rawls,' *Times Literary Supplement*, 25 Feb. 1994, 11–13.

as well as predictable reasons why it is hard to be cautious when the moment arises. Thinking in terms of cultural diversity itself having value may help check universalizing zeal in healthy ways. In the heat of cross-cultural contact, at the moment when a question arises of what *we* are going to do with or about *them,* we're unlikely to be in the best position to notice anything morally worthwhile about *them,* and we're unlikely to notice ways in which our condemnation of them is hypocritical. Starting with a belief that diversity has value may help us to act respectfully where we otherwise would not.[14]

But none of this makes it so. Imperialism, injustice, cruelty, and hypocrisy are all evils, and they're evils that occur often and easily in situations of cross-cultural contact. And each of us has a morally legitimate interest in being left alone, in not having our way of life stamped out. In a world in which there are all too many attempts to stamp out disliked groups and cultures and traditions and mores, people look for a general way to describe the evils of such actions. Saying that diversity is valuable does give an account of what's wrong with such actions; but it's overinclusive. It doesn't distinguish between a language dying off because the state kills all its speakers and a language dying off because its speakers voluntarily abandon it for a language that has wider use. It is always important to remember the terrible ways in which speakers and teachers of minority languages have been persecuted, even when this has allegedly been so that that the minority can enjoy the benefit of wider citizenship. But the enthusiasm for diversity as such takes that caution and misapplies it, overextends it. In so doing it both condemns that which should not be condemned—for instance, the gradual voluntary abandonment of a language—and debases the currency of condemnation, distracting from the real evils target. One sign of this overextension is whether the wrong can only be described in the future tense. It is wrong that the Turkish military does, now, violently shut down Kurdish-language schools and radio stations. The likelihood that in three generations Irish Gaelic will be gone as a native language of the Irish is not a wrong of the same kind; and anti-Procrusteanism allows us to recognize the difference while the valorization of diversity as such does not.

---

[14] For much more sustained consideration of these issues, see Martin Hollis, 'Is Universalism Ethnocentric?' and Seyla Benhabib, ' "Nous" et "les Autres," ' both in Christian Joppke and Steven Lukes (eds.), *Multicultural Questions* (Oxford: Oxford University Press, 1998); Bernard Williams, *Ethics and the Limits of Philosophy* (London: Fontana Books, 1985); Walzer, *Thick and Thin*; and Jeremy Waldron, 'What is a Human Right? Universals and the Challenge of Cultural Relativism,' *Pace International Law Review* 11 (1999), 129–38.

There is a further difficulty with the enthusiasm for diversity, for the protection and preservation of cultural variety. That project depends on there being lots of strong devotees of their own cultures. Unlike preserving biodiversity—a common, but very worrying, analogy—preserving cultural diversity depends on cultivating a certain frame of mind among members of the groups being preserved. And that frame of mind is— necessarily—hostile to diversity at some level. Cosmopolitanism is commonly criticized as being parasitic; but it is the Herderian, the nationalist of all nations, the proponent of cultural diversity, who relies on there being many people in the world who are nothing like himself.

That in turn sharply limits the moral uses of diversity. Sometimes people discuss cultural diversity as a moral resource, as something that offers us the possibility of critically reflecting on our own practices.[15] We ought to protect and preserve cultural diversity, on this account, because it expands our range of options and our ability to think clearly about our own culture and customs. But this is precisely not the attitude taken by people who are in the thick of preserving their own little piece of the allegedly gorgeous mosaic. The moral psychology of belonging to and protecting one's own group is to an important degree incompatible with that critical distance. Given that cultural communities live side-by-side with one another, that they develop in part in contrast with one another, and that they are always—necessarily—concerned with policing the border between insiders and outsiders, treating other cultural communities as a source for ideas about living or for insights about one's own lifestyle is quickly interpreted as a kind of treason, as jeopardizing the integrity of the group.

Moreover, this reaction is most likely to occur in precisely those cases in which morally significant learning might take place. People might react with an interested curiosity when they are devotees of one cuisine coming into contact with another. But when they are devotees of one religion coming into contact with another, or of one comprehensive way of life coming into contact with another, they are extremely unlikely to have such a pleasant and benevolent response. Syncretism sometimes occurs, over the course of generations or centuries. But at any given moment those who live within a culture, a religion, a way of life rarely take intercultural contact as a learning opportunity. A few members on the margins may defect to the other community, or begin trying to hammer out a hybrid identity. But many members, much of the time, harden their attitudes, sharpen points of contrast, and adopt a posture of hostility and enmity.

---

[15] See Joseph Raz, 'Multiculturalism: A Liberal Perspective,' and Amy Gutmann, 'The Challenge of Multiculturalism in Political Ethics, *Philosophy and Public Affairs* 22:3 (1993), 171–206.

None of this requires members of one group or the other being bad people. It's not because they subscribe to some nasty chauvinistic doctrine, even though that's often true. It's not something that only European Christians do, because they're walking around with dualistic mentalities, or anything like that. It's part of belonging, of being deeply committed to a way of life and then having the unnerving experience of encountering something else. People genuinely in the middle of their ways of life adopt a very different attitude from people who self-consciously play at it. For the former, the sort of intercultural contact that occurs in a world of diversity is an occasion for anxiety and hostility, not self-reflection and learning.

Maintaining cultural diversity depends on the activity of many people who are genuinely committed to protecting the integrity of their own group. That means that the protection of diversity depends on behavior that actively discourages one of the great moral benefits that's suggested as attaching to diversity. In order to do it, we have to give up our moral reason for wanting to do it in the first place. That there are theorists and philosophers who barrel ahead anyway seems to be a sign that diversity is being valued essentially and not just instrumentally; and the non-instrumental value of diversity is aesthetic, not moral.

Berlin, meaning for Montesquieu to suffer by the comparison with Herder, observed that Herder 'became convinced that what was true for a Portuguese was not necessarily true for a Persian. Montesquieu had begun to say this kind of thing, but even he, who believed that men were shaped by environment, what he called "climate," was in the end a universalist—he believed that the central truths were eternal, even if the answers to local and ephemeral questions might be different.'[16] But perhaps we need not think the worse of Montesquieu for that. The discrete organic nations by which Herder thought his world was populated might have seemed like units which might embody different moralities. Our world, however, is not populated by nations like that, but by internally heterogeneous and externally overlapping and crosscutting cultural communities, and by individuals who must make their own moral choices, because their cultures do not make them for them.

CULTURAL COMMUNITIES AS PUBLIC GOODS

While nationalism is a distinctive form of the politics of ethnic and cultural identity, set apart by the degree of priority that it claims, it is

---

[16] Isaiah Berlin, 'My Intellectual Path,' 56.

not unique in trying to pick out the one right level of cultural or ethnic community with which persons should identify and to which they should be loyal. The odd logic of picking out one right level of loyalty is vividly illustrated in the attempts to generate (a critic might say 'manufacture,' a supporter, 'forge') emotional attachment to identities like 'Hispanic–American' or 'Asian–American.' Asian–Americans have ancestors who come from countries as different from one another as they are from any others on earth. Asian–Americans include some of the wealthiest ethnic groups in the United States and some of the poorest. They are nearly as religiously diverse as the American population as a whole, ranging from Korean Protestants to Malaysian Muslims to Tibetan Buddhists, to Chinese–Americans without strong formal-institutional religious ties. An Asian–American identity, should one emerge outside of the intelligentsia and activists, would represent an heroic imagining of community, the unifying of many differences. But the putative Asian–American identity accentuates division along another front, between Asian–Americans and other Americans. When the relevant community is the United States, stressing unity or imagining commonality is said to be assimilationist, oppressive, homogenizing. When the community is 'Asian–Americans,' stressing unity is a matter of hanging together in a common enterprise. The United States is too diverse to be imagined as one community, too pluralistic to form a common identity; but 'Asian–American' is not. I do not mean to suggest that the truth is the reverse, that somehow the United States gives a real identity and Asian–American only a fake, manufactured one. It is probably true today that an American identity is more widely felt among the relevant population than is a pan-Asian–American identity, but that is a contingent matter. The point is only there is no particularly good reason to submerge one set of differences in the imagining of an Asian–American identity while insisting that the differences between Asian–Americans and other Americans cannot be submerged in the imagining of a unified American identity.

By the same token, however, there is something peculiar in the common view phrased by Benjamin Barber as 'In America, identity politics have served to define one-half of a hyphenated personality: an "Italian–American" or a [sic] "African–American." '[17] Identity politics has served to define *both* halves, the 'American' which new immigrants seek to become as well as the 'Italian' they seek to retain and remain. As

---

[17] Benjamin Barber, 'Muticulturalism Between Individuality and Community: Chasm or Bridge?' in Dana Villa and Austin Sarat (eds.), *Liberal Modernism and Democratic Individuality: George Kateb and the Practices of Politics* (Princeton: Princeton University Press, 1996), 38.

the discussion of civic nationalism in the last chapter made clear, the shared identity sometimes generated by a common state or a common political history is a particularistic cultural identity. It can't be used as a stand in for 'humanity' or 'universal principles' in order to make ethnic identities seem narrow and particularistic.

It may be that this dilemma is inescapable. Perhaps humans, or humans in modern impersonal societies, have some need for identification with some community larger than the family but smaller than humanity, with something too large for face-to-face knowledge to be generally possible but small enough that we can still identify traits that differentiate 'us' from 'them.' If so, if we have to imagine such communities, then there will inevitably be something arbitrary about the imagining. We will pick some differences and not others to supercede, with nothing making the latter less real than the former (at least to begin with). We have reason not to take the imaginings too seriously, not to give them undue moral weight. At least the contingency should be recognized and acknowledged; we should not be too willing to pick out one level of community and insist on unity within, difference without. But it is the arbitrariness, not the imagination or fiction, with which I am mostly concerned here. I am not suggesting that something which is constructed or imagined cannot be a source of moral obligation. But the arbitrariness of any given imagining of the boundaries of a community means that there will be competing imagined communities, overlapping rivals; and this sharply limits the amount of moral weight we can place on such communities as such, limits the claim of any one community to loyalty, preservation, and so on.

The idea of the possibility of exit from cultural communities looms large in moral thought about multiculturalism and cultural rights. But this is in a sense odd; at least, assessing the voluntariness of remaining in a community by the costs of exiting it seems mistaken. Everything about a culture is an exit barrier. To have a culture whose exit is entirely costless (not just beneficial all things considered, but *costless)* is to have no culture at all. For all but those perfectly bilingual since birth, leaving the culture in which one's native language is spoken for another requires some, and often very great, sacrifice. For most people that sacrifice is not only psychological; the exit or migration requires speaking, listening, reading, and writing in a language other than that in which one most comfortably *thinks*. Every form of communication, everything that requires information or expression, is (subtly or terrifically) more difficult in the non-native language. Similarly, exiting or migrating to a culture whose idioms, stories, imagery, and social understandings are not those with which one was raised is always difficult, always costly. It is not just the lost investment in learning the old culture; economists would tell us to view that as a sunk cost and so not actually a cost to consider in current decision-making. There are new costs to face; it is costly and difficult to learn the new culture, and confusing and difficult to live in it without knowing it well.

Belonging to a cultural community always, necessarily, involves marking members out as different from non-members—both in order to keep the non-members out and in order to keep the members in. The more different a minority culture is or remains, the higher the barrier to exit or assimilation. Not knowing the majority language and not having any liquid assets are not the only such barriers. If one is brought up to think of the majority culture as strange and alien, then one is psychologically conditioned to stay apart from it. Whether one is raised to think that a neighboring culture is decadent or repressive, the gap in standards of behavior constitutes a kind of exit barrier, one that many might find more difficult to overcome than the lack of a language.

Cultural exit or migration entails giving up the familiar for the unfamiliar, the known for the unknown, even the comprehensible for the incomprehensible. The more different the two cultures are, the costlier the transition will necessarily be. Language, religion, history, social meanings, and cultural practices must all be learned anew; and to the degree they are not learned, life in the new culture is lived at a distance *(alienated,* literally).

Refusing to educate children in the language, mores, or laws of a surrounding society; demanding a forfeit of accumulated lands or property; demanding that family and friends shun anyone who leaves the community; these are certainly barriers to exit. But so are learning the community's language, understanding the world in its terms, upholding its practices, and internalizing its morality. These barriers to exit probably cannot be morally distinguished on the grounds that some are deliberately intended to keep members within and others are merely incidental to having a culture at all. Women in conservative cultures often face a serious exit barrier in their cultures' resistance to female education; but if we can really speak of that opposition as having a purpose, it is probably more to ensure the subordination of women who do remain in the community than to ensure their continued presence in the community *per se.*

Conversely, many religious communities have rules and habits which have the intent and effect of setting members apart from outsiders, of keeping members from falling away by making life outside the community seem unclean or repulsive. Among the Amish, or the Roma, or the Jews of the Diaspora, distinguishing cultural values from exit barriers seems virtually impossible. We seek to remain separate from outsiders because they are unholy or unclean; but our rules for holiness and cleanliness forever remind both members and outsiders of the gap between us, making it less likely that we will fall away (aka exit) and less likely that the outsiders would have us.

Robert Goodin has offered a rational-choice account of how and why neighboring cultures that have adopted different norms even on a purely conventional matter gradually increase the importance they place on the distinction.[18] H. D. Forbes's important explanation of ethnic conflict places a great deal of importance on this kind of mechanism, and for precisely the reasons under discussion. The more danger there is of cross-cultural hybridization or assimilation, the more strongly many will emphasize what differentiates two neighboring cultures. (Thus the seeming paradox that increased contact along a cultural boundary makes the individuals involved more tolerant while sometimes making the ethnic groups generally more antagonistic toward each other.)[19] All of this suggests that minorities which seek to resist assimilation are under constant pressure to differentiate themselves from their neighbors in ways that act as exit barriers for their members.

It is thus more difficult than it might seem to use effective ease of exit as a way of morally evaluating cultural communities. If the existence of exit barriers is enough to make us see communal membership as unfree and illiberal, then there is no membership which is not illiberal. Majority or minority, traditional or reformist, with or without expectations of active participation by members, every cultural and linguistic community necessarily makes exit far more difficult than routine choices are.[20]

By contrast, there is a public goods justification of multicultural policies that worries, or is logically committed to worrying, that exit from many communities exit is in an important sense *too easy*. The argument is as follows: Minority cultural preservation is a public good, a large-n prisoners' dilemma. Each member of a minority culture prefers that the culture remain viable—that the language continue to be spoken, that children continue to be raised in the traditions, that all that which

[18] Robert Goodin, 'Conventions and Conversions, or Why Is Nationalism Sometimes So Nasty?' in Robert McKim and Jeff McMahan (eds.), *The Morality of Nationalism* (Oxford: Oxford University Press, 1997).

[19] H. D. Forbes, *Ethnic Conflict*: Commerce, Culture, and The Contact Hypothesis (New Haven: Yale University Press, 1997).

[20] Tamir nicely captures this character of cultural membership choices in her discussion of 'constitutive choices,' *Liberal Nationalism*, ch. 1.

makes the culture unique not die out. But, as long as the culture is a minority culture, each person also has a strong interest in leaving the preservation to others, in gaining for him or herself the advantages of being in the majority.

A common defense of some kinds of cultural rights then goes as follows. There is a collective action or public goods problem with cultural preservation. This problem can only be overcome with some special institutional provision, as is true for many collective action problems. If the institutional provision places some marginal apparent limit on the liberty of members, that is not to be worried over, any more than we worry about taxing people to support national defense. All of them wish for the culture to be preserved, all will be happier if the culture is preserved, and all are happy to give up their liberty to defect out of the culture and migrate or assimilate provided that others do the same. Liberals, at least, dislike overtly paternalistic arguments, and in any event have trouble justifying the idea that continued cultural membership is in the interests of members *whether they like it or not*; but if a collective action argument is available, then they need not resort to such claims.

Imagine a state with two major languages, one spoken by a much larger community than the other. Speaking the majority language brings an increased range of economic, intellectual, and social opportunities; but if everyone ceases to use the minority language for economic, intellectual, and social reasons then it will rapidly fade to the status of a folklore language, not a language in which people can lead complete and modern lives. The specter of the fate of Irish Gaelic hangs over many discussions of language policy. Most observers agree that, despite the best efforts of the Irish Republic's government, Irish Gaelic will never be more than a fading folklore language spoken in shrinking rural areas. It is, to use the metaphors of mortality so common in these discussions, dying a long and slow but inescapable death.[21] If all, or most, cease using the minority language in day-to-day affairs, then the fate of Irish Gaelic awaits it.

Where option 1 = the minority language survives and option 2 = the minority language does not survive, and option *a* = this individual gains

---

[21] See the perceptive discussion in John Edwards, *Multilingualism* (London: Routledge, 1994), chs. 1 and 4, especially the section titled 'Murder and Suicide,' 102–4. When this metaphor is carried over into moral discussions, it is crucial to remember that the death is metaphorical, that even if Gaelic was killed that killing bears no moral resemblance to an Irish genocide. I think that the distinction is forgotten by e.g. George Fletcher, 'The Case for Linguistic Self-Defense,' in Robert McKim and Jeff McMahan (eds.), *The Morality of Nationalism* (Oxford: Oxford University Press, 1997).

access to the benefits of the majority language and option *b* = this individual does not, each individual's preferences are ordered such that (1, *a*) is preferred to (1, *b*) and (2, *a*) is preferred to (2, *b*). The problem of how to rank (1, *b*) and (2, *a*) will be returned to in a moment, but note that the ranking doesn't affect any individual's decision making because no individual actually faces the direct choice between those two. If the minority language does not survive, then one more speaker would not have saved it, and it is rationally preferable to defect to the language that brings the most advantages. If the minority language *does* survive, then the loss of one more speaker won't hurt it in any noticeable way, and so it is still rationally preferable to defect to the dominant language.

To this, the minority cultural advocate adds the following. (1, *b*) is preferred to (2, *a*)—is preferred in fact by most if not all individuals and is morally preferable. The members of the minority culture simply face a prisoners' dilemma. All would be better off if the minority language survived and thrived, if it remained possible to lead rich, complete, satisfying, modern lives, but the rational choices made by each will lead to the language's demise.

Pierre Coulombe puts the point explicitly:

[W]e often forget that the more coercive aspects of [Quebec's language law] Bill 101 do not exempt French Canadians themselves . . . Until they are willing to freely conform to their own rules, French Canadians must be protected against the dangers of assimilation that exist within them, against the temptation to submerge into North American society . . . With community membership come certain duties to respect the good of the community, especially if non-respect leads to the disruption of the community's values that are central to its identity. This justifies constraining unwilling members on the grounds that membership entails certain obligations.[22]

Coulombe goes on to specifically criticize 'those who decide to take a free ride' by educating their children in English to improve their opportunities while hoping that other francophones will educate their children in French and preserve the culture.

Choice of language is not the only choice that can so jeopardize a cultural community, and minority language rights are not the only policy of cultural protection justified as solutions to collective action problems. Many kinds of distinctive cultural practice can be abandoned, one member at a time, by those seeking the advantages of assimilation and hoping that others will keep their original culture intact. Religious codes of conduct and traditional ways of life can be so abandoned. Even

---

[22] Pierre Coulombe, *Language Rights in French Canada* (New York: Peter Lang Publishing, 1995), 123.

intermarriage in some circumstances could be a kind of free riding; each of us marries out of our community, each of us knowing that we cannot individually affect whether the community survives until the next generation, but we would all prefer that the community survive. A cultural community which is importantly geographically based—say, an indigenous community—may face a collective action problem in the sale of land to outsiders. No individual decision not to sell can save the community; but each person sees the likely exodus of all the others, and seeks to sell rather than being the last one left living purposelessly on tribal land. Either collective ownership or a rule forbidding sale of land to outsiders might solve this kind of problem. In the absence of persecution, what typically endangers cultures is the choices of their individual members; and sometimes (or so it is argued) those choices are made strategically rather than out of any genuine shift in cultural sentiment.

Avishai Margalit and Moshe Habertal argue that there is an 'overriding interest' which justifies a basic right to one's own culture (a right that it exist, that its practices continue, that its values not be flouted by outsiders), even if the provision of that right requires both restrictions on the lives of members and burdens on outsiders.[23] They go on to insist that 'a cultural minority cannot be granted control over its members' exit' on the 'pretext that if people begin to leave, then the culture will be destroyed.'[24] But this cannot be reconciled with their affirmation of a right to one's own culture, a right that one's own community continue to exist. No doubt, sometimes the threat of cultural dissolution is invoked as a 'pretext.' There is a point, however, after which exit really does jeopardize the viability of the remaining cultural community. A linguistic community is threatened when too few people speak the language, or operate social institutions in the language. Communities from the Amish to indigenous tribes may be threatened when too few people remain behind to make a communal economy function. Traditional religious communities (like Orthodox Jewry) would not be viable if a large enough number of women exited, or if the highly-educated members who would teach the tradition if they stayed all left instead. If those who remain behind have a right to their own culture, the provision of which justifies coercing both outsiders and insiders, why should insiders-who-wish-to-become-outsiders be exempt from the obligation to preserve the community?

Similarly, Will Kymlicka argues that a secure and stable culture, providing a context for choice, is a primary good to which persons have

---

[23] Avishai Margalit and Moshe Habertal, 'Liberalism and the Right to Culture,' 61 *Social Research* 61 (1994), 491–510.　　　　　[24] Ibid. 508.

a basic right. That is, they have a right that their cultural communities exist and that they be robust enough to be lived in, robust enough that they can give shape to a range of options. The provision of this cultural good justifies what he calls 'external protections' and what I have elsewhere called 'external restrictions'—restrictions on the liberty of outsiders so that they do not jeopardize the culture's existence. Outsiders may be prevented from moving into, or voting in, an area in which members currently predominate. They may be forbidden to purchase members' land, or prevented from spreading the majority language. Kymlicka draws a bright line between such measures and 'internal restrictions,' measures that attempt to preserve the *character* of a culture by coercing members into living in certain ways.

Left unaddressed is the question of whether insiders may be coerced so as to preserve the existence of a culture. But all of the restrictions on outsiders, save possibly the restriction on their right to vote, are restrictions of how they may interact with members—which is to say that they also restrict the liberty of insiders. To prohibit outsiders from buying land is to prohibit insiders from selling it to them. Restricting the language of outsiders may well limit sources of information for insiders. These restrictions, in turn, raise additional barriers to exit; they strengthen the walls among communities. But by the logic of the argument, notwithstanding all of Kymlicka's insistence that the liberty of members not be restricted, these restrictions must be allowed. Indeed, as with Margalit and Habertal, there does not seem to be a reason to actually prevent exit if doing so would keep an otherwise imperiled community viable. Those who would exit would become outsiders, the coercion of whom is morally legitimate to preserve the viability of the community; so why would it not be legitimate to coerce them while they are still members? In any event, lesser barriers to exit are certainly permissible as ways to solve the collective action problem in providing the primary good of a stable cultural framework; they are merely the shadow cast by the external restrictions which Kymlicka explicitly defends.[25] Coulombe is more careful on this point, stressing that Quebec's Bill 101 coerces anglophones and francophones alike, in large part to prevent defection by francophones to English.

There are several problems with grounding multicultural policies in this public goods argument. First, the claim that the members of a culture really do prefer its preservation to the advantages they might gain from

---

[25] See *Liberalism, Community, and Culture*, 193–4, for a brief explicit link between cultural rights and collective action problems.

assimilation is entirely non-falsifiable and non-testable. The behavior of members facing a collective goods problem and the behavior of members who genuinely prefer exit, all things considered, even at some cost to the likelihood of cultural survival, are indistinguishable. This poses a real dilemma for political action to overcome the putative collective action problem, unless we are prepared *ex ante* to rule out the possibility of voluntary widespread assimilation. If there is no way to differentiate between exit being driven by a cultural collective goods problem and exit being driven by a genuine desire to leave, then attempts to solve the collective action problems risk unjustly discouraging the latter kind of exit.

Perhaps something like this is true for all public goods. We cannot, for example, easily distinguish between the free-riding polluter and the polluter who sincerely wouldn't mind if everyone polluted. But there is a striking difference between the cases. If we support environmental protection laws, there is a real sense in which we don't care which motivation the polluter has. We think the polluter would be wrong to be indifferent to widespread pollution; his or her desire to pollute doesn't affect our reasoning. The preservation of cultural communities, however, isn't like that. If cultural communities are valuable because of what they provide for their members (language, conceptual resources, a context in which to make choices, feelings of connection and meaning) and someone sincerely prefers what is provided by another such community, then outsiders don't have grounds for criticizing the way they do in the polluter's case. The non-paternalistic, liberal arguments for protecting cultural communities rely on the knowing that members really do not want to leave, while the argument against pollution is indifferent to the desires of the polluters.

If the continuation of one's ancestral cultural framework were a primary good, the provision of which has lexical priority over other interests persons may have, then perhaps we *could* rule out voluntary assimilation, in the sense of denying that it will occur, or in the sense of preventing it, or both. But, as commentators on Will Kymlicka's *Liberalism, Community, and Culture* have noted, the very most that can be said is that access to *some* cultural framework is a primary good of this kind. If assimilation is genuinely available (i.e. if the gap between the cultures is not too wide to make a successful transition possible and if the majority culture does not prejudicially exclude members of the minority from membership) then undermining the provision of the ancestral minority cultural framework does not deprive members of access to *any* cultural framework. As was the case with national loyalty, the moral picture looks different if persons face a choice between membership in their ancestral culture and alienated life cast adrift from any cultural framework than it does if they face a choice between one culture and another.

Second, even if cultural preservation is a collective good, it may not be an intergenerational public good. That is, even if the living generation prefers to be coerced into preserving its culture, the interests of the next generation might be in rapid assimilation. This is of course treacherous reasoning; it has often been used to inflict grave injustices. Children have been taken from their parents because communal preservation was deemed not to be in their interests, and much damage was done to minority cultural communities without even the benefits of assimilation being genuinely available. American Indian children were forced into English-only boarding schools; Australian Aboriginal children were taken from their families and fostered in white homes. Still, this potential divergence of interests between generations makes cultural preservation an unusual public good at best; there is no such divergence in more conventional collective goods (national defense, clean air).

Both of these problems involve information that seems to be inaccessible. Are current exiters driven by a collective action problem or by a genuine desire to migrate to another culture? If the culture is a public good, is it transgenerational? The third problem also results from a lack of information, though the information in principle might be accessible after careful empirical analysis. Is the culture really in sufficient danger that political action is necessary to overcome the collective action problem, but still viable enough that such political action will actually make cultural preservation possible? The collective action problem only exists if a cultural community is already vulnerable. Many communities—and not only those with national states!—remain large enough that persons do not exit it out of fear of the exit of others. Policies of cultural preservation are then unnecessary at best. But others are already too far gone. Irish Gaelic, for example, apparently cannot be really revived.[26] If the justification of a coercive policy is that it is necessary to provide a public good, the good must actually be provided for the policy to be justified.

---

[26] The resurrection of Hebrew is sometimes mentioned to suggest that, since a language can be brought back from actual extinction (as a non-ceremonial language), surely languages can be brought back from near-extinction. But early Israel was probably uniquely amenable to such cultural engineering. Among other things, modern Hebrew did not face a single competitor the way that Gaelic does in English. The Jews in early independent Israel spoke Yiddish, Ladino, Arabic, and any number of European languages. In circumstances like that a lingua franca is likely to emerge with or without deliberate policy; such policy can set what the language is. In, for example, Ireland, there is no such need, no functional hole for Gaelic to fill.

The second and third problem interact in the following way: if long-term cultural survival is not really an option, then political action designed to keep people in the community does a particular disservice to subsequent generations. It may not reflect their real underlying preferences, as it must if it is to be a non-paternalistic solution to a collective action problem; it would also seem to adversely affect their interests as an outsider understands them.

Again, this requires that we reject the position that my interests are *necessarily* served by my remaining within my ancestral culture. Margalit and Habertal posit just such an 'overriding interest,' which justifies a basic right to one's own culture, even if that requires both restrictions on the lives of members and burdens on outsiders. One of their two primary examples is Orthodox Jewry in Israel. For these Jews there can be no argument that assimilation or cultural migration is genuinely unavailable to them. Unlike indigenous peoples, they do not face a neighboring culture which is opaque to them; and unlike some racial minorities, they do not face a community which would reject their attempts to enter. The argument therefore requires supposing that persons have one and only one culture which is or could be their *own,* as well as denying the possibility or the coherence of the trade-offs persons really do make between the comfort of the familiar and other human goods.

CONCLUSION

One common metaphor in discussions of communal affiliations is of life lived in a series of concentric circles. At the center is self, at the outer edge is all of humanity. In between are family, neighborhood, religion, ethnic group, and nation. Some suggest that our moral obligations are most intense to those in the nearest circles—say, family—and gradually lessen until we get to humanity, to whom we owe only minimal and mostly negative obligations. Others seek to identify some intermediate circle, one of the imagined communities which are too large for face-to-face knowledge but small enough that it feels like it is *ours,* to which we owe the greatest obligations—for example, the nation. The nation is thought to be a potentially self-contained sphere of human life, a unit which can contain everything which is needed to live in the modern world. A linguistic community is thought to define the boundaries of what persons can know or imagine, what choices they can make or what lives they can lead. Encompassing cultures are said to define our personalities and identities.

But there is something misleading about the imagery invoked. The circles are not concentric; they overlap and crosscut. Sometimes nations are larger than ethnic groups, sometimes smaller, and sometimes merely different. Linguistic communities can encompass a fraction of one state or dozens of states. Between family and humanity there are any number of imagined communities to which we belong. Each of them unifies along some dimensions and divides along others; loyalty to any of them requires overcoming some differentiations and accentuating others. And many of the moral choices that persons face, many of the trade-offs that must be made in policies concerned with culture and membership, involve decisions among these crosscutting rival intermediate communities, not merely deciding that we need something between self and humanity.

PART III

Categories and Cases

5

Classifying Cultural Rights

A wide variety of extant and proposed policies seek to accommodate
cultural pluralism; these do not lend themselves to being normatively
analyzed as a single group. On the other hand, many of them do rise or
fall by similar arguments. This chapter seeks to identify those cultural
rights-claims which are morally alike and (as importantly) those which
are unlike one another. It offers a way of sorting those policies which
may facilitate and clarify such arguments.

Normative work on cultural rights is difficult to structure. One can
rarely say with any precision what implications a given philosophical
turn had for the sets of policies being endorsed or disparaged. Arguing
by analogy from one case to another is necessary, but it is also frustrat-
ing without a framework for identifying the traits which made policies
like or unlike in relevant ways.

Drawing purely philosophical distinctions sometimes provides little
guidance in sorting actual institutions or policies. The discussion about
individual and collective rights, for example, important as it is on a
philosophical level, provides little guidance when confronting concrete
policies and rights-claims, some of which seem to fit into neither category, some of which are all-too-easily redescribed as part of either one.
Yael Tamir[1] derives the right of a national group to its own (not necessarily independent) government from the individual right to practice
one's culture, and argues that this derivation means national self-determination should be understood as an individual right. Darlene Johnston
holds that 'the prevalence of collective wrongs such as apartheid and
genocide demonstrates the need for collective rights.'[2] This seems to
redescribe, for example the right not to be murdered by one's government as a group right. Such redescriptions in one direction or the other
are not unique, and the variety of usages of 'collective right'—which can
refer to a right to a public good or a social good, a right which could

---

[1] Yael Tamir, *Liberal Nationalism* (Princeton: Princeton University Press, 1993).
[2] Darlene Johnston, 'Native Rights as Collective Rights: A Question of Self-
Preservation,' *Canadian Journal of Law and Jurisprudence* 2 (1989), 19–34.

only be exercised by members of a collective, or a right which could only be exercised by a corporate collectivity itself, among other poss-ibilities—adds to the confusion. An argument that the only morally important rights are individual ones might still lead to support for a variety of cultural rights-claims (suitably redescribed); an argument that groups can have rights does not prove that any *do*, or which groups have which rights.

On the other hand, sorting rights-claims by the kind of group making the claim[3] clarifies some issues but also makes it difficult to distinguish among the various kinds of claims a group can make. It also, in my view, unnecessarily distinguishes between quite similar claims made by a variety of different groups.

What follows, then, is the set of categories useful in sorting cultural rights-claims. There are clusters of claims which lend themselves to sim-ilar sorts of arguments (pro and con), clusters within which one policy may be taken as precedent for another but across which such claims are much harder to sustain. I have proceeded inductively, from particular cases and arguments to categories. The classification is therefore not a logically exhaustive typology; I am unsure that any such typology captures the range of policies and rights-claims at issue. Usefulness, not truth, is the goal.

For each category, I provide real or proposed examples from the theoretical and empirical literature, and a sketch of the normative issues at stake in such rights-claims. I also identify important clusters within some categories, clusters which raise additional normative issues or which are clearly recognizable patterns of rights-claims actually made. I also indicate what the multiculturalism of fear suggests about the various kinds of cultural rights-claims. Following the classification, I discuss some alternative methods of sorting cultural rights-claims, and some examples of arguments which I think would be clarified by use of a framework like the one presented here.

I have by and large excluded both obviously illegitimate claims—'We have the right to rule you because ruling is part of our culture'—and claims that are simply demands that one's liberal individual human rights be observed—'We have the right that our government not slaughter us.' This classification attempts to sort through the kinds of claims that are seen to be something different from equal

---

[3] As in Ted Robert Gurr, *Minorities at Risk: A Global View of Ethnopolitical Conflict* (Washington, DC: United States Institute of Peace Press, 1993), and Will Kymlicka, *Multicultural Citizenship: A Liberal Theory of Minority Rights* (Oxford: Oxford University Press, 1995). These approaches are discussed in Part III.

Table 5.1: Types of cultural rights-claims

Category	Examples
Exemptions from laws which penalize or burden cultural practices	Sikhs/motorcycle helmet laws, Indians/peyote, indigenous peoples/ hunting laws, Amish/schooling
Assistance to do those things the majority can do unassisted	multilingual ballots, affirmative action, funding ethnic associations
Self-government for ethic, cultural, or 'national' minorities	secession (Slovenia), federal unit (Catalonia), other polity (Puerto Rico)
External rules restricting non-members' liberty to protect members' culture	Quebec/restrictions on English language, Indians/restrictions on local whites voting
Internal rules for members' conduct enforced by ostracism, excommunication	Mennonite shunning, disowning children who marry outside the group
Recognition/enforcement of traditional legal code by the dominant legal system	Aboriginal land rights, traditional or group-specific family law
Representation of minorities in government bodies, guaranteed or facilitated	Maori voting roll for Parliament, U.S. black-majority Congressional districts
Symbolic claims to acknowledge the worth, status, or existence of various groups	name of polity, official name of ethnic groups, national holidays, teaching of history, official apologies

individual rights conventionally understood, but which are still normatively plausible.

Cultural rights-claims and special policies for accommodating ethnic and linguistic pluralism include exemptions, assistance, self-government, external rules, internal rules, recognition/enforcement, representation, and symbolic claims.[4]

---

[4] It has been suggested to me that this classification might also incorporate rights-claims made by or on behalf of, for example, women, the disabled, or gays and lesbians. It has also been suggested to me that if the classification does not prove able to incorporate such claims, it should be adjusted to do so, because of the links between cultural rights and assistance for other oppressed groups. For discussion of those links, see Iris Marion Young, *Justice and the Politics of Difference* (Princeton: Princeton University Press, 1990). If the classification can incorporate such claims, so much the better, but I am not in a position to say whether it can.

EXEMPTIONS

Exemption rights are individually exercised negative liberties granted to members of a religious or cultural group whose practices are such that a generally and ostensibly neutral law would be a distinctive burden on them. Often this is because the law would impair a minority's religious practices, or would compel adherents to do that which they consider religiously prohibited; exemptions are thus often analogous to the status of conscientious objector which exempts, among others, Quakers and the Amish from conscription.

Examples abound. The ceremonial use of wine by Catholics and Jews was exempted from alcohol Prohibition in the United States. The religious use of peyote by American Indians is similarly exempted from many state laws on narcotics and hallucinogens.[5] The Amish in the United States have sought or obtained exemptions from mandatory schooling laws;[6] regulations of private schools like the requirement that schools have certified teachers;[7] participation in Social Security and some states' workers' compensation and unemployment insurance schemes;[8] a requirement that slow-moving vehicles display a standardized reflective symbol;[9] and a variety of health care and

---

[5] The US Supreme Court in *Employment Division, Department of Human Resources of Oregon v Smith*, 494 US 872 (USA 1990) held that the Free Exercise Clause of the First Amendment did not provide constitutional protection for the religious use of peyote. Congress' attempt to provide such protection with *The Religious Freedom Restoration Act* was struck down in *City of Boerne v Flores*, 521 US 507 (USA 1997).

[6] This was granted in *Wisconsin v Yoder*, 406 US 205 (USA 1972); Ontario has informally granted a similar exemption. See Dennis Thompson, 'Canadian Government Relations,' in Donald Kraybill (ed.), *The Amish and the State* (Baltimore: Johns Hopkins University Press, 1993), 239.

[7] See Thompson, 'Canadian Government Relations,' and Thomas Meyers, 'Education and Schooling,' in Donald Kraybill (ed.), *The Amish and the State* (Baltimore: Johns Hopkins University Press, 1993).

[8] The Amish have a religious prohibition on reliance on or participation in organized insurance; Social Security is not an insurance system according to the usual definitions but public rhetoric about it has long referred to it as one. The Social Security exemption was granted to self-employed Amish (a large majority) by legislation in 1965; denied to Amish working for wages by *United States v Lee*, 455 US 252 (USA 1982); extended to Amish employed by other Amish by federal legislation in 1988. Some states have granted analogous statutory exemptions from participation in their unemployment insurance and workers' compensation plans. See Peter Ferrara, 'Social Security and Taxes,' in Donald Kraybill (ed.), *The Amish and the State* (Baltimore: Johns Hopkins University Press, 1993). A similar exemption from the Canadian Pension Plan was granted in 1974 to self-employed Amish, Old Order Mennonites, and Hutterites. See Thompson, 'Canadian Government Relations,' 239–40.

[9] Some Amish objected to the emblem as a worldly symbol as well as to putting bright colors on their carriages. They sought to use reflective tape and a lantern in lieu of the

land-use regulations.[10] A century ago American Mormons sought an exemption from laws against polygamy.[11] Jews and Muslims in a number of states have sought or obtained exemptions from sabbatarian laws, especially Sunday-closing laws for businesses.

Not all exemption claims are religiously based. Indigenous peoples in several countries have sought and obtained exemptions to various hunting, fishing, and land-use regulations, arguing that the rules would unfairly burden their traditional way of life or even their ability to gain sustenance. At various times Afrikaner, Quebecois, and Irish citizens of South Africa, Canada, and the UK have sought exemptions from conscription, saying that they should not be forced to fight on behalf of England. Some exemptions are religious only in an inverse sense to those on the conscientious objection model. For instance, some Muslim states ban the use of alcohol, but exempt non-Muslims from the rule. The exemption is not granted because alcohol consumption is a *duty* of all non-Muslims; it differs from the exceptions to American Prohibition noted above. It is granted because the rule itself is there for an openly religious reason. The state is intimately involved with the majority culture and religion, and considers it appropriate to turn the sinful into the criminal; but by the same token holds that those who do not hold alcohol sinful should not be held criminally liable for it either.

A variety of exemption claims revolve around dress codes and restrictions. Sikhs in Canada have sought exemptions from mandatory helmet laws and from police dress codes, to accommodate the turbans required by their religion. American Orthodox Jews requested an exemption from Air Force uniform regulations to accommodate their yarmulkes.[12]

standard red triangle. They were refused federal protection in *Minnesota v Hershberger*, 110 US 1918 (USA 1990), granted protection under the Minnesota constitution in *State v Hershberger (II)*, 462 NW2d 393 (Minn. 1990).

[10] See Gertrude Huntington, 'Health Care,' and Elizabeth Place, 'Land Use,' both in Donald Kraybill (ed.), *The Amish and the State* (Baltimore: Johns Hopkins University Press, 1993). Other religious groups, notably including Jehovah's Witnesses and Christian Scientists, have also sought and sometimes obtained exemptions from health care regulations.

[11] Their claim was denied in *Reynolds v United States*, 98 US 145 (USA 1878). Muslims in some countries are allowed to have marriages involving one husband and up to four wives, the limit imposed by the Koran; but their case differs somewhat from that of the Mormons. In the United States, polygamy is a criminal offense; what was sought in *Reynolds* was immunity from prosecution, an exemption. The right granted to Muslims will be discussed below under 'recognition and enforcement.'

[12] The claim was denied in *Goldman v Weinberger*, 475 US 503 (USA 1986). Kymlicka discusses these cases at some length. He stresses their integrative capacity; joining the Air Force or the Royal Canadian Mounted Police are acts of belonging rather than of separation. But one could easily find closely analogous examples which lacked the symbolism of belonging; consider dress codes in prisons. Nor are all of Kymlicka's

Muslim women and girls have faced similar situations with regard to the garments they are required to wear, though the most famous of these—the expulsion of Muslim girls from French schools because their headscarves violated rules about the display of religious symbols—is a special case. Exemption disputes involve rules which only accidentally impinge on the minority practice; it's not that the US Air Force bans yarmulkes *per se* but rather that it has a standardized uniform of which yarmulkes would be one sort of violation. But the rule in France was very specifically against anything that would allow one to identify students by religion. The *foulard* is precisely the sort of thing the rule was intended to keep out.[13] One is reminded of the rule that all personal names must be in the state's dominant language, imposed at various times on peoples as disparate as Germanic South Tyroleans in Italy and the non-Han Chinese aboriginal inhabitants of Taiwan. Such rules are intentionally aimed at the minority group, and so it makes little sense to seek an exemption but leave the rule intact. Again, repeal rather than an exemption is what is wanted. These cases obviously have something important in common with those in which an exemption is sought to a rule left otherwise intact; but they differ, too.

Brian Barry argues that for similar reasons exemptions in general make little sense, that either a general law illegitimately violates liberty and should be repealed or it is justified and should be uniformly enforced.[14] But in most cases in which an exemption is demanded or granted, a practice which has a distinctive status and meaning in a minority culture is banned, regulated, or compelled because of the very different meaning it has for the majority culture. The exemption is justified as a recognition of that difference, as an attempt not to unduly burden the minority culture or religion *en route* to the law's legitimate goals.[15] As noted, many are defended as part of the freedom to practice and live according to one's religion, and seek their defense in the broader theory of religious freedom; but all defenses of exemptions

examples of polyethnic exemptions so obviously integrative; exemptions from motorcycle helmet laws or Sunday closing laws do not seem analogous in this respect to the Sikh trying to join the Mounties. Kymlicka, *Multicultural Citizenship*, 114–15.

[13] See Françoise Gaspard and Farhad Khorokhavar, *Le foulard et la République* (Paris: Éditions La Découverte, 1995), 163–212. In fact the situation was worse than that; the rule in effect prohibits worn religious symbols that are not crosses or yarmulkes—that is, it functions *de facto* as a rule against the *foulard,* since public schoolchildren tend not to wear nuns' habits or clerical collars. Leaving the rule intact but granting an exemption for the *foulard* would border on incoherence.

[14] Brian Barry, *An Egalitarian Critique of Multiculturalism* (Cambridge: Polity Press, 2000).

[15] Kymlicka, *Multicultural Citizenship,* 108–15, offers an 'equality argument' which uses reasoning like this.

stress the distinctive meaning which the practice has for the non-dominant group. The fact that exemptions are individually exercised, and that many of the laws in question are so-called 'victimless crime laws,' makes exemptions easy to ground in liberal and libertarian theories emphasizing individual freedom from coercion. But Barry might be correct that the libertarian solution should simply be to abolish the victimless crime laws altogether. Raz thus argues that the exemption for conscientious objectors has been a protection for religious *communities* as much as if not more than a deferral to *individual* conscience, and the argument is easily extended to other exemption rights.[16] Sandel provides a communitarian argument for religious exemptions as exercises of the right to carry out one's communal duties.[17]

If liberty is not all of a piece, however, then even on individualistic grounds what Barry calls the 'rule-plus-exemption' solution might be preferable to either abolishing the rule or refusing the exemption. Some violations of liberty are more serious than others; they intrude closer to the core of a person's dignity, sense of self. Some restrictions are inconveniences, others deep offenses to self. But which is which is not the same for everyone, and cultural and religious understandings help make the difference. Religious rules and understandings make sacred the otherwise profane: a wafer and wine into the blood and body of Christ, or (an example of Michael Walzer's) a butcher block into an altar. The justification of legal restrictions on freedom of action must surely involve the weighing of the importance and legitimacy of the state's goals against the importance of the liberty being restricted. This is reflected in American law in the difference between laws which need only show 'a rational relationship' to 'a legitimate state interest' in order to pass constitutional muster and those which must show 'a necessary relationship' to 'a compelling state interest;' but neither those particular formulations nor the idea of judicial review are necessary for the point at hand. A law might justifiably restrict a minor liberty in the public interest, but at the same time restrict a core religious liberty of a minority. If the state's interest is not one of overriding importance, then the combination of rule-plus-exemption might be the best available solution.

Some state interests, of course, are overriding. Some who sympathize with exemption claims in general maintain that laws that protect the interests of children (e.g. compulsory vaccination or mandatory schooling) are

---

[16] Joseph Raz, *The Morality of Freedom* (Oxford: Oxford University Press, 1986), 252.

[17] Michael Sandel, unpublished paper cited in Tamir, *Liberal Nationalism*, 38–9.

too important to allow for exceptions.[18] And preventing violence and cruelty are undoubtedly moral ends of the highest importance— compelling state interests, in the American legal terminology. There is thus no contradiction between defending many of the exemptions mentioned above and denying the validity of the so-called 'cultural defense' discussed in Chapter 2. Parents having genital cutting performed on their daughters suggest that such ritual cutting should be exempt from child abuse laws; Hmong men argue that their courtship by 'capture' should be exempt from rape and kidnapping laws. Undoubtedly there are distinctive cultural meanings of ritual genital cutting and courtship by capture; but the moral interest being served by the laws against abuse, rape, and kidnapping far outweigh the claimed liberty to practice one's own culture.[19]

Exemptions are criticized as a class for the distinctions they draw in the law; they grant liberties to some which others lack. This is particularly a problem for republican or liberal theories which place over-whelming importance on *equal* liberty. It is also a problem for the conception of the rule of law that emphasizes the general applicability of laws and the absence, as it were, of proper nouns from legitimate law-making. Exemptions are also subject to criticism because they also require the state to identify individuals as members of various groups; perhaps most problematically, religious exemptions can require judicial inquiry into whether a person is a sincere and faithful member of the religion or whether the exemption is being claimed opportunistically. All exemptions, though, require an official determination of the group membership of individuals, a process some might think problematic. On the other hand, exemption rights are wholly immune to the criticism that 'groups cannot be rights-bearers,' for while they are group-differentiated they are not 'group rights' in any meaningful sense.[20]

---

[18] Some liberals who endorse exemption rights generally, including Kymlicka, reject *Wisconsin v Yoder* because of the additional issues raised when an exemption is sought from a law which seeks to protect children. On the other hand, Kukathas both endorses *Yoder* and suggests a similar exemption for Roma (gypsies) in Britain. Chandran Kukathas, 'Are There Any Cultural Rights?' *Political Theory* 20 (1992) 105–39, at 126.

[19] Not all cultural defense claims suggest that a whole class of violent actions should be exempt from the criminal law. Many only treat the offender's culture as relevant to establishing *mens rea* or intent.

[20] See Jan Narveson, 'Collective Rights?' *Canadian Journal of Law and Jurisprudence* 4 (1991), 329–45, and Michael Hartney, 'Some Confusions Concerning Collective Rights,' ibid. 293–314, for the claim that groups cannot bear rights.

ASSISTANCE

Where exemption rights seek to allow minorities to engage in practices different from those of the majority culture, assistance rights are claimed for help in overcoming obstacles to engaging in common practices. Special provision is sought because of culturally specific disadvantages or because the desired common activity has been designed in such a way as to keep members of non-dominant groups out.

The most prominent clusters of assistance rights are language rights; funding for ethnocultural art, associations, and so on; and preferential policies (in, for example, hiring and university admission). All impose a direct cost onto at least some members of the majority or dominant culture; all seek to allow the minority or subordinated culture to do those things which the majority culture can allegedly do already.[21]

Language rights present simple examples; speakers of the minority language seek special provision to allow them to interact with the state or receive state protection and benefits. These include ballots printed in multiple languages; interpreters in court and in administrative agencies, or the appointment of bilingual judges and civil servants;[22] the provision of bilingual or minority-language public education; and offering college entrance exams in more than one language. Voting, using the courts and the schools, having access to the bureaucracy—these are

[21] The language of 'minorities' and 'majorities,' always problematic in the cultural rights debate, becomes especially so when dealing with assistance rights. In a given society different groups may feel excluded from different kinds of activities, and numbers may not be the determining factor. Malaysia has practiced various preferential policies for ethnic Malays *vis-à-vis* ethnic Chinese, a minority which is predominant in business and education. South Africa has implemented widespread affirmative action policies for its black majority. For a similar reason, 'dominant' and 'non-dominant' are unsatisfactory. Often a group which is predominant is business is disadvantaged in politics; this has been true of Indian, Chinese, Jewish, and sometimes Arab populations around the world. On the other hand, 'dominant/non-dominant in the relevant sphere' and 'unfairly disadvantaged/unfairly advantaged in the relevant sphere' are unwieldy, and I shall continue to use the imprecise language of majorities and minorities.

[22] See Sergij Vilfan, 'Introduction,' and Lode Wils, 'Belgium on the Path to Equal Language Rights up to 1939', in Sergij Vilfan *et al.* (eds.), *Comparative Studies on Governments and Non-Dominant Ethnic Groups in Europe, 1850–1940*, iii: *Ethnic Groups and Language Rights* (New York: New York University Press, European Science Foundation, 1993), on the wide variety of ways in which minority language-speakers can seek to be accommodated in courts and administrative procedures. Issues include not only the right to speak one's own language in court but the language of the overall proceedings; not only the right to speak to a civil servant in one's own language but the right to have correspondence from the state in that language; not only the right to be a member of the civil service but the question of the language in which intra-civil service communication is to be conducted.

common activities which speakers of the minority language are effectively prevented from engaging in. Overcoming that obstacle requires special provision which imposes a cost; interpreters are expensive, a requirement that judges or civil servants be bilingual even more so, and there is a direct cost associated with printing ballot papers in more than one language. Supporters of assistance rights maintain that these costs are less important than the injustice which would result if minority-language speakers were denied access to the activities in question. Bruno De Witte summarizes the general argument in favor of such assistance rights, which he refers to as rights of linguistic equality (as opposed to mere linguistic freedom, the right to speak one's own language):

The freedom to use one's own language in addressing [judicial or administrative] authorities is ineffective if those authorities have no corresponding duty to understand and act upon that language; and with 'negative' rights, no such duty can be imposed upon them. Indeed, in the absence of such a duty, the individual members of the administration or the judiciary could themselves invoke their own linguistic freedom against that of the citizen with whom they deal. In the context of administrative and judicial usage, the primary interest of minorities *is* the recognition of a form of linguistic equality rather than linguistic freedom.[23]

Subsidies to a variety of cultural and linguistic institutions and associations are also common. It is argued that the majority culture, simply by being in the majority, has its cultural integrity and heritage protected for free, as it were, while other cultural groups have to create, maintain, and fund institutions like private schools, fraternal associations, museums, art galleries, theater companies, community newspapers, cultural clubs, and so on in order to preserve their cultural integrity to anything like the same degree. Special state measures to ease that burden are assistance rights. These can include direct subsidies to ethnic associations, special tax deductions for contributions to such associ-ations, the provision of tax credits, vouchers, or direct subsidies to cultural private schools or the parents of children who go there, and so on. Kymlicka also argues for support for 'ethnic associations, magazines, and festivals,' seeing them as a logical extension of state funding for arts and culture generally and possibly as security against discrimination in the allocation of such funds.[24] Carrying the logic of these assistance rights farther, Yael Tamir suggests the provision of cultural vouchers which could be donated to a wide variety of cultural institutions.[25]

[23] Bruno de Witte, 'Conclusion: A Legal Perspective', in Sergij Vilfan *et al.* (eds.), *Ethnic Groups and Language Rights* (New York: New York University Press, European Science Foundation, 1993), 303.

[24] Kymlicka, *Multicultural Citizenship*, 31,123, 223–4 n. 15.

[25] Tamir, *Liberal Nationalism*, 54–5.

With the possible exceptions of the language of public education and subsidies for private education,[26] the most controversial and explosive assistance rights are preferential policies. They are also extremely common worldwide. Affirmative action, preferential hiring and admissions, quotas and set-asides are present in various places in private employment, the civil service, bank loans, the military, universities, the awarding of government contracts, and land allocation.[27] For reasons which are either systematic and permanent or at least in theory contingent and temporary, members of one group are held to be at a disadvantage in competing for the resources or positions in question, a disadvantage which these assistance rights attempt to overcome.[28]

The explosiveness of preferential policies comes in part because the costs of the policy are apparently concentrated on the marginal members of the non-preferred group, those who are better-qualified or more competitive than some of those members of the preferred group are awarded the positions or resources. In this they differ from language rights or funding for ethnic associations; those assistance rights do have costs, but they are dispersed among a society's taxpayers. They are also highly controversial because of their open departure from principles of merit and equal treatment, although Iris Marion Young argues that such principles are themselves biased and unequal.[29]

Language rights and cultural subsidies (though not preferential policies) are immune to fears about identifying individuals on the basis of group membership; such identification is not generally necessary for their exercise. Arguments for the separation of culture and state, or against the legitimacy of claims for cultural support, *do* impact on language rights and cultural subsidies.[30] Many assistance rights are integrationist and so

[26] On the centrality of the question of education to ethnic and nationalist disputes worldwide, see Ernest Gellner, *Nations and Nationalism* (Oxford: Basil Blackwell, 1983); Janusz Tomiak and Andreas Kazarnias, 'Introduction,' and Knut Eriksen, *et al.*, 'Governments and the Education of Non-Dominant Ethnic Groups in Comparative Perspective,' in Janusz Tomiak *et al.* (eds.), *Comparative Studies on Governments and Non-dominant Ethnic Groups in Europe, 1850–1940*, i: *Schooling, Educational Policy, and Ethnic Identity* (New York: New York University Press, European Science Foundation, 1991).

[27] See Thomas Sowell, *Preferential Policies* (New York: Basic Books, 1991), and Donald Horowitz, *Ethnic Groups in Conflict* (Berkeley: University of California Press, 1985), 653–80.

[28] Of course, a crucial part of the defense of such programs is showing that the stipulated disadvantage is real and that the policy is not simply a way for a politically powerful group to extend its influence into other spheres.

[29] Young, *Justice and the Politics of Difference*, 192–225

[30] See e.g. Narveson, 'Collective Rights,' 344–5. Kymlicka, *Multicultural Citizenship*, 108–15, and Tamir, *Liberal Nationalism*, 145–50, arguing for (among other cultural rights) assistance rights, maintain that arguments for a separation of culture and state are untenable.

not subject to charges of separatism; this is the case for multilingual
ballots, for example, which allow all to participate in a common political system. On the other hand, funding for minority-language schools,
newspapers, radio stations, and so on, while allowing the minority to do
the same sorts of things as the majority, do not encourage the two
groups to pursue their activities *together* and do not seem integrationist.

As ought to be clear, some differences in justification necessarily
surround the clusters of assistance rights; but they are importantly similar as well, in ways which make them dissimilar to other kinds of
cultural rights-claims. All assistance rights involve costs to members of
the majority culture (though these are not costs in liberty; policies
imposing such costs require different justification and are discussed
separately under 'external rules'), and those costs must be justified. All
involve the aspiration or the desire to do things which members of the
majority already or easily do, and are therefore not typically subject to
criticism on grounds of leading to or encouraging separatism.[31] Unlike
exemptions, which are readily defended in terms of liberty and only
indirectly in terms of equality, arguments about assistance rights are
almost always arguments about equality. They are opposed on the
grounds that they single out members of specific groups for receipt of
unequal benefits; they are supported on the grounds that members of
the minority culture face an unfair inequality in their chances to do or
participate in something.

The *unfairness* of the inequality is an important part of the argument;
it is typically stated that the inequality comes from historical injustice,
actions of the state or of the majority group, or from the bare status of
being a minority, rather than from choices made by individual members
of the group.[32] Note that this does not mean assistance rights are all

---

[31] The provision of bilingual education, or state support for minority-cultural schools,
are an important exception to this; this may suggest that such policies are better understood as part of another category, though it is unclear which that would be. If the cultural
community can tax its own members and provide its own schools, a form of self-government would seem to exist. Perhaps bilingual education provided by the state should be
understood as an assistance claim while schools provided or assisted by the state which
intend to keep students in the minority culture (for instance, through minority monolin-
gual education) should be understood as part of self-government; but that, too, would
seem strange as a description of a policy which provided tax deductions for contributions
to private minority-language schools or which provided vouchers to attend them.

[32] On the fairness or unfairness of various advantages and disadvantages accruing to
cultural and ethnic groups, see Robert Simon, 'Pluralism and Equality: The Status of
Minority Values in a Democracy,' and Joseph Carens, 'Difference and Domination:
Reflections on the Relations Between Pluralism and Equality,' in J. W. Chapman and
Alan Wertheimer (eds.), *NOMOS XXXII: Majorities and Minorities* (New York: New
York University Press, 1990).

thought to be *temporary*, although preferential policies are very often temporary in principle (even if not in practice). The argument for language rights, for example, would only yield temporary conclusions if the minority language group were made up of a group that was expected to assimilate entirely (and, if the group is made up of immigrants, not to be replenished by newcomers). Even if members of the minority were all rightly expected to learn the majority language, supporters of language rights could argue that it is unfair to force them to speak, read, listen, or write in a second language when (for example) defending themselves in court. Permanent assistance rights are typically sought when the disadvantage is a result of the simple status of minority, rather than a result of a history of injustice.

SELF-GOVERNMENT

Self-government claims are the most visible of cultural rights-claims and among the most widespread; ethnic, cultural, and national groups around the world seek a political unit in which they dominate, in which they can be ruled by members of their own group. These political units might be joined with others in a confederation, or they might be cantons, states or provinces in a federal system, or they might be fully independent. They might instead occupy a distinctive status not quite like that of other political units; this is true for the semi-sovereign Indian nations of the United States. Examples range from Quebec to KwaZulu, from Eritrea to Tibet; Slovakia, Scotland, Kurdistan, Catalonia, Brittany, Kashmir, the Basque lands, and the Jura canton in Switzerland do not begin to exhaust the list of places where self-government has been demanded or granted. The normative claims are similar in all of these cases: there ought to be a government which members of the group can think of as their own. They should not be ruled by aliens. Borders ought to be drawn, and institutions arranged, to allow the group political freedom from domination by other groups.

Self-government claims are ordinarily treated as distinct from other cultural rights-claims, and the normative issues they raise are well explored elsewhere (including, in part, in Chapters 2 and 4); I shall not rehearse them at length here.[33] None the less, a few points should be

---

[33] Secessionist claims for full independence are dealt with most thoroughly in Allen Buchanan, *Secession: The Morality of Political Divorce from Fort Sumpter to Lithuania and Quebec* (Boulder, Colo.: Westview Press, 1991), and Margaret Moore (ed.), *National Self-Determination and Secession* (Oxford: Oxford University Press, 1998), but also in Harry Beran, 'A Liberal Theory of Secession,' *Political Studies* 32 (1984), 21–31;

emphasized. The justification of self-government claims is unique in that it requires addressing questions of territory and borders. These claims are also more about government structure, and less about what private persons may do, than most cultural rights-claims. The incidental effects on minorities within minorities raise distinctive issues—distinctive even from policies *designed* to affect such local minorities, external rules); the question of whether those minorities in turn have a right to self-government is a perennial one.

The link between rights of cultural practice and self-government rights are not easy to draw, though Tamir tries to ground self-government rights in an extension of the individual right to practice one's culture; and even she recognizes the need for a separate argument showing the importance of having a public sphere of one's (culture's) own. The language of individual rights is more commonly thought irrelevant to self-government claims, except to condemn them if the self-governing group is thought likely to be illiberal or undemocratic.

Where a self-government claim or right is neither about full independence (Lithuania) nor about a general system of federalism (Switzerland) but is instead about a distinctive self-governing status within a larger state (Indian tribes, Puerto Rico) the issues raised may differ somewhat from those in the other cases; on some accounts it is thought easier to justify two separate states than it is to justify differentiated citizenship within one state.

In the Introduction and in Chapter 3 I argued that there cannot be a general right to self-government, but that self-government is justified in response to violence and exclusion by the currently ruling state.

EXTERNAL RULES

In some cases, it is claimed that protecting a particular culture requires restrictions on the liberty of nearby nonmembers. One of the most

Anthony Birch, 'Another Liberal Theory of Secession,' ibid. 596–602; Avishai Margalit and Joseph Raz, 'National Self-Determination,' *Journal of Philosophy* 87 (1990), 439–61; Cass Sunstein, 'Constitutionalism and Secession,' *University of Chicago Law Review* 58 (1991), 633–70; and Kai Nielsen, 'Liberal Nationalism, Liberal Democracies, and Secession,' *University of Toronto Law Journal* 48 (1998), 253–95. See also Crawford Young, *The Politics of Cultural Pluralism* (Madison: University of Wisconsin Press, 1976), 460–504. Federalism, confederalism, and regional autonomy as specific responses to ethnic pluralism are less well explored in the normative literature, but see Wayne Norman, 'Toward a Philosophy of Federalism,' in Judith Baker (ed.), *Group Rights* (Toronto: University of Toronto Press, 1994). The comparative literature on self-government short of secession is much larger; see Horowitz, *Ethnic Groups in Conflict*, 601–28 for an overview.

prominent of such external rules has been Quebec's Bill 101, which originally banned commercial signs in English and now mandates that they carry French translations if they are not in French. The province has other language laws including one requiring that businesses with more than fifty employees be run in French.[34] Kymlicka argues that preserving American Indian culture requires creating areas 'in which non-Indian Americans have restricted mobility, property, and voting rights.'[35] The restrictions on mobility and property rights take the form of 'denying non-Indians the right to purchase or reside on Indian lands;'[36] the proposed restriction on voting rights would (where the property and mobility restrictions are not in effect) require a three-to-ten year residency requirement before non-Indians gained the right to vote for or hold office in regional government.[37] On many US tribal reservations, residents who are not members of the tribe can never gain voting rights.

There are similar examples of external rules in other contexts. Quebecois as well as Indians have sought the power to limit the settlement of immigrants in their area. Where ownership or sovereignty do not already grant such control, an aboriginal veto over mining or development on tribal land would serve as an example of an external rule,[38]

---

[34] See Charles Taylor, *Multiculturalism and the Politics of Recognition* (Princeton: Princeton University Press, 1993), 52–5. The overruled Toubon law in France might have provided a similar example, and would have illustrated that in a global society it is not only minorities within a state which can feel culturally endangered. On the other hand, unlike in Quebec, the English threat (if that's what it is) in France comes not primarily from anglophones but from francophones adopting Anglicisms, and the Toubon law was seen as focused on members rather than nonmembers, so it is probably not analagous to the Quebec case and better understood outside the framework of external rules.

[35] Will Kymlicka, *Liberalism, Community, and Culture* (Oxford: Oxford University Press, 1989), 136.

[36] Ibid. 146. The inalienability of native land (or, more precisely, its alienability only to the Crown or its successor) has been a recurrent rule in the Anglo-settler colonies. As Kymlicka notes, it is both a restriction on nonmembers and a restriction on members. The degree to which it is one or the other depends in part on whether the rule is that native lands cannot be bought and sold *at all* or that they cannot be sold to or bought by *non-indigenes*. There is also variation in whether the rule simply prevents individual sales or whether even the tribe as a whole is incapable of selling even part of its land.

[37] Ibid. 147.

[38] This is the state of the law in Australia. Aborigines there do not have self-government or sovereignty; and ordinary landowners in Australia do not have either ownership of subsurface minerals or the right to refuse access to mining interests. Legislation recognizing Aboriginal land rights (in the Northern Territory in 1976, nationwide in 1993) granted special rights and powers to native title-holders to control or veto mining; this is an external rule, a limitation on the rights miners would have elsewhere in Australia. If all landowners had such rights, no special provision for Aborigines would be needed; that is, the ordinary common-law rule governing relations between landowner and miner need not be thought of as a cultural right. I argue against the Australian situation, in favor of the common-law rule granting all landowners mineral ownership and veto

as would extraordinary powers to control mining or development on nearby but non-tribal land. Allen Buchanan seems to suggest that the Amish and Mennonites be given the power to keep pornography and other 'cultural influences that threaten to undermine the community's values' out of the areas near their settlements.[39] In a slightly different vein, hate-speech laws come under this heading.

External rules are often argued to be an extension of the cultural community's right of self-government; the power to limit outsiders is compared with the comparable power held by states (such as the power to pick and choose among would-be immigrants). Some critics of Kymlicka suggest that external rules can *only* be justified in such a way, that is, with reference to the specific, partially independent status of the communities in question.[40] Similarly, Buchanan seeks to promote external rules as a viable alternative to secession, letting cultural minorities have state-like powers to protect their societies without the need to become independent states.

One thus might say of the right to impose external rules that it is derivative of the right to self-government, and that only a group with the latter right has the former. (This by itself, on Kymlicka's more recent account, would take the Amish out of the running.) The question of which external rules are legitimate might then be reduced to the question of what rules states themselves can legitimately impose on nonmembers. Even on this theory, some account is required of what those rules are, and whether the rules a small, culturally endangered state may impose on nonmembers are different from those which may be laid down by a large state which is not so endangered. If no such difference is stipulated, then the justification for external rules simply reduces to the justification of self-government (and of the claimed right

rights. Jacob Levy, 'Reconciliation and Resources: Mineral Rights and Aboriginal Land Rights as Property Rights,' *Policy* 10:1 (1994), 11–15; and 'The Value of Property Rights: Rejoinder to Brennan and Ewing,' *Policy* 10:2 (1994), 44–6.

[39] Buchanan, *Secession,* 59. The Amish themselves have never sought such a power; to do so would violate their own norms. They believe that Christians should have nothing to do with the violence and the power of the state, which is 'worldly'. Indeed, they ordinarily refuse to act as plaintiffs in court; seeking to control and direct the power of the criminal law would be unthinkable. Buchanan refers to the 'government of a territorially concentrated religious community such as the Amish or Mennonites' as analogous to Indian tribal governments, which is mistaken; the relevant religious authorities would be extremely resistant to seeing themselves as force-wielding governments.

[40] John Tomasi, 'Kymlicka, Liberalism, and Respect for Aboriginal Cultures,' *Ethics,* 105:3 (1995), 580–603; John Danley, 'Liberalism, Aboriginal Rights and Cultural Minorities,' *Philosophy and Public Affairs* 20 (1991), 168–85. Kymlicka himself seems to have come around to this view; he now argues for external rules only on behalf of national minorities (all of which, on his view, have a right to self-government) and using the analogy between the powers of such groups and the powers of states.

of all states to control, for example, immigration). If there is such a difference—if an Indian tribal government may restrict non-Indians in a way that the United States could not morally restrict, say, resident aliens, or if strenuous requirements for voting are thought legitimate near Indian lands but not in Estonia—then the appeal to self-government cannot do all of the justificatory work, and one of the arguments described below will be needed.

If external rules are not simply derivative from self-government, if some groups without valid self-government claims can none the less impose external rules legitimately, the supporter of an external restriction must argue for the priority of a culturally related end *over the liberty of nonmembers*, which is what makes external rules distinct in the kind of justification they require. What this entails obviously depends on the status of liberty in the general political philosophy of which the cultural-rights theory forms a part. This might be done by arguing that the liberty lost is of no very high value; this is part of the approach in defending hate-speech laws. Or it might be done by stressing the importance of cultural membership to the exercise of liberty at all, and then limiting the external rules to those necessary to protect the good of cultural membership.[41] An argument about the externalities of nonmembers' actions is also likely to play an important role; this is most evident in the case of an indigenous veto on mining or development, but forms a necessary part of any argument for an external rule: your exercise of your freedom has the side-effect of damaging my culture. External rules can be argued against by reversing any of these steps; liberty (or the particular liberty at stake) might be argued to have a greater importance, the cultural good might be argued to have a lesser (moral) importance, or the existence or magnitude of the externalities might be disputed (thus denying the necessity of the external rule for the protection of the culture).[42]

In Chapter 3 I argued that a supposed generalized good of cultural

---

[41] This, or something close to it, was Kymlicka's original approach, and seems still to carry that part of the justification for external rules which cannot be borne by the appeal to self-government.

[42] Narveson, 'Collective Rights?' clearly embraces both of the first two arguments: liberty is extremely important, and the preservation of a culture, while perhaps valuable, is not morally important enough to give rise to a right. Kukathas, 'Are There Any Cultural Rights?' seems to use both as well. Tamir, *Liberal Nationalism*, 38–42, stresses that, since cultural membership is partially chosen, it should not be 'entirely isolated from "the market of preferences." ' For Rawlsian liberals, identifying culture as chosen deprives it of the sort of moral status which could trump liberty claims, which is why Kymlicka, *Liberalism, Community, and Culture,* takes pains to identify a culture as a 'context of choice' rather than the result of choices.

preservation could not justify external restrictions. I also suggested that the letter in fact often restrict members at least as much as they restrict non-members, since they characteristically restrict forms of interaction between the two, weighing relatively more heavily on the members of the smaller group.

RECOGNITION/ENFORCEMENT

It is fairly common for cultural communities to seek to give their traditional law a status in the law of the land, to seek to have their members bound by the traditional law of the community rather than the general law of the wider state. Very often, these claims seek to have the general law recognize a culturally specific way of establishing certain rights which are established otherwise by the general law. A simple, and fairly innocuous, example, is the authority granted to religious officials in some states to perform legally binding marriages.[43]

An extremely wide range of issues are caught up in the question of recognition for traditional law, but among the most common are land rights, family law, and criminal law. James Crawford notes that the doctrine that Australian Aborigines (whether aware of it or not) were subject to British rather than tribal law 'involved the denial of land rights and the non-recognition of traditional marriages as much as the refusal to recognize Aboriginal tribal laws as a defense to crimes defined by British law.'[44]

Indigenous groups in Australia and in the United States have sought legal recognition for their criminal punishment systems, which recognition would imply both that the offender should not be punished again by the state and that the tribal punisher should not be criminally liable (for example, when the tribal punishment includes a spearing).[45] Some Muslims in India have sought (and won) legal standing for Muslim family law, and have generally argued that Muslims should be bound by the *sharia* rather than by general Indian

---

[43] In other states—France and Germany, for example—the religious ceremony lacks legal standing, and must be supplemented with a civil ceremony before a secular civil official.

[44] James Crawford, 'Legal Pluralism and the Indigenous Peoples of Australia,' in Oliver Mendelsohn and Upendra Baxi (eds.), *The Rights of Subordinated Peoples* (Oxford: Oxford University Press, 1994), 181–2, footnotes omitted.

[45] See K. E. Mulqueeny, 'Folk-law or Folklore: When a Law is Not a Law. Or is it?' in M. A. Stephenson and Suri Ratnapala (eds.), *Mabo: A Judicial Revolution* (Brisbane: University of Queensland Press, 1993).

law in civil matters—though they accept the need for a general criminal law.[46] A British court refused such recognition to traditional Indian rules about arranged marriages.[47] In some states polygamous marriages in accordance with Muslim law are recognized and given full legal status as marriages. This differs from a simple exemption from criminal laws against bigamy, and one could easily support the exemption claim while opposing the recognition claim. Granting the recognition claim has implications for the whole array of legal privileges that adhere to marriage in most states. Those privileges, including preferential tax treatment, extension of health insurance, default rules about power of attorney, child custody, and property allocation after a divorce or a death *in testate,* are often shaped and supported on grounds of public policy rather than justice. Those public policy arguments, formulated in the context of two-person marriages, might or might not make any sense in the context of plural marriages. Of course, a claim in justice might then be made saying that unequal treatment of different family arrangements was unjustified; but this is a different kind of argument from that saying that one ought to be free to have religiously but not legally binding plural marriages without facing criminal penalties.

At the base of indigenous land-rights claims is the notion that the legal system of the settlers ought to recognize the property systems established according to native law, and that if a particular group owned a particular piece of land under traditional law they ought to have a valid title under settlers' law as well. The Australian High Court case *Mabo v Queensland (no. 2)*[48] puts this problem in stark form: Could Australian law recognize and incorporate the property law of the Mer people of the Torres Strait Islands, or must it be bound by the doctrine of *terra nullius* which held Australia to be legally unowned? Many land-rights cases in Canada and the United States are one step removed from this question, and seek to undo seizures of land which were either illegal even according to settler law or which violated treaties which recognized native title. The root issue is the same, however, although the British in North America recognized native ownership much earlier than they did in Australia. Still, many Indian nations in North America did not sign treaties with the settler

---

[46] See Veena Das, 'Cultural Rights and the Definition of Community,' in Oliver Mendelsohn and Upendra Baxi (eds.), *The Rights of Subordinated Peoples* (Oxford: Oxford University Press, 1994).
[47] Kukathas, 'Are There Any Cultural Rights?', 133.
[48] *Mabo v Queensland (no. 2)*, 175 CLR 1 (Australia 1992).

governments, and their land-rights-claims are straightforward recognition claims.[49]

A recognition of a property-law system need not be only or even primarily about landownership; other issues include hunting and passage usufruct rights over land, and fishing and other marine rights. A related question is that of intellectual property. Some Australian Aborigines have sought to have the copyright law extended to protect folklore and art which Aboriginal customary law holds may only be told or reproduced by certain persons or groups.[50]

In general, legal standing might be given to a tradition's method of performing marriages; its rules about conduct within marriages; its method of obtaining a divorce; its rules about relations between ex-husband and ex-wife; its way of defining a will, or its laws about post-mortem allocation of property; its expectations about the support of the indigent; its arbitration of civil disputes or its judgments in criminal matters; its methods of establishing property rights and its rules about use of property; its hunting and fishing rules; its evidentiary rules or procedures;[51] and so on. Arguments for doing so often refer to the

---

[49] Tully explicitly argues for indigenous land rights as part of an argument for the recognition of indigenous legal systems. James Tully, 'Aboriginal Property and Western Theory: Recovering a Middle Ground,' *Social Philosophy and Policy* 11 (1994), 153–80. Shepherd provides an interesting discussion of the Han Chinese settlement of Taiwan and conflicts over the recognition of the land tenure system of the island's indigenous inhabitants; *modulo* the difference between English and Chinese law, the history and issues are remarkably like those in North America, Australia, and New Zealand. John Shepherd, *Statecraft and Political Economy on the Taiwan Frontier 1600–1800* (Stanford: Stanford University Press, 1993), 241–56. Where land rights-claims are based on the illegality of the seizures under instruments of the dominant legal system (the Proclamation of 1763, Indian treaties) it seems to me that no special issues related to culture or ethnicity are raised. Any problems raised are problems in the theory of restitution. This is also the case in the current return of seized property to dispossessed blacks in South Africa and dispossessed Asians in Uganda.

[50] See Kamal Puri, 'Copyright Protection for Australian Aborigines in the Light of *Mabo*,' in M. A. Stephenson and Suri Ratnapala (eds.), *Mabo: A Judicial Revolution* (Brisbane: University of Queensland Press, 1993). Standard copyright law is poorly suited to accommodate any intellectual property in such works because of, *inter alia*, its restriction to work with one or a small and identifiable group of authors and its exclusion of purely oral works. These rules have good reasons, and are thought important to preserving freedom of speech and intellectual and artistic freedom; but, Puri argues, those reasons and those categories reflect parochially western understandings about what it means to create a work of art.

[51] As, for example, when testimony which takes the form 'I know this is my land because my father told me so, and he told me that his father told him, and . . .' is accepted from members of a group which relies on oral tradition rather than written evidence, instead of being rejected as hearsay. This is true in Canada, Australia, New Zealand, Papua New Guinea, and several of the formerly British states in Africa; I do not know the state of the law on this matter in the United States. See B. A. Keon-Cohen, 'Some Problems of Proof: The Admissibility of Traditional Evidence,' in M. A.

cultural non-neutrality of the state's general laws; to the importance of not upsetting settled expectations and plans (involving property, inheritance, norms about marriage, and so on); and to the unfairness of holding people accountable to an unfamiliar law or, worse, leaving them accountable both to the state's law and to the traditional one (which can carry sanctions like ostracism even if it is not given legal status). Too great a disjunction between the law on one hand and real practices, expectations, or shared understandings on the other is argued to be unfair; if correct, this provides strong support for recognition/enforcement claims.[52] Additionally, the more formal and less substantive the issue is from the wider society's perspective (which may not correspond with the minority's!), the easier it seems to justify recognition. On few philosophical accounts would the words spoken at a wedding ceremony be of great significance; that is not true for the question of what rights women have in the subsequent marriage.

Crawford, citing a report of the Australian Law Reform Commission, notes a variety of drawbacks to recognition and enforcement (though he ultimately endorses many such rights-claims).

The recognition of . . . customary law has often meant its limitation or confinement. It has also been used, on occasions, as a smokescreen to avoid consideration of issues such as autonomy, including the autonomy to change or even to abandon customary ways. The spectre is that of the exhibited Aborigine, recognized as long as recognizably 'traditional.'[53]

Crawford also notes fears about morally unacceptable punishments (e.g. spearing); women's rights; loss of Aboriginal control over laws and traditions; and divisive and discriminatory legal pluralism. Most arguments against recognition/enforcement claims build on one or more of these fears. It is thought the very essence of discrimination to have entirely different legal codes applying to members of different cultures. The law whose recognition is sought is often religious, typically customary and traditional in some strong sense, so women's rights—or basic human rights more generally—are thought to be endangered.

Stephenson and Suri Ratnapala (eds.), *Mabo: A Judicial Revolution* (Brisbane: University of Queensland Press, 1993). See also *Baker Lake v Minister of Indian Affairs* (1979 Canada) 107 DLR (3rd) 513; *Simon v R* (1985 Canada) 24 DLR (4th) 390; *Milirrpum v Nabalco* (1971 Australia) 17 FLR 141.

[52] This argument is obviously compatible with certain communitarian visions (for example, Walzer's theories about the importance shared understandings). The argument is not limited to communitarian philosophies, though. In another context, Tamir warns that a government and a legal code disconnected from the culture of the ruled creates the risk of 'alienation and irrelevance,' 'the enfeeblement of formal law and the marginalisation of government activities.' Tamir, *Liberal Nationalism*, 149.

[53] Crawford, 'Legal Pluralism,' 179.

Concerns about protection of basic rights are perhaps relevant to recognition of family and criminal law in a way which they are not to the recognition of claims for land rights. Land-rights claims are more often argued against on grounds of distributive justice, that is, that it would be unjust to if thus-and-such a small percentage of the population owned so many thousands of square miles of land.[54] Of course, such an argument might be made opportunistically, and many who make it about land would be unwilling to look too deeply into what percentage of a country's population held what portion of its liquid assets. Yet the argument can also be made sincerely.[55]

Different justificatory problems are involved if the traditional law is to have *exclusive* jurisdiction over members, or whether they can choose which legal system to use. In the former case—epitomized by the millet system in Ottoman Turkey—concerns about the basic rights of members are highlighted; if the customary law is reactionary, repressive, or discriminatory, members have no opportunity to escape or work around it.[56] Where members can choose—as in the case of the Aborigine or Indian who must consent to face tribal rather than general criminal sanctions—an inequality of treatment is created which may require justification. A member of the dominant group who commits a crime must face the dominant system's legal judgment; members of the non-dominant group might make an opportunistic decision, choosing the legal system expected to be more lenient. There is the further complication that not all parties to a dispute will necessarily choose the same legal system; if Muslims can choose between Muslim family law and the general family law, one spouse might seek a divorce under the *sharia* with the other seeking divorce under the general law, creating disputes as to who will be

---

[54] They are also sometimes argued against on the grounds that recognition raises the question of what other aspects of the minority legal system must be incorporated into the dominant legal system; as Crawford notes in the passage quoted above, the legal rationale for excluding Aboriginal criminal law from Australian law was the same doctrine as that used to exclude recognition of Aboriginal land rights. Tully's argument would also seem to suggest that once land rights are conceded there is a live question about the legal status of other parts of minority customary law.

[55] As it is at as in Kymlicka, *Multicultural Citizenship*, 219–21 and Tamir, *Liberal Nationalism*, 40–1. Kymlicka, I think, understates how much a distributive egalitarianism argues against land-rights-claims and how much real land-rights-claims are based on recognition rather than distribution.

[56] The concern for the protection of the basic rights of members animates Kukathas's rejection of exclusive recognition/enforcement of customary family or civil codes as well as Kymlicka's. Kukathas, 'Are There Any Cultural Rights?' 128–9 and 133; Kymlicka, *Multicultural Citizenship*, 39–42. On neither account, I think, is it clear whether recognition without exclusive jurisdiction is being condemned as well.

bound by which obligations.[57] Again, the more purely formal the right claimed is, the less weight these concerns hold. If a customary marriage is recognized but considered legally identical to a civil-law marriage, if native title confers rights no different from freehold title despite its different origins, then the ability to move between legal systems is unlikely to create problems (though these situations of partial recognition may face other difficulties, political and/or theoretical).

Arguments for recognition and enforcement claims are sometimes closely linked with arguments for self-government, and it is true enough that at least some recognition/enforcement rights are likely to go along with any move to self-government; the legal system of the new unit will probably be based in part on the traditional rules and expectations of the newly self-governing group. But it is important to note the separability of the issues. Recognition/enforcement rights-claims, for one thing, involve no necessary claim to territory, and no request to govern non-members. They can be made even when cultural groups are thoroughly intermixed. Furthermore, granting recognition/enforcement claims does not necessarily give members of the group any special standing in the determination of their laws; often, it is up to courts of the general society to decide when customary law has or has not been followed. Indeed, since these rights-claims are precisely about gaining recognition from the general legal system (for the group's marriages, property laws, and so on) outsiders may be given more power over the group in a very real sense, hardly what one expects from self-government. Even enforcement of traditional criminal law, which might be seen as a clear case of self-government rights, seems a great deal less like self-government if the general courts must authorize it, monitor it, and decide on its limits. On the other hand, where a group seeking self-government is not very traditional, or is highly differentiated internally and has no one set of rules regarded as authoritative, or does not differ in its traditional rules from the dominant group, self-government may include very little by way of recognition/enforcement; it may be a simple matter of seeking to control the language of government operations and public schooling, and bringing the capital closer to home.[58] Self-government and autonomy claims are about the structure of government and the identity of the governors; recognition/enforcement claims are about

[57] On the other hand, these disputes might not be any more complicated than those arising because of competing jurisdictions in a federal system.
[58] The secession of the Czech Republic and Slovakia from each other would seem a polar case. No claim was made that the Czechs were disrupting traditional Slovak law, or that independence would allow Slovaks to live according to their own traditional rules.

the content of the law. One faces concerns about borders, territory, and the status of non-members; the other faces concerns about the justice of the treatment of members. A general system of recognition/enforcement of minority cultural law might resemble federalism in that it creates multiple legal orders within the state; but accepting recognition claims does not force one down a logical or moral road to federalism, and vice versa. The *reductio* of recognition rights might be the millet system but it is not secession.[59] The next two chapters are primarily about recognition and enforcement claims, and devote further attention to how they differ from self-government claims.

INTERNAL RULES

Many rules and norms governing a community's members are not elevated into law. There are expectations about how a member will behave; one who does not behave that way is subject to the sanction of no longer being viewed as a member by other members. This sanction may take the form of shunning, excommunication, being disowned by one's family, being expelled from an association, and so on; ostracism of one sort or another usually stands as the ultimate punishment for violating an internal rule. The content of the rules varies enormously; one might be excommunicated for blasphemy or disowned for marrying outside one's own cultural group. Many are at least in part religious, but as the (common) rule against intermarriage shows, they need not be.[60]

On most liberal or democratic accounts, these rules would be clearly unjust if they were imposed by the state. Controversy arises over how

[59] Special treatment may be required for non-territorial, non-customary self-government, sometimes called non-territorial federalism or 'the personality principle.' Bauer and Renner proposed such a system for Austria-Hungary. See Tom Bottomore and Patrick Goode (eds.) *Austro-Marxism* (Oxford: Oxford University Press, 1978). While this work is often referred to as offering possible solutions to difficult problems, there has been little development of the basic ideas into concrete policies, and so I do not try to fit them into this framework.

[60] The old American taboo against 'miscegenation' between blacks and whites differs dramatically from more common forms of the rule against intermarriage, in that it was motivated entirely by racism, a vision of superior and inferior groups, and a fear of 'pollution.' On the other hand, many cultural groups in plural societies are concerned about the continuation and strength of their culture across generations; intermarriage is frowned upon not so much because outsiders are dirty or inferior as because of a responsibility to make sure that the next generation grows up in the culture and a fear that mixed marriages do not provide such cultural integrity. Even if the outsiders are thought well of, they are thought unlikely parents of future group members.

to view them when they are enforced by informal or formal but non-coercive sanctions. A state may not reserve decision-making offices for men; may the Catholic Church? The state may not punish someone for his or her choice of spouse; does the same injunction apply to parents? The state may not deprive someone of citizenship for changing religions; but should a religious group, or a religiously-centered cultural group, be allowed to deprive someone of membership for such a conversion? More generally: is ostracism or expulsion to be taken as normatively different from punishment? Are associations, families, and churches subject to the same moral constraints on their actions that states are? Obviously, one's general theoretical stance about family arrangements, freedom of association and disassociation, and religious freedom will largely determine one's response to internal rules. A theory which argues that only internally democratic associations have any claim to respect from a democratic state will likely have little patience for internal rules, as will one which sees the family as a political institution and a site of unjust oppression under majority and minority culture alike.

Liberal accounts may be more sympathetic than (for example) strong democratic or feminist ones. Kymlicka, who condemns 'internal restrictions'—'where the basic civil and political liberties of group members are being restricted'[61]—goes on to say that

> Obviously, groups are free to require such actions [as church attendance or adherence to traditional gender roles] as terms of membership in private, voluntary associations. A Catholic organization can insist that its members attend church. The problem arises when a group seeks to use governmental power to restrict the liberty of members. Liberals insist that whoever exercises political power within a community respect the civil and political rights of its members, and any attempt to impose internal restrictions which violate this condition is illegitimate.[62]

The strength of this qualification is unclear, though. Kymlicka later criticizes 'minority cultures [that] discriminate against girls in the provision of education, and deny women the right to vote or hold office . . . [or that] limit the freedom of individual members within the group to revise traditional practices,' and says that '[t]hese sorts of internal restrictions cannot be justified or defended within a liberal conception of minority rights.'[63] Does this mean that the right of Catholicism or Orthodox Judaism to keep women out of [some] religious offices cannot be justified or defended? That when the Amish and Mennonites limit the freedom of members to revise traditional practices (and still remain

---

[61] Kymlicka, *Multicultural Citizenship*, 36.   [62] Ibid. 202 n. 1
[63] Ibid. 153.

members) that they are committing rights-violations? Such would seem to be the case, based on Kymlicka's discussion of the Hutterites, a communal religious group which expelled members for apostasy and refused to divide up their communal assets in order to give a share to the ex-members. This, Kymlicka thinks, is a denial of religious freedom for it imposes a high cost on abandoning one's religion at will.[64] This high cost is characteristic of internal rules; the child disowned for inter-marriage or for abandoning the faith is in a similar position to the ex-Hutterites. Similarly, we are told that liberalism 'precludes a religious minority from prohibiting apostasy and proselytization.'[65] If such rules constitute abridgments of the freedom to marry or freedom of conscience, then internal rules stand condemned as a class.[66]

Kukathas, on the other hand, clearly makes full use of the idea of free-dom of association.[67] Indeed, he carries it beyond the range of internal rules as described here, defending the right of the Pueblo *state* to ostra-cize those who abandon their tribal religion. My suggestion here is that, on their own terms, both Kymlicka and Kukathas have made a category mistake. Kymlicka sees internal rules as rights-violations where, based on his argument, he ought to see only associational freedom. Kukathas sees what is really a state as merely a voluntary association entitled to enact internal rules. I will return to this point in Part III.

In Chapter 1, under 'Internal Cruelty,' I argued that internal rules which are violent or cruel ought to be proscribed, but that there is other-wise good reason for leaving internal rules unhampered.

REPRESENTATION

In order to secure protection of their interests or rights, in order to prevent discrimination or ensure certain privileges, in order to have a

---

[64] Kymlicka, *Multicultural Citizenship*, 161.   [65] Ibid. 161.

[66] As should be clear, I find Kymlicka's arguments here puzzling, not because they condemn internal rules but because of the way in which that condemnation occurs. I'm not sure what it *means* to tell a religious group that it cannot prohibit apostasy. Must the person who openly rejects the faith continue to be welcomed as a member of it? It is simple enough to say that the *state* cannot prohibit apostasy, that the millet system was unjust; but Kymlicka says more than that. The rule may be that a religion cannot be so central or dominant a part of a person's life that abandoning it is very costly. That is clearly a rule for which one could articulate a defense, though it would require a stand-ard for measuring the size of the costs. But it would hardly be a *liberal* standard.

[67] Chandran Kukathas, 'Are There Any Cultural Rights?' and 'Cultural Rights Again: A Rejoinder to Kymlicka,' *Political Theory* 20 (1992), 674–80.

say in the actions of the state, ethnic minorities often seek some form of guaranteed representation in the state's decision-making bodies, especially but not only legislatures. The mechanisms for this vary. Sometimes it takes the form of a straightforward quota; in Zimbabwe's first decade of black rule, 20 per cent of parliamentary seats were reserved for whites, and three out of the nine seats on Quebec's Supreme Court are reserved for judges from Quebec. Sometimes the number of seats reserved varies with the number of people choosing to vote on the reserved electoral roll rather than the general one; Maori representation in the New Zealand parliament has some of this flexibility. An effort might be made to create 'majority-minority' single-member legislative districts; this has long been the approach used in the United States to increase black representation in Congress (though its days seem to be numbered). In party-list systems, parties might have formal or informal commitments to have a certain portion of their candidates come from particular groups. Proportional representation, perhaps with a formula weighted toward smaller parties, might be adopted with the intention of letting the various parts of a plural society be represented; cumulative voting might be adopted to allow minorities to concentrate their votes.

Levine observes that 'the issue central to proposals for according blacks (and perhaps other disempowered groups) special electoral rights is not quite the same as in affirmative action or 'reverse discrimination' debates. There the crucial consideration is justice. In evaluating claims for group rights to electoral power, the principal concern is democracy.'[68] To put it another way: the justice and effectiveness of majoritarian democracy are called into question when its assumption of shifting and alternating majorities is violated. Each group, it is argued, should *sometimes* be in the winning coalition; and ethnic minorities often find themselves permanently locked out from decision-making.[69] This is thought unfair according to democratic theory's own terms, and likely to produce either ethnic conflict or oppression.

Other arguments for representation are possible. Kukathas argues that

there may sometimes be good reason to design political institutions to take into account the ethnic or cultural composition of the society. Yet there is no reason

---

[68] Andrew Levine, 'Electoral Power, Group Power, and Democracy,' in J. W. Chapman and Alan Wertheimer (eds.), *NOMOS XXXII: Majorities and Minorities* (New York: New York University Press, 1990), 215–52.

[69] See Lani Guinier, *The Tyranny of the Majority: Fundamental Fairness in Representative Democracy* (New York: Free Press and Macmillan, 1994), 3–6, 41–156; Arend Lijphart, *Democracy in Plural Societies* (New Haven: Yale University Press, 1979), 25–41; Kymlicka, *Multicultural Citizenship*, 131–51.

to see this as inconsistent with liberal theory, which, at least since Montesquieu, has recognized the importance of the(*sic*) institutions conforming to the nature of the social order.[70]

But these are, on Kukathas's view, questions of institutional design, that is, how to design those institutions which will most effectively protect individual rights; 'group rights play no part in the justification of the mechanisms that uphold the modus vivendi.'[71]

Three sets of issues are involved in most arguments for representation, issues easily blurred but important to separate. One is the presence of members of the minority group; one is the chance for members of the minority group to choose representatives; and one is protection of minority group interests. These need to be argued for (or against) separately, and they imply different kinds of arrangements.

When parties in a party-list system set aside a certain number of their seats for members of a group, or the group will have *members* in the legislature but not necessarily chosen *representatives*. Here the focus is on the identity of the legislators rather than the identity of the electors. The same is true if a number of seats are set aside for minority group members, but everyone votes to decide who will occupy those seats. This is a kind of affirmative action for legislators, and might even be best understood as an assistance right rather than a representation right.[72] To the extent that such a system builds on the arguments for representation, it does so by assuming that *any* members of the minority group will represent the interests of that group.[73] To a large degree, though, such a system must be understood as overcoming the burdens faced by would-be legislators (e.g. a tradition of drawing candidates from professions or regions dominated by the majority). It is subject to the normal arguments (pro and con) of the affirmative action debate.

In other cases, the concern is less the disadvantage faced by members of the minority who wish to hold legislative seats than on the disadvantage faced by the minority in electing its own representatives. That is, the focus is on the identity of the electors rather than on the identity of the officials; examples include the Maori voting roll; the pre-coup Fijian constitution with voting rolls for Fijians, Indians, and others (mainly

[70] Kukathas, 'Are There Any Cultural Rights?' 131.   [71] Ibid. 132.

[72] Kymlicka makes related points; *Multicultural Citizenship*, 141–42, 148–9.

[73] If the argument for guaranteeing seats in the legislature rested on the idea that deliberation is improved and more ideas heard when there is greater diversity among the deliberators, then this would be a democracy-based representation claim rather than one about affirmative action. Of course, often both arguments are made simultaneously. The strength of the deliberation argument depends in part on the structure of the legislature; if it is based on strict party discipline, with decisions made by party leaders rather than by caucus, the argument would be difficult to sustain.

British);[74] and racially gerrymandered districts. Iris Marion Young argues that 'a democratic public should provide mechanisms for the effective recognition and representation of the distinct voices and perspectives of those of its *constituent groups* that are oppressed or disadvantaged.'[75]

Finally, one might worry that even with representatives of a minority group in place—even if they occupy a disproportionate number of seats—they could simply be outvoted time after time. Mechanisms to offset this danger are analyzed by the consociational school and include formal or informal requirements to have grand coalition governments; Switzerland's seven-person executive council and rotating presidency; pre-civil-war Lebanon's reservation of the most important government positions according to cultural/religious status; Belgium's requirement that linguistic legislation be approved by a majority of parliamentarians from each linguistic group, and similar proposals for minority vetoes; and so on. Lani Guinier's recent work is focused on ways to solve this problem. Donald Horowitz suggests that this goal might be at odds with the two discussed above.

[G]roup rights—or really, special group privileges [referring to guaranteed representation] . . . provide illusory security, easily pierced. Even if they continue to function, they consign minorities to minority status. Unless they offer a minority veto—in which case the urge to abolish them will grow—they ratify the exclusion of the minority from power. So, in the first respect, group rights provide too much—benefits that are disproportionate and are, on that account, unlikely to survive. And, in the second respect, group rights provide too little, for they do not aim at minority participation at the seat of power.[76]

Horowitz maintains that such representation undercuts the need to form multiethnic coalitions and thus increases the likelihood that the winning coalition will simply take no account of a minority group's interests. If this is so, then it becomes all the more important to separate out the various arguments involved in representation claims, for it may be that one must choose among them.[77]

---

[74] See Vernon Van Dyke, 'The Individual, the State, and Ethnic Communities in Political Theory,' *World Politics* 29 (1979), 353.

[75] Young, *Justice and the Politics of Difference*, 185; emphasis added.

[76] Horowitz, *A Democratic South Africa? Constitutional Engineering in a Divided Society* (Berkeley: University of California Press, 1991), 136.

[77] Horowitz thus suggests e.g. single transferable vote systems, which he thinks encourage alliances across ethnic boundaries at voting time. Consociationalists disagree, and argue for proportionality at election time and trans-ethnic alliances at the elite level. If their argument is correct, then allowing direct minority-group representation is compatible with, indeed is a crucial part of, ensuring protection for minority group interests.

Two complementary arguments are commonly deployed against representation rights-claims. One is that such claims falsely impute a unity of viewpoint based on ethnicity; that is, they assume that all members of the minority group share the same political ideas and interests. It is also argued that claims for representation assume clear *differences* of interest and viewpoint *among* groups. (It is sometimes further argued that this assumption is self-fulfilling, that is, that granting representation will encourage political cleavages along ethnic lines.)

Some representation schemes are also open to the charge that they require officially identifying voters on the basis of race, in the way that South Africa did under its 1983 (ostensibly) triracial constitution. Many plans for representation, though, have no such requirement. Changing an electoral system in order to protect minorities—for example, adopting cumulative voting or proportional representation—might be done *in order* to protect ethnic minorities, but yield protection for any politically cohesive minority, acting through their parties and votes rather than through a separate voting roll.

SYMBOLIC CLAIMS

Many ethnocultural disputes are over issues which do not directly affect anyone's ability to enjoy or live according to their culture, or the distribution of political power among groups. They concern such matters as the name of a polity, its flag, its coat of arms, its national anthem, its public holidays, the name by which a cultural group will be known, or the way a group's history is presented in schools and textbooks.[78] These symbolic disputes are about claims to recognition—recognition as a (or 'the') founding people of the polity, recognition as a group which has made important contributions, recognition as a group which exists with a distinct and worthwhile identity.

While language-rights-claims in courts, in schools, on ballot papers, and so on are typically claims of assistance rights, the demand to have a minority language be made one of a state's 'official' languages (or the demand to eliminate or prevent the category of 'official languages' altogether) is a symbolic one, albeit one that might have an important impact on the whole range of assistance language-claims. The one kind of claim is about the ability of persons to interact with the organs of the

---

[78] See Horowitz, *Ethnic Groups in Conflict*, 127 for examples in addition to those discussed below.

state; the other is about the very *identity* of the state. It is worth noting again that the more symbolic claim is not necessarily considered less important than the apparently more substantive one. From the majority culture's perspective, the cost associated with hiring interpreters or bilingual employees, or with printing documents in multiple languages, might be borne much more easily than a challenge to the official status of the *Staatvolk*. From the minority culture's perspective, the absence of interpreters at a particular government office might be viewed as an inconvenience, whereas the elevation of the majority tongue to official status, or the denial of that status to the minority language, might be viewed as an open declaration that some are not wanted as members of the state.

The symbolic nature of these claims is seen in pure form by the successful (in 1938) drive to have Rhaeto-Romanic declared a national language of Switzerland. Rhaeto-Romansh was *not* made a language of state business; German, French, and Italian remained the only languages with that role ('official' languages). Laws did not have to be translated; courts, legislative assemblies, and the army had no new requirement to operate even in part in Rhaeto-Romansh. Native speakers had the right to address courts and authorities in their own language, but they had had that right long before, as well. The constitutional amendment yielded almost no *practical* changes, but it meant that Rhaeto-Romansh speakers were recognized as one of the constituent peoples of Switzerland. This symbolic outcome was what was most desired by petitioners, who were indeed at pains to point out that they were *not* requesting that theirs be made a language of state business.[79]

The variety of symbolic claims and disputes is vast. Australia's Aborigines have argued for a clause in that country's constitution recognizing their prior presence; Quebec has demanded official recognition as a 'distinct society.' Both of these changes are sought in part because it is thought they would pave the way for other, more concrete cultural rights; but the recognition is sought for its own sake as well. Many symbolic claims lack even that role as a possible first step to more concrete policies. Aboriginal and American Indian groups have argued against the symbolism of Australia Day and Columbus Day celebrations. In 1994 the Australian government began referring to Macedonians as 'Slav Macedonians' in order to placate Greek–Australians upset over the recognition of Macedonia; this in turn

[79] Bernard Cathamos, 'Rhaeto-Romansh in Switzerland up to 1940,' in Sergij Vilfan *et al.* (eds.), *Ethnic Groups and Language Rights* (New York: New York University Press, European Science Foundation, 1993), 98–105.

outraged Macedonian–Australians and led them to claim that they had a right not to be renamed by the state.

Symbolic claims are impossible to commend or condemn as a class, since they may well be contradictory; one group's request for recognition as a founding people runs into another group's desire for recognition as unique. Both sides in a dispute about a polity's symbols make claims for recognition. Sometimes these disputes can be compromised, as described by Claus Offe:

On March 29, 1990, Slovak deputies of the Czechoslovak Federal Parliament entered a motion that the name of the state should from now on be hyphenated as 'Czecho-Slovakia' (as it was written in the inter-war period) rather than Czechoslovakia. The Czech majority voted in favor of the compromise that the spelling proposed by the Slovaks should be used in Slovakia, but the unhyphenated version should be used in the Czech Lands and abroad. This decision was perceived by the Slovak public as deeply insulting, and the elimination of the hyphen was protested the next day at a mass rally in Bratislava by a crowd of 80,000 people. In this case, a compromise could be actually be found. On April 12 the parliament changed the official state name to Czech *and* Slovak Federal Republic.[80]

I discuss symbolic claims much more fully in Chapter 8.

DISCUSSION

Gurr sorts cultural rights-claims into demands for exit, autonomy, access, and control, with various further subdivisions.[81] Exit is full secession, that is, the attempt to gain a fully independent state. There are obvious reasons to treat such secessions separately from internal self-government or federalist arrangements. I have lumped secession and internal self-government together under 'self-government,' because they have much in common with each other which they do not have with other cultural rights-claims, but I do not deny that they must be considered separately for a variety of purposes. This does *not* mean that internal self-government ought to be lumped in with other rights-claims, and this is what Gurr does. His category of 'autonomy' includes rights from every category in my classification.[82] What seems to mark autonomy off as a separate category is that it includes the demands which might be

---

[80] Claus Offe, *Ethnic Politics in European Transitions* (Bremen: Center for European Law and Policy, Papers on East European Constitution Building No. 1, 1993), 7 n. 5
[81] Gurr, *Minorities at Risk*, 294–312.   [82] Ibid. 299.

made by a group which might otherwise secede, or by indigenous groups. All the demands which Gurr considers autonomy claims are anti-assimilationist; but that is the extent of what they have in common. Something of the same is true for access, 'recognition and protection of [certain kinds of cultural groups'] interests within the political framework of a plural society.'[83] Assistance, representation, and exemptions are all clearly included, and they lack even a common orientation toward integration or separation. What they do have in common is that they are claimed by those groups which are not candidates for secession, are not indigenous, and do not seek to gain control over other groups.[84]

Kymlicka sorts cultural rights-claims into self-government, polyethnic rights, and representation, with a crosscutting distinction between external protections and internal restrictions.

The self/government/polyethnic distinction, I think, largely matches Gurr's autonomy/access distinction. Both focus on the kind of group making the claim. Kymlicka's category of national groups includes Gurr's ethnonational and indigenous groups; Kymlicka's ethnic groups would seem to include at least Gurr's disadvantaged contenders and ethnoclasses. Both distinctions stress the separatist nature of one kind of claim and the integrationist or cooperative nature of the other.

Kymlicka wishes to emphasize that the legitimate claims of immigrant ethnic groups do not create a slippery slope to self-government while defending self-government for groups like the Quebecois and Indian tribes. Similarly, Gurr wants to identify the clusters of claims which seem to march together in the world. This approach has its uses but also has limits, especially as a framework for normative work. It divides like rights-claims, and it lumps together claims which might be *made* together but which must be *justified* separately. Is the Native American Church's peyote exemption really more like tribal self-government than it is like the right of Jews and Catholics to ceremonial wine during Prohibition? In one sense, yes; the peyote and self-government claims are both made by Indians. This chapter has tried to show that this is not the kind of similarity which is most important for normative political work, and that the affinity between the peyote and alcohol cases make it much more plausible to argue for or against them together

---

[83] Ibid. 306.

[84] Gurr's 'control' lies, I think, outside the framework of this chapter; it is defined as the aim to establish or maintain hegemony. Groups seeking control seek to preserve or obtain power over other groups, unequal economic privilege, a state which imposes a particular religious view, and so on; the category is constructed so as to only include claims which are clearly illegitimate on almost any general normative account. Gurr seeks to describe the possible aims of real groups in the world, not just those aims which raise interesting moral issues; hence the difference.

than to separate them and argue peyote along with self-government. Similarly, recognition claims are scattered through several of Kymlicka's categories, depending on who makes them and on whether the law being recognized restricts group members. There may be good reason to grant legal recognition to the customary laws of indigenous peoples but not to the customary laws of immigrants; but I submit there is also good reason to treat that outcome as the answer to a single question, 'What should be the legal status of cultural customary law?' If not, there is at least something useful in being able to identify the kinds of rights to which national minorities are entitled but ethnic groups are not without referring to categories defined as 'the rights of national minorities' and 'the rights of ethnic groups.' In empirical work, too, clarity may be gained by being able to specify (for example) the kinds of rights-claims immigrant ethnic groups tend make without reference to a category defined as the claims made by non-national, non-indigenous ethnic groups. Common terms for the kinds of policies at stake would allow us to *then* identify the kinds of claims which will be made (or should be recognized) for this or that kind of group.

Kymlicka's internal/external distinction seems to me insufficiently precise, as the (often-argued) case of the Pueblo exclusion of Protestants from communal resources and functions makes clear.[85] Here what I have identified as self-government, recognition, and internal rights stack on top of one another. The Pueblo are a self-governing semi-sovereign nation. They are also a cultural community bound together by custom, including religious customs which allocate common duties and benefits. Someone who converts out of the traditional religion and withdraws from religious obligations is ostracized and denied access to collective resources; this is a common form of internal rule. Abandoning religious beliefs and customs may well lead to an American Jew being excluded from functions of her former community, and might even lead to ostracism on an informal basis.

American Jews, however, do not form a state. On a theory like Kymlicka's in which exclusion from one's cultural membership is a serious harm, Pueblo converts are in danger in a way that Jewish ones are not. Non-believing Jews have long since adapted Jewish tradition into a different but still distinctively Jewish cultural tradition, and the Jewish apostate still has access to that cultural community. Given current institutions,

---

[85] See, among others, Frances Svensson, 'Liberal Democracy and Group Rights: The Legacy of Individualism and its Impact on American Indian Tribes,' *Political Studies* 27 (1979), 421–39; Kymlicka, *Liberalism, Community, and Culture*, 195–9 and *Multicultural Citizenship*, 152–170; Kukathas, 'Are There Any Cultural Rights?' 121–3 and 'Cultural Rights Again.'

though, Pueblo identity means to be a member of a tribe (a citizen of a particular kind of self-governing polity), to keep a set of customs (abide by a set of internal rules), *and* to follow customary law (recognized as the law of the polity). It is this stacking of cultural rights, this vesting of different kinds of powers in the same body, which complicates the matter. One could argue in favor of internal rules, self-government, and recognition separately and still condemn this stacking of them; but a simple differentiation into 'internal' and 'external' does not allow for that.

Kymlicka and Kukathas take the Pueblo as a clear example of their disagreement; but I am not sure that their arguments (as opposed to their stated opinions on this case) bear them out. Kymlicka has, it seems to me, provided an argument against internal rules *linked with* either recognition/enforcement rights or self-government; the stricter the cultural rules, the more space there must be between them and state enforcement. He has also (briefly) argued for the legitimacy of internal rules *simpliciter*.[86] Kukathas has argued for the legitimacy of internal rules, and briefly argued against internal rules linked with recognition/enforcement.[87] If I am right, then their arguments on this point have failed to meet each other; what one condemns, the other has not actually defended.[88] But this cannot be made clear without disaggregating the idea of cultural autonomy or self-government in something like the way done here.

A classification such as this one is subject to criticism from two directions: that it has multiplied categories unnecessarily, and that it has created categories which are too broad to be useful. Existing sorting devices—Gurr's, Kymlicka's, the individual/collective distinction—mostly seem to me to commit the second error, which I suppose means that I am most likely to have committed the first. In fact, I fear that some of my categories may be too broad as they stand, that perhaps exemptions must be disaggregated into religious and non-religious, or that preferential policies need to be separated from other assistance claims. I have tried to note such distinctions without increasing the number of basic categories so much as to make the classification unwieldy, but such a balancing act is likely to be imperfect.

---

[86] Kymlicka, *Multicultural Citizenship*, 202 n.1

[87] On the second point see Kukathas, 'Are There Any Cultural Rights?' 133. As was noted above under 'Internal Rules,' this means I think Kukathas got the particular case of the Pueblo wrong on his own terms; he has argued for the legitimacy of internal rules but has not met the additional hurdle of linking internal rules with self-government to allow for a state-imposed religion. That is, he has seen an association where there is really a state.

[88] The same is not true of their disagreement about external rules and assistance claims.

To the charge that this classification is already unwieldy or inelegant, I reply that we confront policies which are different in kind. We have little reason to think that, for example, representation, exemptions, and symbolic claims can be argued for or against as a group; their common ethnic or cultural referent is not enough to warrant treating them together. Even if one wishes to endorse *every* rights-claim discussed in this chapter, it is not enough to argue for the importance of ethnocultural groups and the injustice or oppression faced by some such groups; that is only the first step. Subsequent steps require different kinds of arguments for different kinds of policies. The same holds true if one wants to condemn all of these claims; no single argument will do the job. Some policies require identifying individual citizens by ethnic group, but many do not. Some may be precedent for secession or Balkanization, but others are not. Some infringe on members of other groups, but others need not. Some might be described as collective rights and thus shown to be incoherent on an individualist morality; but others cannot.

This chapter has tried to provide a common language in which the cultural rights debate might be conducted. It has also tried to show the need for *some* such language, for some general differentiation of cultural rights-claims which might be used by theorists of different orientations, even if *this* classification cannot do the necessary work.

6

Incorporating Indigenous Law

INTRODUCTION

If a history of cruelty, a legacy of violence and injustice, is important to our evaluation of cultural rights-claims, there can be few better claimants to special consideration than indigenous peoples. Until the horrors of the twentieth century, there was probably nothing with which to compare the vast scale and scope of the mistreatment inflicted on the original inhabitants of the Americas and other colonized lands. While sometimes there is anachronism involved in the moral judgement of long-ago actions, this is not the case here. The cruelty and injustice were recognized as such by its contemporaries, ranging from Bartolomé de Las Casas and Francisco de Vitoria in the sixteenth century to Kant and Montesquieu in the eighteenth, and beyond.[1]

Not all indigenous peoples have been treated with the same savagery; whatever the complaints of Scandinavia's Sami peoples, they do not include the enslavement and genocide practiced in the Spanish conquest of the Americas. Violent expropriation of lands has been all too common around the world, however, almost whenever indigenous peoples have come into contact with expanding modern states and empires. In the Americas, Australia and New Zealand, and South Africa, but also in Siberia, northeastern India and western Myanmar (Burma), Scandinavia, and Taiwan, the refusal to recognize the legitimacy of indigenous land claims has been central to the violent histories of contact between indigenous and other cultures. And the refusal to recognize land claims was often part and parcel of a refusal to recognize indigenous law in general.

---

[1] See Bartolomé de Las Casas, *The Devastation of the Indies*, trans. Bill Donovan (Baltimore: Johns Hopkins University Press, 1992 [1552]); Francisco de Vitoria, 'On the American Indians,' in Anthony Pagden and Jeremy Lawrance (eds.), *Political Writings* (Cambridge: Cambridge University Press, 1991 [1539]); Immanuel Kant, *The Metaphysics of Morals*, in Hans Reiss (ed.), *Kant's Political Writings* (Cambridge: Cambridge University Press, 1970 [1797]); Montesquieu, *Les Lettres Persanes*, ed. Laurent Versini (Paris: Garnier-Flammarion, 1995 [1721]) and *De L'Esprit des Lois* (Paris: Garnier-Flammarion, 1979 [1758]).

162   *Categories and Cases*

Today indigenous minority groups often seek (or have already secured) recognition of their customary legal systems in the law of the wider state. On land use and possession, marriage and family life, inheritance, and a variety of other issues indigenous peoples have legal traditions of their own. They do not wish to see those traditions supplanted or ignored by the laws of the states in which they live.

States can respond in a number of ways. To do as the colonizing powers did and refuse to recognize indigenous law or the rights arising from it at all is utterly unjustifiable. There is, however, a range of more appropriate responses, a variety of policies and legal systems that recognize or incorporate indigenous law in different ways. Once the decision has been made to make *some* accommodation of indigenous law, there remain serious questions about how this is to be done, how best to balance goals like respect for indigenous traditions, protection of the rights of indigenous persons, legal clarity and simplicity, and peaceful and cooperative coexistence with the wider society.

This chapter describes three broad kinds of incorporation of indigenous law: common law, customary law, and self-government. These modes of incorporation have different internal logics, different moral and political implications, and different resulting legal rights of indigenous people. The chapter discusses those differences with reference to the experience of some societies that have incorporated indigenous law in these various ways.

Indigenous law incorporated within the common law is not quite recognized as *law* at all, but as a social situation which creates the kinds of facts which trigger the law of the wider society. The state recognizes indigenous forms of common law rights and statuses. Indigenous land rights might gain legal status though the concept of adverse possession, and indigenous marriages might gain legal status through the concept of common-law marriage.[2]

More status is given to indigenous law, and accordingly less to the idea of law common to all citizens, when indigenous law is incorporated as a separate system of customary law, parallel (or at least not entirely subordinate) to the common law. In this case the standards to be invoked, the concepts to be applied, the meanings to be imputed are

---

[2] I should note at the outset that my use of terms like 'common law incorporation' or 'common law recognition' does not correspond to the usage of James Tully in his important recent works 'Aboriginal Property and Western Theory: Recovering a Middle ground,' *Social Philosophy and Policy* 11 (1994), 153–80, and *Strange Multiplicity: Constitutionalism in an Age of Deep Diversity* (Cambridge: Cambridge University Press, 1996). Tully generally advocates what I refer to as customary law recognition, in which indigenous law is considered a system parallel to the common law rather than being subsumed within it.

those of the indigenous legal tradition. Legal decisions are to be reached in accordance with the demands of customary law, however modified or constrained that law might be.

Indigenous law is accorded the greatest status when self-government forms the foundation of the recognition of indigenous law, which implies that indigenous peoples have at least in principle been recognized as sovereign nations. Indigenous law is respected in a way analogous to the respect accorded the laws of foreign states.

As I will argue at greater length below, the fact that one model accords greater status to indigenous law than another does not necessarily mean that indigenous people have more or preferable rights under that model. Customary incorporation characteristically yields legal rights to use traditional lands as they have traditionally been used; that is, it generates usufruct rather than proprietary rights. Common law incorporation, on the other hand, characteristically generates stronger property rights in the form of collective freehold[3] ownership; as far as the law of the state is concerned, indigenous people are free to use their land traditionally or otherwise and still retain it as their own land.

Most states use elements of more than one mode of incorporation; but there are differences of emphasis. The self-government mode of incorporation is most important in the United States, and is also significant in Canada. Customary incorporation plays at least some part in most states that accord any status to indigenous law, but South Africa relies on it almost exclusively.[4] Australia places greater emphasis than other states on common law incorporation.

I do not intend to deny the important historical, legal, and logical connections among these three ways of incorporating indigenous law. All three found some expression in the nineteenth-century opinions of John Marshall in US Indian cases. The common law and customary law modes have enough in common that an advance in one is often taken as

---

[3] In this chapter I generally use the term 'freehold' except when the courts of a given state use 'fee simple.' The differences between these terms for private property ownership (i.e. the slightly more general character of 'freehold') are not particularly relevant to any of the questions being addressed.

[4] For the discussion of South Africa in this chapter, I have drawn heavily on T. W. Bennett, 'The Equality Clause and Customary Law,' *South African Journal on Human Rights* 10 (1994), 122–30, and *Human Rights and African Customary Law* (Cape Town: Juta & Co./ University of the Western Cape, 1995). See also Kim Robinson. 'The Minority and Subordinate Status of African Women Under Customary Law,' *South African Journal on Human Rights* 11 (1995), 457–76; A. J. Kerr, 'Customary Law, Fundamental Rights, and the Constitution,' *South African Law Journal* 111 (1994), 720–35; Lynn Berat, 'Customary Law in a New South Africa: A Proposal' *Fordham International Law Journal* 15 (1992), 92–128; and A. C. Myburgh, *Papers on Indigenous Law in Southern Africa* (Pretoria: J. L. van Schaik, 1985).

precedent for the other. All are responses to similar sets of facts and circumstances. But without disputing any of this I still suggest that there are three different logics, that (for example) conceiving of indigenous land rights as ownership, customary use, and sovereignty are importantly different and in some ways incompatible.

Typically, these three different logics of incorporation have emerged through different mechanisms. Common law incorporation has characteristically taken place judicially, for example, and self-government has typically been recognized in treaties. There is, however, no necessary correspondence between the logic of incorporation and its mechanism.[5] Legislation as well as judicial decision has moved Australian law toward the common law logic. Customary incorporation often takes place through a state's constitution rather than through judicial recognition of a parallel system of law. And treaties with indigenous peoples, while they are a common incident of recognizing indigenous peoples as sovereign, are neither necessary nor sufficient for the self-government mode of incorporation. Sometimes (e.g. New Zealand's Treaty of Waitangi) a treaty is the mechanism for *surrendering* the sovereignty that has been recognized.

In some sense common law recognition accords the least status to indigenous law and self-government recognition the most; it might seem sensible to begin the discussion with one of those and move steadily to the other end of the scale. Customary recognition, however, in some ways provides the conceptual framework for all three modes, and common law and self-government will be easier to discuss after customary recognition.

CUSTOMARY LAW

The relations of [Indians] to their ancient sovereign or government are dissolved, but their relations to each other, and their customs and usages remain undisturbed.[6]

[T]here are indigenous peoples whose legal conceptions, though differently developed, are hardly less precise than our own. When once they have been studied and understood they are no less enforceable than rights arising under English law.[7]

---

[5] I had failed to notice this before Patrick Macklem pointed it out, resulting in significant confusion in an earlier draft of this chapter.

[6] Justice Badgley in *Connolly v Woolrich*, 1 RLOS 253 (Quebec, 1869), upholding an Indian customary marriage.

[7] Lord Sumner, *Re Southern Rhodesia*, AC 211 (1919). This passage immediately follows the passage made famous and infamous by its use in *Milirrupum v Nabalco*, 17 FLR 141 (1971 Australia) at 151, insisting that some indigenous people are 'so low on the scale of social organization' that there is no point in imputing ownership of land to them.

Incorporation of indigenous law as customary law was common throughout the British Empire, and remains so in its successor states.[8] In customary incorporation, the state recognizes the survival of law based on customary rules and usages of the indigenous community, without conceding sovereignty to that community. That is, indigenous people have the right to be governed by their own traditional law, without having the right to self-government. They may marry, inherit, adopt children, hunt, fish, and use their lands as they did before colonization. The sovereign state might claim the right to override customary law by explicit legislation, just as it can legislatively override the common law. For example, the constitution of Hawaii says that

The State reaffirms and shall protect all rights, customarily and traditionally exercised for subsistence, cultural and religious purposes and possessed by *ahupua'a* tenants who are descendants of native Hawaiians who inhabited the Hawaiian Islands prior to 1778, subject to the right of the State to regulate such rights.[9]

In the absence of such an override, though, customary law is presumed to remain in effect. The British routinely restricted the customary law of the inhabitants of its colonies by preventing its operation when it violated (British interpretations of) the principles of 'natural justice.' A distant descendant of that restriction is the limitation of customary law by a written constitution or bill of rights. While the South African constitution of 1996 explicitly provides for and protects the various indigenous systems of customary law, it also holds that those systems are subject to that constitution's bill of rights.[10] These constitutional provisions have been given specific form in legislation legally recognizing customary African marriages, even when, for example, they are polygamous;[11] but child marriages have been banned, and polygamous unions require the consent of *all* spouses.

Land rights are central to all three modes of incorporation, and the

---

[8] For the most part, in this chapter I discuss states operating under the English common law, due to my greater familiarity with English legal concepts than with e.g. Roman ones. But I do not think that any of the three modes of incorporation is specific to English law. Occupancy can give rise to property rights under Roman law, and this is a key aspect of common law incorporation. Self-governing incorporation is possible in any state that considers its indigenous population sovereign; customary incorporation is possible in any state that recognizes the indigenous law without recognizing indigenous sovereignty. For examples of customary incorporation in non-common-law states, see the Constitution of Paraguay, Chapter V, and the Constitution of Guatemala, §66.

[9] Constitution of the state of Hawaii, Article XII, section 7.

[10] See §211 for the recognition of customary law and §39(2) for the limitation by the bill of rights

[11] Recognition of Customary Marriages Act, Act 120 of 1998.

differences among the three models can be clearly seen by their differing treatments of land. Under customary recognition, the questions of what lands indigenous people have rights to and of what rights they have to them are both answered with reference to indigenous custom and law. This notably means that indigenous land rights include neither freehold nor sovereignty, but specific rights of usage and exclusion, for example, rights to fish, hunt, forage, hold religious ceremonies, occupy, and/or exclude others. As Justice Brennan of the Australian High Court put it in his *Mabo* opinion,

Native title has its origin and is given its content by the traditional laws acknowledged by and the traditional customs observed by the indigenous inhabitants of a territory. The nature and incidents of native title must be ascertained as a matter of fact by reference to those laws and customs.[12]

For more than a century Canadian courts have held that customary indigenous law continues to affect such matters as marriage, divorce, and inheritance. A customary marriage, for example, was held to be a legally valid marriage as early as 1867 in *Connolly v Woolrich*.[13] While the trial court suggested that there was a continuing Indian right of self-government and so moved down the path toward the self-government mode of incorporation, the court of appeals (in the passage which began this section) flatly denied that and grounded its affirmation in the validity of indigenous customary law.

Indigenous law can be incorporated as customary law by the general courts or by specifically indigenous ones. Often, both will be true to some degree within the same state, so that (for example) a dispute between two indigenous persons will be handled in the first instance by indigenous institutions and, if it is subsequently taken to the general courts, the latter will attempt to apply customary laws as best it understands them.

In addition to land use and family law, customary criminal law may be incorporated by the state, which may grant customary authorities the authority to punish offenses against customary law. This is extremely controversial, and is most likely to invite concerns about human rights-violations, as in the 1994 case of an Australian judge who authorized the customary punishment of a spearing through the leg in lieu of a punishment by the state.[14]

In North America, however, customary mechanisms of punishment

---

[12] *Mabo v Queensland (No. 2)*, 175 CLR 1 (Australia 1992), 429.
[13] *Connolly v Woolrich*, 17 RJRQ 75 (Quebec 1867).
[14] See David Foster, 'Bloody Justice,' *The Independent Monthly*, May 1994, 30–6, and Wanda Jamrozik, 'White Law, Black Lore,' ibid. 37–8.

are more likely than those of the general law to emphasize restitution and/or reconciliation. In 1994 two members of the Alaskan Tlingit tribe were sentenced to banishment on coastal islands where they were both to gain rehabilitation through living off the land and cut timber to sell to pay for restitution for the medical bills of the man they had beaten and robbed. A Washington state judge gave formal approval to the banishment, though both men were required to serve prison time as well.[15] Canada has given some legal standing to the 'sentencing circles' of First Nations communities, communal procedures involving both victim and offender and typically resulting in fines or restitution (or, more rarely, banishment for a period of time) rather than imprisonment.[16]

COMMON LAW

In some territories . . . a customary system of real property law might not have existed, or might be incapable of proof. If the territory was inhabited, this does not mean that the indigenous people living there would have no legal rights to the lands occupied by them after the Crown acquired sovereignty. In this situation, English law would apply to give them a 'common law aboriginal title'.[17]

The common law mode of incorporation recognizes customary ways of using powers or establishing legal situations for which the dominant culture has a different set of procedures. A customary marriage might be recognized as creating a real marriage in law, bringing with it all of the benefits the state has attached to that legal status. Customary wills, gifts, property conveyances, or even establishing of initial property rights can be the subjects of such recognition. These are typically recognitions not of customary ways of making law, or of the content of customary law, so much as customary ways of establishing legal conditions and situations. Woodman and Morse refer to such incorporation

---

[15] Only a small fraction of the restitution owed has yet been paid, one of several reasons why the experiment has not been regarded as a success and is unlikely to be repeated in the United States for some time.

[16] In contrast to the criticism of the brutality of the Australian spearing, North American critics have complained that banishments and restitution are too lenient compared with prison. After a Cree man was sentenced to a year-long banishment in the woods followed by three years probation for sexual assault, the *Toronto Sun* editorialized, 'where can we sign up for punishments like that?' 'Memory Lapses,' *The Toronto Sun*, Opinion/Editorial section p. 1, Wednesday 31 May 1995.

[17] Kent McNeil, *Common Law Aboriginal Title* (Oxford: Clarendon Press, 1989), 192.

as recognition of 'norms of validation.'[18] Thus, common law incorporation might recognize customary marriages as common-law marriages,
meriting some or all of the privileges which the law accords to marriage;
but not recognize, for example, polygamous marriages where these are
authorized by customary law but not by the general law. Common law
incorporation would generate no *right* to inherit according to customary rules of succession, but would grant the expectations formed by
custom the same status as other expectations of support have in the law
of estates. No state relies exclusively on common law incorporation, but
it plays an important part in Australian law.

Turning again to the central issue of land rights: common law indigenous title is grounded in the facts of indigenous occupancy of land.
Indigenous ownership of traditional lands is recognized; but what is
recognized is *ownership*. As far as the law of the general state is
concerned, it does not matter whether the indigenous people traditionally used their land for cultivation, hunting, gathering, fishing, or religious ceremonies; they own it. As Justice Toohey put it in his *Mabo*
judgment, 'It is presence amounting to occupancy which is the foundation of the title and which attracts protection.'[19] At common law the
fact of possession significantly contributes to a claim of ownership, and
the fact of occupancy contributes to a claim of possession. While the
Mabo decision did not quite wholly articulate or endorse a common law
understanding of native title, the subsequent Native Title Act (1993)
moved Australia even more toward common law recognition by allowing native title to be traded for freehold, even when alienation was not
possible under customary law.

While generally the collective freehold ownership of common law
incorporation offers wider control over land to indigenous landholders than do customary rights, there is an important qualification to be
made. The common law logic has no space for exemptions from
general regulations concerning land use, hunting, fishing, or the environment. If the customary use of the land is restricted or prohibited by
a general statute, common law recognition may not offer any defense.

---

[18] Bradford Morse and Gordon Woodman, 'Introductory Essay: The State's Options,'
in Bernard Morse and Gorden Woodman (eds.), *Indigenous Law and the State*
(Providence: Foris Publications, 1988).

[19] *Mabo*, 486. Toohey admittedly goes on to say that 'presence on land need not
amount to possession at common law in order to amount to occupancy.' He mentions
the argument of Kent McNeil that indigenous occupancy *does* amount to possession and
accepts that this might be correct; but he is unwilling to make this the foundation of
indigenous title. Justices Deane and Gaudron rely even more closely on a common law
understanding of native title, though they endorse the rule that native title is inalienable
(*Mabo*, 439). I discuss inalienability at greater length below.

Something similar is true in other areas of law. Common law incorporation offers those married according to indigenous law all the legal privileges of marriage according to the general law—or at least all the privileges of common law marriage—rather than limiting the rights of customarily married couples to those they held under customary law. (Income tax benefits were not a right arising under customary law for married couples; common law recognition allows customary marriages to attract the benefits that the state accords to all marriages.) As noted above, however, it need not allow for any special rights, privileges, or duties which arise under customary law but which are prohibited by the general law, such as a right to enter into polygamous marriages.

The widely cited Australian Law Reform Commission (ALRC) report on the recognition of Aboriginal law largely recommended incorporation within the common law, with some elements of customary law.[20] The comprehensive statute proposed by the commission explicitly stated that customary law was to be recognized as a matter of fact, not as a matter of law.[21] Recognition for a variety of purposes such as marriage and inheritance was described as 'functional.' Customary marriages were to be recognized for a variety of specified purposes within Australian law (e.g. the tax code), not declared to be valid marriages *tout court*. Expectations of support arising because of custom were to be granted the same standing as other reasonable expectations of inheritance, but the customary law of inheritance was not itself to be incorporated. Customary criminal law was to be taken into account by the Australian judicial system; it was not to replace it.

Incorporation through the common law leaves very little space for recognition of indigenous criminal law. 'Little,' however, is not quite 'none.' Certainly, common law incorporation means that indigenous persons are subject to the general criminal law. This is unlike the customary and self-government modes, in which there is at least some presumption that matters between indigenous persons are to be governed by indigenous law. Still, indigenous criminal law needs to be recognized at least as a matter of fact by the courts. In many cases

---

[20] Australian Law Reform Commission, *The Recognition of Aboriginal Customary Law* (Canberra: AGPS, 1986).

[21] When a court recognizes a body of law *as law*, that body of law is directly binding. When a body of law is recognized *as a matter of fact*, the law being applied remains unchanged; the alien body of law is taken into account as a set of circumstances that help answer the questions of which laws have been triggered, which laws apply. The ALRC did not recommend that the Australian courts become forums for the adjudication of customary law, only that they take customary law and Aboriginal adherence to it into account when deciding questions of common law.

matters such as intent and reasonableness cannot be wholly determined without reference to the indigenous law.

The ALRC recommended further accommodation of the general criminal law to Aboriginal law, still considerably short of customary incorporation. (For one thing, the proposed legislation explicitly stated that Aboriginal law was to be recognized as fact and not as law.) Thus, it urged that persons be able to refuse to testify in the general court if their testimony would reveal that they had violated Aboriginal law. Moreover, judges were to be empowered to empanel single-sex juries if a defendant had to reveal matters about Aboriginal law which the other sex was forbidden to know. It also made extensive recommendations regarding judicial discovery of the content of Aboriginal law; the ALRC intended for common law incorporation to be taken seriously.

The distinctness of the common law mode of recognition is often overlooked. It is commonly said that *Mabo* brings Australian law into line with the law of states like Canada, New Zealand, and the United States; but this is not quite right. Australia has relied more heavily than the other states on incorporation through the common law, while the other states use various mixtures of all three types (but are especially distinguished from Australia by their recognition of indigenous sovereignty, discussed below). Commentators as distinguished and knowledgeable as Henry Reynolds and Garth Nettheim have fallaciously assumed that *Mabo* is compatible with or even entails recognition of some form of Aboriginal sovereignty. Reynolds asks

If, as the High Court determined, indigenous land rights and land law survived the arrival of the British why didn't other aspects of the local law? If property rights continued until they were extinguished in a clear and plain manner why didn't other elements of Aboriginal law, custom, and politics? If interest in land ran on into the colonial period and beyond why didn't the right of internal self-government?[22]

Nettheim similarly suggests that

There seems ... no reason why the High Court's approach should not be extended from real property to intellectual property, or into the area of criminal justice, or into the domain of self-government. If the laws of Aboriginal peoples have survived for some purposes, there is no reason in principle why they may not have survived for other purposes.[23]

[22] Henry Reynolds, *Aboriginal Sovereignty* (Sydney: Allen & Unwin, 1996), 9.
[23] Garth Nettheim, 'Mabo and Legal Pluralism: The Australian Aboriginal Justice Experience,' in Kayleen Hazlehurst (ed.), *Legal Pluralism and the Colonial Legacy* (Brookfield, Vt.: Avebury Press, 1995).

If, however, I am right that there is a distinct common law mode of incorporation, then there is no inconsistency between, say, *Mabo's* finding in favor of land rights and the subsequent finding in and *Coe v Commonwealth* and *Walker v NSW* that there is no surviving Aboriginal sovereignty.[24] 'Interest in land' has status within the common law; 'the inherent right of internal self-government' does not.

Australian law seems to fluctuate between common law and customary incorporation. The *Mabo* court was divided on the basis of native title, with Brennan considering it customary, Gaudron and Deane finding that customary title was extinguished with the English acquisition of sovereignty, then 'reignited' as common law native title, and Toohey adopting an intermediate position that emphasized occupancy.[25] *Walker* and *Coe* decisively rejected any claim that Aboriginal law and especially Aboriginal sovereignty survived colonization, but the *Wik* judgment seems to treat at least some native title as grounded in customary rights rather than common law title.[26]

SELF-GOVERNMENT

The Indian nations had always been considered as distinct, independent political communities . . . The constitution, by declaring treaties already made, as well as those to be made, to be the supreme law of the land, has adopted and sanctioned the previous treaties with the Indian nations, and consequently admits their rank among those powers who are capable of making treaties. The words 'treaty' and 'nation' are words of our own language, selected in our diplomatic and legislative proceedings, by ourselves, each having a definite and well-understood meaning. We have applied them to Indians, as we have applied

---

[24] *Coe v Commonwealth*, 118 ALR 193 (Australia 1993); *Walker v NSW*, 126 ALR 195 (Australia 1994). In *Coe* a request was made (and denied) for a declaration of the sovereignty of an Aboriginal tribe. In *Walker* a criminal charge against an Aboriginal man was contested on the grounds that the general criminal law was inapplicable to Aboriginal peoples who had not requested or accepted it, that only customary criminal law could be applied. This claim, too, was rejected: 'Such notions amount to the contention that a new source of sovereignty resides in the Aboriginal people. Indeed, *Mabo (No.2)* rejected that suggestion.' Section 2. I do not think that Chief Justice Mason was right to suggest that recognition of customary criminal law necessarily violates the very ideas of a criminal law and of equality before the law; but he was certainly right that Australian law under *Mabo* does not extend such recognition.

[25] See discussion in K. E. Mulqueeny, 'Folk-Law or Folklore: When a Law is Not a Law. Or Is It?' in M. A. Stephenson and Suri Ratnapala (eds.), *Mabo: A Judicial Revolution* (Brisbane: University of Queensland Press, 1993), 168.

[26] *Wik Peoples v State of Queensland*, ALR 129 (Australia 1996).

them to the other nations of the earth. They are applied to all in the same sense. (John Marshall, *Worcester v State of Georgia*)[27]

A quite different relationship between the settler state and indigenous peoples is posited by the self-government model. There, indigenous peoples are considered (semi-sovereign) states or (domestic dependent) nations, self-governing except with regard to foreign affairs and alliances.[28] The self-government mode of incorporation is most prominent in the United States and Canada.

The self-government model grants or recognizes what neither of the other two models does: territorial sovereignty. It is the only mode to recognize a *lawmaker* in addition to, or instead of, *laws*. The tribal governments are acknowledged as legitimate rulers (or at least legitimate intermediate rulers) over indigenous people. Put another way, indigenous people are seen as having a right to give themselves laws rather than simply to live according to their laws.

Land rights grounded in the self-government model thus look more like political territory rather than like private property, which explains why such land is often seen as inalienable. Indigenous peoples have sovereignty, and only other sovereigns stand as their equals. Private persons can no more purchase indigenous lands than they could purchase sovereign power over England.

[T]he Crown (or other European crowns) was the only agent with the authority to negotiate with the Aboriginal peoples, considered as nations, and to secure non-Aboriginal title to property in North America.[29]

In the United States it is typically the case that the tribal governments which have sovereignty over their territory do not have title to it as property; the land is owned by the United States government which holds it in trust for the tribe.[30] Indeed, on many reservations individual non-Indians own much of the land, without legal detriment to Indian sovereignty—though at some periods there was much political detriment, and the non-Indian landowners were the opening wedge for the ultimate undermining of sovereignty.

---

[27] *Worcester v State of Georgia*, 31 US 515 (United States 1832).
[28] On the distinction I draw in Ch. 4 between the recognition and enforcement of minority law and self-government, the treaty mode is an instance of the latter, while the other two modes are instances of the former.
[29] Tully, *Strange Multiplicity*, 170.
[30] This is not true for all tribes; the Five Civilized Tribes, the Senecas, and the Pueblos all own title to their lands as well as having sovereignty. See Sharon O'Brien, *American Indian Tribal Governments* (Norman, Okla.: University of Oklahoma Press, 1989), 215.

At least since Marshall's time on the Supreme Court, the self-government mode of incorporation has held a prominent place in the law of the United States. While the federal government has cyclically strengthened and weakened the powers of tribal governments, they have always been recognized as being of some importance.[31] Some sovereignty, some rights of self-government, have generally been considered to reside in Indian tribes. Tribal governments are to a significant degree free from interference by the various states. They may establish criminal courts (to try only Indians), family courts, marriage laws, and land use laws. They may allow commercial gambling even when that is prohibited by the state within which the tribal reservation is located. Tribal laws are incorporated into the general law in a manner similar to the incorporation of one state's law by another. The two legal systems must acknowledge the validity of one another's acts, grant those acts 'full faith and credit' (in the terms of the Constitution), and cooperate or at least reach agreement on jurisdictional matters. Disputes between the legal systems are regulated by the federal courts, since indigenous sovereignty is always subordinate to federal sovereignty, but the federal courts are often obliged to protect Indian law against state incursions.

Canadian law has ordinarily not gone quite as far down this path as American law. If tribal governments in the United States have powers close to those of states, tribal governments in Canada have tended to be more like municipalities. Under the Indian Act, provincial laws generally do apply to Indians and other indigenous people; and band councils have delegated authority over matters like traffic regulations, building codes, and public health.[32] Representatives of Canada's First Nations have long argued that their rights of self-government are inherent rather than delegated, and are much more extensive than is recognized in the Indian Act.

This pattern changed dramatically with the August 1998 signing of an agreement between the Nisga'a nation, on one hand, and the governments of Canada and British Columbia, on the other. This agreement, the first modern-day Canadian Indian treaty, not only secures possession of 750 square miles to the Nisga'a. It also provides for the creation of a new level of self-government, a level with powers much more extensive than those of the Indian Act band councils. The treaty has yet to be ratified, but is already being pointed to as a possible precedent for agreements between Canada and fifty other First Nations whose claims taken together cover most of British Columbia.

---

[31] See the overview of this history, in O'Brien, *American Indian Tribal Governments*, chs. 4–5.   [32] Indian Act, §§88, 81.

The creation of Nunavut changed the pattern even more significantly for the Inuit. On 1 April 1999, the eastern half of what was the Northwest Territory became a separate, partially self-governing territory, Nunavut—a territory that has an Inuit majority. The creation of Nunavut was part of a negotiated settlement of land and sea claims between the Inuit and the Canadian government. Nunavut will comprise about one-fifth of the Canadian land mass, and title to about one-fifth of Nunavut itself is being restored to the Inuit as a result of the agreement. Ownership and sovereignty remain distinct, however, and non-Inuit continue to be able to own land, subject to the regulations of the Nunavut and federal governments.

Customary law and customary rights sometimes superimpose on common law recognition and common law rights rather than strictly replacing them. Similarly, treaties can be superimposed over both. In Canada, for example, the fact that many tribes have land rights recognized by treaty does not change the fact that tribes without treaties may have common law or customary title.

For a decade and a half there was considerable activism in support of a treaty (or 'Makaratta') between the Australian government and Aborigines.[33] A prominent group of non-Aboriginal Australians formed an Aboriginal Treaty Committee in 1979 to lobby for such action. In 1982 a Senate committee recommended an amendment to the Constitution which would give the Commonwealth the power to enter into a 'compact' with Aborigines. By 1987 then-Prime Minister Bob Hawke supported the idea, urging that a treaty or compact be agreed upon in time for the bicentennial of English settlement in 1989. Instead, in 1991 the Council for Aboriginal Reconciliation (CAR) was created with a ten-year mission to promote greater understanding between Aboriginal and non-Aboriginal Australians, possibly leading to a final written document by the hundredth anniversary of Australian federation in 2001.

The treaty movement had its greatest momentum before *Mabo*, and supporters typically assumed that a treaty would be a, or the, way to secure native title. Non-Aboriginal critics, like then Opposition Leader John Howard, accepted the link between a treaty and land rights and used this as an argument against a treaty. (By contrast, Aboriginal critics saw a treaty as most likely symbolic and a distraction from the struggle for land rights.)

[33] See Department of the Prime Minister and Cabinet [of Australia], *Aboriginal Reconciliation: An Historical Perspective* (Canberra: AGPS, 1991); and Ken Baker (ed.), *A Treaty With the Aborigines?* (Melbourne: Institute of Public Affairs, 1988).

Subsequent developments, however, have shown this to be a mistake; native title can be grounded perfectly well within the common law, without a treaty. Given *Mabo*, the Native Title Act, and *Wik v Queensland*, any treaty of more than symbolic value would seem to involve primarily self-government rather than land rights. As the deadline for the CAR's work draws nearer, Australia may have to confront the question of whether to continue developing common law and customary law incorporation or to switch emphases dramatically to self-government. The latter course of action seems unlikely.

INCONSISTENCIES AND HYBRIDS

The point of distinguishing the three modes of incorporation is not to recommend one over the others, or even to suggest that no state can coherently use more than one of them. One reason for distinguishing these categories, however, is that the failure to do so has often been unfairly disadvantageous to indigenous peoples. That is, they have received the worst of two or more categories at the same time; the inconsistency in their treatment has not been random and neutral but detrimental.

In *Baker Lake v Minister of Indian Affairs*, Justice Mahoney laid out a plausible test for common law native title. He said that claimants of such title must prove that they and their ancestors were members of an organized society; that the organized society occupied the specific territory over which the title was claimed; that the occupation was to the exclusion of other organized societies; and that the occupation was an established fact at the time of colonization. No reference here is made to customary law in any form; these criteria clearly test occupation and possession, not the existence or content of Indian law. That Mahoney was thinking in terms of common law title is further borne out by his *dictum* that 'the coexistence of an aboriginal title with the estate of the ordinary private landholder is readily recognized as an absurdity.'[34] There is nothing absurd about the coexistence of a customary usufruct right with freehold title; but of course one title of exclusive possession cannot coexist with another. Yet Mahoney held that the Inuit of Baker Lake, who satisfied his four criteria, held only a right to hunt and fish over the land, not a right to possess the land or to exclude others from it. This he seems to have based on his supposition that only rights to

---

[34] *Baker Lake*, 565.

hunt or fish existed under *customary* law; but he did not otherwise refer to the existence of Inuit law, much less prove what it contained. Under *Baker Lake,* then, Indians and Inuit land rights are incompatible with 'the estate of the ordinary private landholder;' this is one of the disadvantages of common-law title. That title includes too much to coexist with private property, and so has often been extinguished where customary usufructury rights might have continued to exist. Yet *Baker Lake* aboriginal title has all the disadvantages of customary title as well; it is limited to (the judicial reading of) the traditional uses of the land. Having met the burden of proving exclusive occupation, the Inuit did not gain the right to exclude or to occupy!

Similarly, the self-government mode of incorporation, and its underlying logic of territorial self-government, logically implies recognition of indigenous criminal law, and recognition that tribal governments have authority to punish anyone on tribal land who violates that law. Since the 1978 Supreme Court decision *Oliphant v Suquamish Tribe,*[35] however, the United States has held that tribal governments have *no* authority over non-members in criminal matters, even in the case of crimes committed against Indians on reservation territory. The jurisdiction of Indian law is held to include only Indians, as if that law were personal customary law. The disadvantage to Indians of this inconsistency is not only formal or procedural. When a non-Indian commits crimes against an Indian on a reservation, only a federal court may try the case. US Attorney General Janet Reno has noted the real difficulties this has created for the maintenance of law and order on reservations. Federal prosecutors rarely make the prosecution of misdemeanors a priority, and federal courts are typically located far from the reservations over which they have jurisdiction.

As a result, misdemeanor crime by non-Indians against Indians is perceived as being committed with impunity. This implicit message of lack of accountability deters victims from reporting crimes, and police from making arrests because they know there will be no prosecution. This, in turn, encourages the spread of crime and ultimately, the commission of even more serious crime.[36]

Some recent Canadian and Australian jurisprudence on land rights has attempted to hybridize the customary and common law modes; I do not think that it has succeeded, and it has repeated with greater sophistication some of the disadvantages of *Baker Lake.* In *Mabo,* the Australian High Court held that the content of native title varies

---

[35] 435 US 191 (USA 1978)
[36] Janet Reno, 'U.S. Department Of Justice Commitment To American Indian Tribal Justice Systems,' *Judicature* 79 (Nov.–Dec. 1995), 113–17.

depending on the content of Aboriginal customs and traditions. In this respect *Mabo* native title appears to be customary; but it is entirely extinguished with freehold private property over the same land, the burden that logically follows from common law title. In other respects *Mabo* came close to fully articulating a jurisprudence of common law title, especially insofar as it rejected any linkage between the survival of native title and the continuation of traditional or customary ways of life. If Aborigines have a customary right to possess a piece of land and to exclude others from it, their continued enjoyment of that right does not depend on the maintenance of customary religious practices or of the technological or of economic conditions of their ancestors. Moreover, Aborigines were recognized to have the right to do much with their land which was not part of their traditions. The break, however, was incomplete: native title was held to be inalienable, on the grounds that the traditional Aboriginal understanding of land did not allow for its sale. Thus Aborigines were prevented from the sale of any piece of their land, and (perhaps more importantly) prevented from using it as collateral for mortgages or credit. So, in *Mabo* as in *Baker Lake*, indigenous rights were extinguished like common law title, without gaining the full legal rights of that title.

The recent Canadian case of *Delgamuukw v British Columbia*[37] explicitly tries to rationalize this discrepancy. Chief Justice Lamer's majority opinion argues that the Delgamuukw and Haaxw indigenous peoples who argued for aboriginal title as fee simple ownership,[38] and the British Columbian government which argued that aboriginal title was nothing but a cluster of customary use rights, were both mistaken.

> The content of aboriginal title, in fact, lies somewhere in between these positions . . . its characteristics cannot be completely explained by reference either to the common law rules of real property or to the rules of property found in aboriginal legal systems. As with other aboriginal rights, it must be understood by reference to both common law and aboriginal perspectives.[39]

To be specific: aboriginal title

> is a right in land and, as such, is more than the right to engage in specific activities which may be themselves aboriginal rights. Rather, it confers the right to use land for a variety of activities, not all of which need be aspects of practices, customs and traditions [. . .] However, that range of uses is subject

---

[37] S.C.J. No. 108 (Canada 1997).
[38] To be specific, they accepted the jurisprudence holding that aboriginal title was inalienable but otherwise argued that it included full fee simple ownership. I return to inalienability below.   [39] Paragraphs 111, 113.

to the limitation that they must not be irreconcilable with the nature of the attachment to the land which forms the basis of the particular group's aboriginal title.[40]

Lamer argues that the nature of the aboriginal attachment to land is, among other things, premised on the transfer of the land from generation to generation. The limitation to which he refers thus prevents activities ranging from strip mining to the spoilage and wasting of the land to the sale of the land.

I don't mean to deny that *Delgamuukw* is a very favorable ruling for Canada's First Nations, or that it is conceptually much clearer than much of the jurisprudence that preceded it. Yet one is left wondering why the court goes so far but no farther in renouncing the status of guardian of indigenous traditions and understandings. Aboriginal title is considered a title to the land, one which includes the right to do much that was not traditionally done and not dependent on any continuity of customs or practices. Why the stop short of recognizing fee simple rights?

Part of the answer seems to be that Canadian courts, like their Australian counterparts, view the law as absolutely settled on the inalienability of aboriginal or native title, and think that they must articulate doctrines which make sense of this settled point. The major sources for this position, however, are the Proclamation of 1763 and the United States Supreme Court decisions of John Marshall—both grounded in the self-government mode of incorporation or in the recognition of Indian nations as foreign sovereign units. The exclusive right of purchase of Indian lands which Marshall found vested in the United States had more to do with their status as partially foreign states than with the traditional communal character of land tenure, more to do with the right of each 'discovering' or colonizing power to exclude the others than with the protection of indigenous custom.[41]

By contrast, the Nisga'a treaty holds that 'the Nisga'a Nation owns Nisga'a Lands in fee simple, being the largest estate known in law.'[42] As far as Canadian law is concerned, the Nisga'a are free to do as they wish

[40] Paragraph 111.

[41] This is especially true of the last of Marshall's important Indian opinions, *Worcester v Georgia*. The earlier *Johnson v M'Intosh* did make reference to the communal character of traditional title as part of a secondary argument; but in that opinion, unlike in *Worcester*, Marshall viewed the Indians as having little more than a right of occupation. *Johnson* may be good precedent for customary incorporation, as *Worcester* certainly is for the self-government mode; but neither is binding on or even particularly relevant to the common law mode. *Worcester v State of Georgia*, 31 US 515 (USA 1832); *Johnson v M'Intosh*, 21 US 543 (USA 1823).

[42] Nisga'a Final Agreement, chapter 3, section 3.

with their lands, including selling the fee simple title; they do not lose sovereignty over the land when they sell the title. (I return to the issue of separating ownership from sovereignty in the next chapter.) The Nisga'a Constitution and Nisga'a law can constrain alienation, but federal and provincial law cannot. The Nisga'a may register their land as inalienable with the federal government, but retain discretion to withdraw that registration and return the land to fee simple ownership.

RELIGIOUS LAW

The standing given in some countries to the law of religious minorities, or the laws of all religious groups, is in important ways similar to the incorporation of indigenous law.[43] Israel and India are well-known examples; family law, inheritance law, and the like are specific to each religious community. There have been disputes about the relationship of those religious legal systems to the civil law, including disputes over the right of the civil system to override the religious law in the event of human rights-violations.[44]

Religious law most often lends itself to customary incorporation. In certain minor ways common law recognition is possible, as when a state recognizes all religious leaders as having the authority to create (legally identical) marriages. Religious minorities might be recognized as national minorities with rights of self-determination and self-government, as Serbs and Croats have sought within the Bosnian state; but this accords no particular standing to the *content* of religious law. By contrast, the state of Kelantan in Malaysia and the state of Zamfara in Nigeria have explicitly made the Islamic *shari'a* the basis of their general legal codes, for Muslims and non-Muslims alike. That is, they have melded customary and self-government incorporation, subjecting all to criminal sanctions for violating the local understanding of Islamic religious law. (In more extreme ways, the governments of Saudi Arabia, Iran, and Afghanistan of course do this as well.) That this violates the basic liberty of nonbelievers in those places should be clear. The

---

[43] It is interesting to note that indigenous custom has sometimes been categorized as 'religion' in order to deny it the standing of 'law.' See *Milirrupum v Nabalco*.

[44] J. N. Matson notes some of the historical links and parallels between British recognition of Muslim law in some colonies and British recognition of indigenous customary law in others. See Matson, 'The Common Law Abroad: English and Indigenous Laws in the British Commonwealth,' *International and Comparative Law Quarterly* (1993), 753–79.

exclusvely customary incorporation of religious law, however, is more morally defensible, if still legitimately debatable. India serves as a useful example.

At the time of British colonization, Muslim law was in force through large parts of the north of India. Britain constrained the Muslim princes and allowed more or less free reign to Hindu practices; the Muslim criminal law in particular was entirely superseded. But Islam was not pushed out of law altogether; Muslim 'personal law' was allowed to govern relations among Muslims. Some similar provisions were made for Sikhs, Buddhists, Jainists, Christians, and the tribal peoples of the northeast, but the size and centrality of the Muslim minority makes it a case of particular interest. Islam has a rich and complex legal tradition which originated outside the Hindu sphere of influence (unlike, say, the Sikh or Buddhist religions), and continuation of Muslim personal law into post-independence and post-partition India has sometimes been a matter of serious controversy. The Indian state openly considers the reform of Hindu social traditions and practices a legitimate state purpose; customary Muslim leaders strenuously deny that it should view Islamic law in the same light.

Muslim men may marry up to four women at a time, the limit prescribed in the Koran. They may also divorce their wives at will (divorce by *Talak*), and need not follow judicial divorce proceedings; Muslim wives seeking divorce against the will of their husbands must show cause. Muslim couples may divorce extrajudicially by mutual consent, a power not available to others. The apostasy of a Muslim man from Islam results in the automatic dissolution of a Muslim marriage, though the same is not true for the apostasy of a Muslim woman.[45]

The support of divorced wives has been a contentious issue. The Muslim law in force holds that an ex-husband must ordinarily support an ex-wife for three months after the divorce and children raised by the ex-wife until they are two years old as well as returning the wife's dowry. The criminal law holds persons of means responsible for the support of their indigent relatives, including aged parents, handicapped adult children, and ex-wives. In the important and controversial *Shah Bano Begum* case, the Supreme Court in 1985 held that the relevant section of the criminal code was applicable to Muslims. Legislation passed in response effectively reversed that judgment. Now Muslim men

---

[45] At least one commentator has argued that this last was a legislative violation of the relevant Islamic law, sacrificing religious authenticity to the control of women who might otherwise apostasize in order to gain a divorce. Vrinda Narain, 'Women's Rights and the Accommodation of "Difference:" Muslim Women In India,' *Southern California Review of Law and Women's Studies* 8 (1998), 43.

are liable for support only for three months, unless at the time of divorce both husband and wife declare that they would rather be governed by the general criminal code. Responsibility for support of an indigent Muslim ex-wife now lies with those relatives who would be able to inherit from her under Muslim law (parents, siblings, adult children), not with the ex-husband.[46]

Only one-third of a Muslim's property may be disposed of by will. Daughters receive only half the share of sons on inheritance.[47] Non-Muslims cannot inherit from Muslims, except when they are apostates. This may not apply to testamentary disposition of property; but that cannot exceed one-third of the estate in any event.[48]

In general, land and property law is not included under 'personal law,' an obvious difference from the indigenous cases. In one significant respect, however, personal law determines the rules concerning land holdings. When two or more Muslims jointly own a piece of land, or when one owns land and another has some legal right concerning it (e.g. a right of passage over it), or when one owns land and another owns an adjoining plot, there is a right of pre-emption of sales. When one Muslim seeks to sell his or her (share in the) property, the co-owner, possessor of a non-proprietary right, or owner of adjacent property must be given the opportunity to buy it first. When there are a number of Muslims with such interests, the Muslim seeking to sell land (or other real property) must get all of them to refuse explicitly to buy the land before selling to an outsider. Those exercising their right of pre-empting a sale do not actually have to buy the land in order effectively to block the sale. If they refuse either actually to purchase the land or explicitly to waive their right to do so, then any outside purchaser is faced with the prospect of litigation which may well be lost. All of this results in a kind of community veto over sales to outsiders, and indeed the point of pre-emption is to allow a community to retain its character.[49] This device perpetuates communal concentration ('segregation' to critics, 'the viability of communities' to sympathizers) in a way similar to rules that members of indigenous tribes may only sell their lands to other tribe members.

Muslim criminal law in general does not have legal standing, and on matters defined by the Indian state as criminal, confessional differences are typically not observed. That is not to say that there are no distinctions

---

[46] A. M. Bhattacharjee, *Muslim Law and the Constitution* (2nd edn., Calcutta: Eastern Law House, 1994), 150–9, 179; Veena Das, 'Cultural Rights and the Definition of Community,' in Oliver Mendelsohn and Upendra Baxi (eds.), *The Rights of Subordinated Peoples* (Oxford: Oxford University Press, 1994), 125–37.   [47] Ibid. 180
[48] Ibid. 109–17   [49] Ibid. 163–75, 180.

drawn. A Hindu man who marries more than one woman not only does not have a legally valid plural marriage; he is subject to criminal prosecution for bigamy. The criminal code of India, not merely its family civil law, dictates that adequate alimony be paid from a divorced husband to a divorced wife; this is no longer applicable to Muslims. But there is no Muslim community which is entitled to inflict coercive punishment for violation of its rules, no Muslim jurisdiction to compete or conflict with the general jurisdiction in criminal cases, no talk of having Muslims police Muslims and deal with lawbreakers internally—much less self-government that would allow criminal jurisdiction over local non-Muslims.

The legal foundation for recognition in India is entirely statutory. The key piece of legislation is *The Muslim Personal Law (Shariat) Application Act 1937*; important revisions and additions came in *The Dissolution of Muslim Marriage Act 1939* and *The Muslim Women (Protection of Rights on Divorce) Act 1986*. Substantial case law has developed around the statutory provisions, of course; but there is no constitutional right to confession-specific personal laws. Indeed, the Constitution of India instructs the 'State [to] endeavour to secure for the citizens a uniform civil code throughout the territory of India' (§44). Britain established the custom of allowing multiple systems of personal law, but the custom has legal standing only insofar as it was codified and the codification remains in force. There is substantial dispute over the degree to which the fundamental rights provision of the Constitution limits the various systems of personal law; but there is no question that the Indian legislature could eliminate all recognition if it saw fit. The relevant statutes often make reference to Muslim (or Mohammedan) law, leaving to the courts the task of identifying that law. The courts in turn are inclined to defer to the *Hadith* and the *Imamia*. The latter are authorized traditional commentaries on and interpretations of the Koran, the former often-apocryphal extra-Koranic statements attributed to Mohammed. This relieves them of having to directly engage in Koranic interpretation.[50] Courts also rely on previous courts' declarations of what the relevant Muslim law

---

[50] These are similarities between constitutional interpretation and interpretation of a religious text. Sanford Levinson analogizes calls to abandon the accretions of caselaw and interpretation, to return to the text of a constitution, to Protestantism and to similar movements in Judaism and Islam. Approaches to constitutional interpretation that emphasize precedent or other extra-textual sources of authority (like the statements made by constitutional founders outside the constitutional text, e.g. *The Federalist Papers*) are, he suggests interestingly similar to Catholicism, to Talmudic Judaism, and to Islamic thought that relies on the *Hadith* and the *Imamia*. *Constitutional Faith* (Princeton: Princeton University Press, 1988), 16–53.

requires. This is customary incorporation; until and unless India abol-ishes the confessional personal legal codes, the courts are supposed to rule according to their understanding of the relevant religious laws.

The 1937 legislation instructs courts to apply Muslim law to personal relations between Muslims. There is legal controversy about some of the implications of this. Muslim law dictates that a marriage be dissolved when the husband apostatizes; but when he has apostatized, he is arguably no longer Muslim and it is unclear whether Muslim law should still apply as far as Indian law is concerned. In some areas Muslims can opt out of Muslim law; for example, a couple at divorce may declare themselves bound by the general code and not by Muslim law. But there is no general Indian code of personal law, only enact-ments of Hindu and Muslim (and Sikh and Buddhist and . . .) personal laws. There are some statutory provisions for how to handle a case that falls between the cracks, but often it is a matter for judicial discretion.

The British courts retained the right to interpret, apply, and limit customary law in Africa, and to do the same with religious customary law in India. By contrast, the Ottoman millet system and its successors in contemporary states like Israel and Lebanon do not allow secular courts to interpret religious law. Religious officials and institutions within each community, such as rabbinical courts, have the final author-ity which the British system reserved for British courts. Religiously specific courts raise the danger of giving too much secular power to reli-gious officials, like Israel's Chief Rabbinate; but the general courts might distort religious law, as the Indian courts have been accused of with reference to Muslim law. Of comparable importance is whether there is a general civil code accessible to those who wish to opt out of the religious courts. There is not in Israel, and in India there is only for certain very limited purposes. In both states, however, there are vocal advocates of such a code. Opponents of the civil power of religious offi-cials in Israel, for example, continue to fight for a civil code of marriage which would allow non-religious or inter-religious marriages—both of which are currently legally impossible.

If we are more concerned with preventing internal cruelty and abuses of power than with procedural authenticity—and the multiculturalism of fear argues that we should be—we have good reason to prefer the British–Indian model. If, however, we have strong reason to suspect bad faith or lack of sufficient knowledge on the part of the dominant group's courts, as was arguably true of British courts in Africa and was certainly true of apartheid-era courts in South Africa, we have reason to prefer leaving interpretation in the hands of the community whose customs are being interpreted. In either case, both the concern to protect individual members of communities and the need for a stable legal framework that can survive intermarriage, assimilation, secularization, and so on call for a civil code accessible to all who choose it.

EVALUATIONS AND LIMITATIONS

One could agree with everything that has been said until now and not agree with what follows; the conceptual distinctions made could be valid even if all of the evaluations made below are invalid.

Much of what is accomplished by common law incorporation, and some of what can be accomplished with customary incorporation, can also be accomplished by individualization of the law generally. For example, a state with mandatory primogeniture might allow a minority with other traditions to abide by their customs allowing women or subsequent sons to inherit—a form of customary recognition. But it might also abandon mandatory primogeniture in favor of the purely testamentary disposition of goods; this would allow members of the minority as well as members of the majority to follow rules other than primogeniture. Now, it might still be the case that neither members of the majority culture nor members of the minority culture thought that the legitimate disposition of goods was determined by choice; both might think that there is a binding cultural rule which they must follow in drawing up their wills. But that is no different from laws on freedom of religion which claim to allow people to practice whatever religion they choose even if no one experiences either inherited belief or conversion as a *choice*.

Marriage law—in particular, *divorce* law—has been individualized to a certain degree in some states by the growing use of prenuptial agreements. Some of what minorities seek through the incorporation of customary marriage law might be accomplished with further individualization of marriage contracts, including the ability to set in advance the permissible terms of divorce. Louisiana has, controversially, increased the number of available options by one; couples may choose to enter 'covenant marriages' from which divorce is more legally difficult. If still wider discretion were granted, then the perceived need for the incorporation of culturally-specific legal codes might well be less.

Even some unusual property rules (e.g. the Indian Muslim rule of preemption, some indigenous inalienability rules) could be generated under a regime that allowed restrictive covenants on land titles. Something similar is true of many demands for exemptions from general laws;

repeal of the law accomplishes the same purpose. Jews and Catholics do not need special exemptions from Prohibition for their ceremonial wine once Prohibition is repealed; Sikhs do not require exemption from motorcycle helmet laws if none such are in place.

I think this is a strategy worth pursuing. It allows for cultural differentiation without freezing any particular customary understandings or communal affiliations into law. There are a few reasons, however, for thinking that this will not always be enough (though of course one might think that it is all that is morally justifiable). Every system of law has default rules, rules that come into play when a problem has not been foreseen or provided for in advance. Testamentary disposition does not solve the problem of what to do in cases of intestacy; and when two cultural communities have significantly different family patterns and expectations, the minority may well seek incorporation of its rules for intestacy. Similarly, even the most elaborate of prenuptial agreements cannot predict every subject of dispute in a divorce. Courts must have rules on which to fall back; and those rules may be dependent on one cultural understanding of family obligations but be quite inappropriate in another. The ALRC recommended allowing not only customary Aboriginal wills but customary intestate inheritance and even challenges to wills on the basis of legitimate customary expectations; this sort of result obviously could not be reached simply by allowing individual choice of law to rule.

Will Kymlicka has noted a Catch-22—I do not think it is a paradox— in the problem of developing a shared sense of citizenship in multinational states.

Self-government rights . . . do pose a threat to social unity. The sense of being a distinct nation within a larger country is potentially destabilizing. On the other hand, the denial of self-government rights is also destabilizing, since it encourages resentment and even secession. Concerns about social unity will arise however we respond to self-government claims.[51]

The dilemma is not limited to self-government rights as I describe them here. Self-government and customary recognition both partially legally detach indigenous peoples from the state and the general law, and so potentially undermine their sense of belonging to that state. Common law recognition, on the other hand, may well not satisfy the feeling among indigenous peoples that they ought to be recognized as distinct peoples. It may leave many members of indigenous communities feeling alienated and distant from a state that does not grant them their

---

[51] *Multicultural Citizenship*, 192.

due. Perhaps they will never feel like full citizens in a state which does not fully acknowledge their distinctive status.[52]

It is important to note one more aspect of the impasse. Even partial detachment from the state can undermine the feeling, however weak it may be to begin with, among non-indigenous peoples that their indigenous neighbors are fellow citizens, engaged in a common social or political enterprise. That is, if social unity and shared citizenship are important goals—if we really care about the experienced feelings of shared citizenship rather than some unanswerable questions about which collectivities individuals *ought* to feel loyal to—they cannot only be measured with reference to the feelings of indigenous citizens. Now, even if indigenous peoples were simply resident aliens trapped in states not of their own making, or citizens of enclave polities surrounded by those states (think of Lesotho and South Africa), those states would owe them much better treatment than they have often received. Even such aliens have a right not to be exterminated, not to have their goods expropriated, not to have their children stolen away. And even such aliens would have a right to restitution or compensation for many of those past wrongs. But they would *not* have any right to special representation in the political organs of the state, or to ongoing non-compensatory financing by that state, or to special assistance in entry into the life of the wider society. Why would anyone offer affirmative action in the civil service or universities to such aliens, if their just moral claims have essentially to do with separateness? If non-indigenous citizens are made to feel that indigenous peoples aren't really part of the state, then they will have little reason to support such integrative benefits. This does not get us any closer to solving the problem Kymlicka notes; indeed, it takes us farther away.

It seems to me, though I cannot show this in any scientific fashion, that this dilemma of membership afflicts New Zealand somewhat less than it does Canada, the United States, or Australia, to say nothing of

---

[52] Chandran Kukathas has argued that the liberal state has no legitimate concern with social unity in this sense, that my sense of my own identity is none of the state's business. I am sympathetic to his worries about making social unity and identity-shaping too central to our political morality; I don't think that the liberal state should try to shape its citizens' identities so that identification with the state takes some unmitigated *priority* over identification with other collectivities. But surely the liberal state legitimately can be *as* concerned as churches, ethnic groups, and the rest with the identity of their members; it may try to ensure that there is *some* attachment, though it is of course constrained in the means it may use. See Chandran Kukathas, 'Liberalism, Communitarianism, and Political Community,' *Social Philosophy and Policy* 13 (1996), 80–104, and 'Cultural Toleration,' in Ian Shapiro and Will Kymlicka (eds.), *NOMOS XXXIX: Ethnicity And Group Rights* (New York: New York University Press, 1997).

more deeply-divided states like South Africa and India.[53] But if this is true, it is probably true for non-replicable reasons. The Maori can be convincingly understood as one people with status as co-founder of the state, while the indigenous peoples of the other states are much more diverse among themselves. New Zealand can have Maori and English as joint official languages. Canada could not make every indigenous language an official language and have that status retain any meaning.

Similarly, the Treaty of Waitangi arguably does involve a voluntary waiving of sovereignty on the part of the Maori. Even complete compliance with the treaty on the part of the New Zealand government wouldn't create differentiated citizenship. The British did not think that Australia's Aborigines were competent to sign treaties, and the North American treaties generally retained or merged rather than waived sovereignty. So the feeling of shared citizenship between Maori and Pakeha (if I'm right that there is such a feeling) flows from a real jointness of the polity that may not be available to the other states under discussion.

I do not suppose that this classification, or any classification, can cut this knot; the problem is a real one that can't be clarified away. But I can suggest some additional considerations to be put into the balance. Transparency, simplicity, and clarity are virtues of a legal system, though of course a legal system must also be complicated enough to take many morally relevant nuances and details into account. The incorporation of customary law undermines all these virtues; it multiplies the fundamental legal philosophies as well as multiplying jurisdictions and interpreters.

Perhaps these problems are easily manageable. After all, civil law and common law jurisdictions coexist in the United States (Louisiana adheres to the civil law) and Canada; South Africa has always relied on both common law and Roman–Dutch legal systems; and Switzerland survives and thrives with its marriage of Roman and German legal traditions. Customary law might coexist with English law just as easily. We have, however, some reason to doubt this. The European legal traditions have common roots; the civil law and the common law, for example, have both been critically influenced by Roman legal traditions. That substantially aids mutual comprehensibility between the two traditions. No such common roots exist between European and indigenous traditions. Adding to the difficulties are the multiplicity of customary laws within a

---

[53] South Africa's constitution and current official self-understanding—'We, the people of South Africa . . . believe that South Africa belongs to all who live in it, united in our diversity'—describe the hope of shared citizenship rather than a formula for attaining it, much like the American *E pluribus unum*.

state; customary law is not Indian or Aboriginal but Cree or Navajo or Pitjantjatjara or Waanyi. As jurisdictions and legal concepts multiply, the comprehensibility of the legal system as a whole can be maintained only by restricting the range of activities subject to customary law.

Legal transparency also aids in social and cultural mobility. Those bound by a system of customary law which is itself difficult and complicated to master will be that much less likely to invest the time to learn about the law of the wider state, their rights under that law, and the possibility of using it rather than customary law for some purposes. I think that such mobility, the possibility of accessing the law of the wider state, is important for any sense of shared membership in that state. It is certainly important for the freedom of those living in customary cultural communities. The possibility of a choice of jurisdictions is one of the advantages, or compensations, that liberal multiethnic states can offer indigenous peoples whose ancestors did not voluntarily join those states. And the more often customary legal incorporation is used instead of common law incorporation, and the more complex and differentiated customary law is, the less real that choice of jurisdictions becomes.

Self-government incorporation might present fewer such difficulties, though it depends in part on what decisions the sovereign indigenous peoples make about their laws. In general, though, this kind of recognition creates a legal environment similar to federalism, the complications of which are well-known but also manageable. Territorially based federalism has well-known advantages and disadvantages regarding the promotion of a shared identity. It sometimes creates a base and a structure for future secession; but it sometimes gives members of ethnic minorities an institutional tie to the political order.

The point of common law incorporation, of course, is to recognize indigenous rights within a common legal and conceptual framework, so it creates the fewest difficulties of legal complication; though it certainly also gives indigenous peoples less reason to think that they have been recognized as fully distinct. In some sense common law incorporation can bolster a common citizenship only to the degree that the sense of political separateness is already weak. If the distance felt from a given state by the indigenous people in that state has to do with the discriminatory application of the general law, the denial of land rights, and the actual suppression of custom, then common law incorporation can be a viable solution.

Each mode of incorporation has further virtues and drawbacks as measured by liberal democratic principles. Common law incorporation preserves the possibility of one law before which all can be equal, once that law has been understood in suitably generous ways. It eliminates (or at least mitigates) the culturally discriminatory aspects of the general law, without limiting the access of indigenous people to the rights offered by that law. On the other hand, it clearly subordinates indigenous law and generally leaves the law of the settlers' state as the framework for all legal relations. The common law model does not attempt to undo historical wrongs (such as conquest), except insofar as it demands compensation for unjust takings of indigenous property in land.

Customary law recognition involves the fewest legal fictions; indigenous traditions are not forced into either the concepts of European common law or those of European international law but are recognized (as far as possible) on their own terms. Customary recognition also emphasizes the traditional aspect of indigenous traditions, however, and leaves little space for innovation, reform, or democratic alteration even by indigenous people themselves. Customary recognition may bind indigenous people to old ways, and even make their rights conditional on their adherence to the old ways.

For example, holders of common law title own their land under few conditions. The greater the reliance on customary law, however, the greater the conditionality of ownership might become. Customary law might identify who has rights to use a piece of land for what purpose; but it also identifies who has what *responsibilities* to the land, and what uses are impermissible for anyone. A legal regime in which indigenous peoples held their lands primarily under customary law rather than common law title, and which took customary law seriously, would result in indigenous peoples being significantly more restricted in the use of their lands than other members of the society are in the use of theirs. It is arguable that, under such a regime, refusal to fulfill responsibilities about land logically entails a forfeiture of rights to the land. Using such reasoning, the Queensland Aboriginal Land Rights Act makes customary Aboriginal responsibilities for land an essential part of the land claims process.

A land claim application must include, among other things, a statement of the responsibilities in relation to the land that the claimants agree to assume if the land is granted because of the claim. If the claim is made on the ground of economic or cultural viability, the claim must also include a statement of the specific proposal for the use of the land claimed . . . The deed of grant must specify . . . the responsibilities that the group of Aboriginal people have agreed to assume in relation to the land.[54]

---

[54] Graeme Neate, 'Looking After Country: Legal Recognition of Traditional Rights To and Responsibilities For Land,' *University of New South Wales Law Journal* 16: 1 (1993), 161–222, at 196, 197.

Enforcement of customary law by the criminal law system of the state can even more obviously bind members to observance of traditional rules. Will Kymlicka terms rules binding members of minority cultures to their cultural traditions 'internal restrictions' and criticizes them as incompatible with liberal principles.[55] While I do not think that all such internal rules are illiberal, we surely have some grounds to worry if the state enforces such customary norms or makes legal rights conditional on their observance.

This problem may be exacerbated by customary legal enforcement by state courts (rather than by a parallel system of indigenous courts). The state courts typically have only the blunt instrument of a 'natural justice' exception with which to override customary law, and no mechanisms for its reform or evolution. Outsiders have limited access to the kind of information that would allow a judge to say, 'this has been the rule, but that is the underlying principle, and in new circumstances the principle can be better satisfied with a new rule.' While the common law changes and grows by judicial action, the judiciary is likely to take a more static view of customary law, in part because they have a better chance of being true to the customs if they do, in part because if the indigenous law isn't customary then it has no particular standing on this model.

The converse of the fear that state recognition will artificially freeze customary law is that such recognition will distort the customs.[56] Whether the state courts are the only forums for adjudication of customary legal claims or the forums of last resort, final authority for the interpretation of indigenous law is taken out of indigenous hands. Sometimes the distortion is intentional, as it seems to have been by the apartheid regime's codifications of African customary law. But even the best-intentioned of interpreters may be handicapped by being raised in (and having legal training in) a different cultural background.[57]

This problem may be inescapable under customary incorporation; the problem of the freezing of customary law can at least be mitigated

---

[55] Will Kymlicka, *Multicultural Citizenship* (Oxford: Oxford University Press, 1995), ch. 3.

[56] See Gordon Woodman, 'How state courts create customary law in Ghana and Nigeria,' in Bradford Morse and Gordon Woodman (eds.), *Indigenous Law and the State* (Providence: Foris Publications, 1988).

[57] All of this, of course, assumes that lawyers and judges are much less likely to be members of indigenous cultures. That is a contingent fact, but so far a generally true one. Bruce Clark offers that fact as a reason why indigenous leaders in Canada might prefer political negotiation to forcing judicial recognition of (what he claims are) existing rights of self-government (*Native Liberty, Crown Sovereignty: The Existing Aboriginal Right of Self-Government in Canada* (Montreal: McGill-Queen's University Press, 1990), 4).

in its effects. A general, liberal legal code accessible to all, and accessible on a case-by-case, issue-by-issue basis, helps make exit or partial exit possible for members of customary communities. If there is not a liberal civil code, or if members of some communities do not have access to it because the state considers them bound by customary law, then the possibility of exit (and the check it creates on group membership) does not exist. Although Kymlicka and Chandran Kukathas disagree to a certain extent about the validity of conservative rules within a minority group when exit *is* possible, they certainly unite in condemning such rules when it is *not*.[58]

Conversely, *if* the law of the wider state is easily accessible to indigenous people,[59] customary recognition might help promote liberal goals in a way similar but preferable to federalism. Offering a choice of jurisdictions, a choice of laws, over a wide range of activities creates a kind of competition among legal systems. Under federalism, some change of place is typically necessary in order to move from a more to a less restrictive law. Since customary law is personal, not territorial, if indigenous people can choose the law under which they live—and especially if they can choose on a case-by-case, issue-by-issue basis—pressure might be placed on both legal systems to more closely match their needs and choices. On the other hand, this assumes that there is some valid mechanism for the change or reform of customary law, which we have seen to be a difficult assumption to make.

A self-government foundation is most in accordance with norms concerning the right of peoples to self-government; it also leaves the least space for liberal human rights constraints. Only the self-government model accords to indigenous people the right to determine their political status as they see fit. Only the self-government model allows them to stand as the final interpreters of their own law. And only the self-government model allows them to change and reform their laws as they see fit. Assuming that the tribal governments are internally democratic, self-government seems to meet democratic requirements at least as well as common law incorporation and rather better than customary law.

Liberal values are somewhat less well served. When an indigenous sovereign violates individual rights—by restricting religious liberty, by

[58] See Chandran Kukathas, 'Are There Any Cultural Rights?' *Political Theory* (1992), 105–39, and 'Cultural Rights Again: A Rejoinder to Kymlicka,' ibid. 674–680; Kymlicka, *Multicultural Citizenship*, ch. 8.

[59] Customary recognition might itself make the wider law less accessible in fact, even if it is formally available, because of the difficulty in learning about one's rights and duties under two or more deeply different legal systems.

unjustly discriminating against women, and so on—the logic of the self-government model gives the wider state little space to intervene. As Kymlicka puts it, recognizing the self-government rights of a national minority (a category which includes indigenous minorities) requires liberals in the wider state to view rights-violations within the minority nation the same way they would view rights-violations in, say, Saudi Arabia: something to be criticized and agitated against, but not something they have legitimate authority to prevent. Joseph Carens suggests that this might be for the best, in a discussion of the possible application of the Canadian Charter of Rights and Freedoms to indigenous governments, because

people are supposed to experience the realization of principles of justice through various concrete institutions, but they may actually experience a lot of the institution and very little of the principle.[60]

That is, the ostensibly liberal institutions of the wider state (e.g. courts) have done such a poor job of promoting liberal values with respect to indigenous people that we have reason to deny those institutions jurisdiction. If this is so, it only says that self-government is the least-bad alternative from a liberal perspective given current constraints, not that it is an affirmative good.[61]

Some argue that a self-government or sovereignty model is the only one which is logically coherent. How can laws be recognized without recognition of a lawmaker? How can indigenous ownership of land be acknowledged without acknowledging indigenous sovereignty over that land? These questions in a sense assert what they attempt to prove: the reality and continuing validity of indigenous sovereignty. If there is no such sovereignty, of course, there is nothing inconsistent about not realizing it. But if we suppose that at the moment of settlement Europeans did or should have viewed indigenous peoples as sovereign nations under the terms of European international law, even that does not prove the existence of continuing sovereignty. If adverse possession is a good rule for ownership,[62] it is an indispensable rule with regard to sovereignty. Even in the complete absence of any legally valid extinguishment of sovereignty, full sovereignty cannot be thought to endure unexercised

[60] Joseph Carens, 'Dimensions of Citizenship and National Identity in Canada,' *The Philosophical Forum* 28 (1996–7), 111–24, at 117.

[61] Will Kymlicka has suggested that one solution to this problem might lie in indigenous peoples submitting to international human rights conventions and tribunals, thereby gaining the advantages of judicial review without having to submit directly to the state that has broken promises to them in the past.

[62] I argue that it is, especially in a multicultural society, in the next chapter.

forever. A case can be made for the rights of living members of cultural minorities to self-determination, or to secession in certain circumstances; but that case cannot simply be based on the putative sovereignty of their ancestors. And I argued in Chapters 1 and 3 that the case must be made instrumentally in terms of defense of liberal values or protection from violent states, because any general defense of an inherent right to self-government rests on implausible claims about the external reality of some category like 'nation.'

At the risk of over-repetition, I am not sure that it makes sense to try to identify 'the best' or even 'the preferred' mode of incorporation; but it does make sense to identify the characteristic dangers, difficulties, and opportunities of each. Customary incorporation without a commonly accessible civil law is dangerous to members of the indigenous community.[63] Customary incorporation *with* a general civil law creates dangers of opportunistic choice of jurisdiction; but the possibility of such choice is generally salutary and the danger of, for example, an indigenous criminal opportunistically choosing the more lenient jurisdiction can be taken into account. Territorial self-government carries well-known dangers concerning the treatment of local minorities, possible incentives for secession, and the protection of individual rights. Common law incorporation risks understating the distinctiveness of indigenous peoples.

Neither is the joining of all three modes a solution. The risks that a territorial government will be oppressive are hardly lessened by making it sole owner of as well as sovereign over all of its land, or by justifying its authority in terms of its ability to preserve forcibly customary ways of life.

From the perspective of indigenous groups, consistency is a virtue; inconsistency, at least, has too often been to their disadvantage. From the perspective of the wider state, clarity and simplicity are advantages; I've argued that they are advantages for the indigenous minority as well. All of these needs, at least, common law incorporation can satisfy. Elements of customary incorporation are often necessary; but the more customary law is constrained by the possibility of members opting out of it, perhaps the more like common law incorporation it becomes. For contingent historical reasons, some indigenous communities have clear legal claims to consistently observed self-government rights; but those rights are not and should not be too tightly linked with the other modes

---

[63] Jeremy Waldron notes elsewhere, though using different terminology, that it is also dangerous to the peace of the wider community. See 'When Justice Replaces Affection,' in *Liberal Rights* (Cambridge: Cambridge University Press, 1993).

of incorporation. Where there is not yet a strong claim or need for self-government—as in Australia—it seems to me that it can be treated as a last resort, after good-faith efforts have been made to meet indigenous aspirations and needs through common law and then customary incorp-oration.

From the perspective of a multiculturalism of fear, these considera-tions weigh heavily on the side of common law recognition, and limit customary recognition to cases in which there is a general civil law available. Territorial models of ethnocultural self-government are systematically prone to conflicts over borders and the local minorities problem. The nonterritorial models, by contrast, actually diminish the incentives for certain kinds of conflict. Local minorities are obviously less aggrieved than under a territorial model; the indigenous (or reli-gious) minority gains legal rights which diminish its members' sense that only their own state can protect them. However, nonterritorial custom-ary recognition, when that recognition excludes access to any civil code, creates dangers of its own.

In Chapter 2 I differentiated between internal cruelty within cultural communities and the problem of developing a framework for interaction among cultural communities. In truth, the two often run together, espe-cially when members exit their communities or when they seek the protec-tions of the laws of the larger state or a neighboring community. When the leaders of a cultural community maintain that a particular person is bound by custom and the person denies it, a framework or a process for resolving the dispute is needed. The state or the other community cannot treat the problem as purely internal to the first community; whether it is internal or not is one of the issues being disputed.

In the British Columbian case *Thomas v Norris,* David Thomas successfully sued several other Coast Salish Indians for assault, battery, and false imprisonment when they forcibly initiated him into a tradition known as Spirit Dancing. Thomas was held in for four days, during which

> eight men . . . took turns digging their fingers into his stomach area and biting him on his sides. This kind of ritual was repeated daily, four times each morn-ing and four times each afternoon . . . He was given 'about a cup of water each day.' He was never given any food . . . He was then whipped or beaten with cedar branches, hard enough to raise welts on his skin.[64]

The defendants maintained that such initiations were part of a Coast Salish tradition, which they had the right to practice under the

---

[64] *Thomas v Norris,* 2 CNLR 139 (British Columbia 1992), 142.

Canadian Constitution's guarantees of indigenous rights. According to that tradition as it was described in court, initiations are sometimes consensual but need not be. Thomas

> never authorized anyone to have him initiated into the society, and he did not want to be a member of the society. He knew very little about the religion of the Coast Somenos people. He was not, and is not, really interested in learning about their culture. He was not brought up in it and lived off the reservation. What little exposure he had to it came through hearing his great grandmother talk about it.[65]

Claude Denis maintains that 'what went wrong' was that the right of the Coast Salish people 'to deal with problems in their own way was denied by the Canadian state,' and that someone 'whom they claim as a member of their community, took the situation out of their hands and brought it to a Canadian court.'[66] This was, he supposes, a case of what I have called internal cruelty (a concept he is at pains to relativize[67]), a case that was wrongly decided because outsiders should not have intervened. But who counts as an outsider with regard to David Thomas's life is part of what was at stake in the case. Thomas, although legally a member of an Indian band, seems not to have viewed himself as a member of the Coast Salish cultural community in any strong sense. And initiating someone into a tradition supposes that they are not already fully part of it. No matter how strong Indian self-government becomes, the question of Thomas's membership isn't one on which the Canadian state could remain silent or neutral. Others 'claim' Thomas 'as a member of their community'; he denies that he is so, at least completely or sufficiently. Even in the case of two equal communities living side-by-side—that is, even if the Canadian state did not have the final legal authority that it does—neither community can claim final, unreviewable authority over whom it will include as a member. When someone seeks asylum or refuge from one of the communities, the other has to say *something,* yes or no. It has to pass judgment. The two communities may formally negotiate a framework for resolving disputes between their systems; they may develop a body of custom and precedent for adjudication. But they cannot simply take every claim the other makes as final.

The laws and legal traditions of neighboring communities—including

---

[65] Ibid. 142–3.
[66] Claude Denis, *We Are Not You: First Nations and Canadian Modernity* (Peterborough, Ontario: Broadview Press, 1997), 77. Denis refers to the case and the parties with pseudonyms.
[67] Ibid. 68–71.

indigenous minorities and the states in which they live—come into
contact, and potential conflict. The conflicts may be simple: a patrilin-
ear culture and a matrilinear culture may make competing claims on the
child of a mixed marriage; or one culture recognizes the validity of intermarriage and the other does not. Or they may vastly complex, as when
English–Australian law attempts to come to terms with the intricate
patterns and rules among Aboriginal Australians about which tribe may
use what land for what purpose at what time. In the next chapter I focus
on the question of land, including indigenous land rights. In the case of
land as in the case of marriage, and in the case of rules about membership, interaction is sure to take place across communal lines, and mutual
adjustments are likely to be necessary. What is needed, again, is a framework of legal recognition, a common law for mediating between the
conflicting laws, which steers a middle course between the imposition of
a single cultural model and the impossible quest for cultural autarky.

7

Blood and Soil, Place or Property: Liberalism, Land, and Ethnicity

THE NEGLECT OF TERRITORY

Contemporary normative theorists of nationalism and ethnicity[1] typically conceptualize nationhood and ethnicity as primarily cultural. That is, they have to do with ways of life, with languages spoken and tales told and values embodied and worth recognized. Nationhood and ethnicity are not understood as political matters; nor are they thought to concern material goods in any important way. In this chapter I argue that nationalism and indigenous ethnic politics cannot be well understood without reference to at least one material good: land. Nationalist and indigenous movements conflict with each other and with liberal societies about the control and possession of land but also about its social meaning, the kind of good that it is. Culturalist accounts of ethnicity may be more easily reconcilable with liberalism and with each other; but a liberal political theory which is concerned to mitigate or minimize ethnic conflicts must develop a framework for thinking about disputes over land.

In *Liberalism, Community, and Culture*, Will Kymlicka puts forward an account of linguistic culture as providing a context for choice, a

---

[1] I have in mind theorists including Will Kymlicka, Yael Tamir, and Charles Taylor, all of whom are discussed below. See Kymlicka, *Liberalism, Community, and Culture* (Oxford: Oxford University Press, 1986) and *Multicultural Citizenship* (Oxford: Oxford University Press, 1995); Tamir, *Liberal Nationalism* (Princeton: Princeton University Press, 1993); Taylor, *Reconciling the Solitudes: Essays on Canadian Federalism and Nationalism*, ed. Guy Laforest (Montreal: McGill-Queens University Press, 1993) and 'The Politics of Recognition,' in Amy Gutmann (ed.), *Multiculturalism: Examining the Politics of Recognition* (Princeton: Princeton University Press, 1993). I think that territory is neglected in a number of other accounts as well. For an two exceptions, both of which I think are broadly compatible with what I say here, see Margaret Moore, 'The Territorial Dimension of Self-Determination,' in Margaret Moore (ed.), *National Self-Determination and Secession* (Oxford: Oxford University Press, 1998), and Jeff Spinner-Halev, 'Land, Culture and Justice: A Framework for Collective Recognition,' *Journal of Political Philosophy* (forthcoming).

background against which persons can autonomously choose and revise their life plans. A stable linguistic culture is a Rawlsian primary good, not part of the good life but a precondition for it. Members of the majority culture in a state like Canada have that primary good provided, as it were, for free. But the culture of a minority comes at a cost, and the smaller the minority, the higher the cost. Members of the minority either have to devote their own resources to preserving what members of the majority get for free, or they face the loss of a basic primary good. As a matter of justice, this disadvantage should be made up for; minority cultures should be shored up and kept stable so that individuals have stable contexts for choice. By contrast, the character of the culture, its conservatism or traditionalism or liberalism or modernity or religiosity or atheism, these are the result of choices members of the culture make about the good life. A culture has no right to remain conservative against the wishes of its members. So while the state can limit the liberty of outsiders to prevent their undermining the existence of the culture, it cannot limit the liberty of members to prevent them from modernizing it.

Against this background, Kymlicka discusses policies designed to protect the culture of the Quebecois and the cultures of Indians and Inuit. For Indians, Kymlicka argues that there is justification for keeping tribal land collectively owned and inalienable, and for preventing the free migration of non-natives into native areas.

But something does not follow here. There is no right to live traditionally, only a right to keep the culture stable and intact. But land, for Canada's indigenous peoples, has to do precisely with living traditionally. Hunting and fishing rights are claimed over even larger areas than any kind of traditional ownership. To forbid division and alienation of land restricts the liberty of non-natives to buy some land, but there is a great deal of other land for them to buy. On the other hand, it restricts the ability of the Indians and Inuit to sell, or to use land as collateral, almost entirely. This looks exactly like a restriction on the liberty of members in order to preserve the character of the culture.

No land rights can be secured by the culture as context of choice argument; neither can any land-use rights, like hunting and fishing rights. This theory may sanction rights to state-supported schools in the native languages, or rights to tribal self-government of various kinds, but not land rights. Rights to hold, preserve, and use land, however, are central to the political aspirations of indigenous peoples.

Yael Tamir characterizes nationalism as primarily cultural and only secondarily political. That is, the nationalism which she thinks is reconcilable with liberalism is not, as Ernest Gellner once defined nationalism, the principle that the boundaries of that nation and the state should coincide; the expression and living of one's culture, not its political standing, constitute nationalism. The primacy she accords to culture, language, and way of life in her account minimizes the dangers of nationalist conflict; one of the ways it does that is by ignoring the importance of land and territory.

> We still need to clarify the use of the term 'living within one's nation.' This could sound like a territorial claim, suggesting that individuals must live in physical proximity to other members of their group, but in the modern world this is not necessarily the case ... As the phenomenon of modern diasporas proves, a national community could in fact have more than one public sphere and need not occupy a continuous territory ... Although written far away from Dublin, *Ulysses* is part of the Irish culture it portrays. While writing Ulysses, Joyce was in a metaphysical sense 'living within his community,' and could have claimed he never left home.[2]

Tamir argues that nations need a public space in which they can live their culture, but it is never exactly clear either how it is public or how it is space. It seems that the ability to publish books drawn from the cultural tradition, even if half a world away, is sufficient. At no point does Tamir concede that nations require land. States do, and she counts as a dispositive argument against state-seeking nationalism that there isn't enough space in the world for every nation to have its own state.

This misses something fundamental. Say that the wide open spaces that remain in much of the world—from Montana and Alberta to Western Australia to Patagonia—were opened up for new nation-states. Inspired by the twentieth-century transplantation of Jews to Palestine, millions of Kurds resettle in North Dakota, Bosnian Serbs go to Saskatchewan while Bosnian Croats go to Australia, and so on. All of Tamir's theoretical aspirations could be satisfied. Every culture could have its public space in which to manifest. And, plausibly if not certainly, every nation could have its state. States, after all, never had to be as big as was generally thought, and have even less need for great size in an integrated global economy; surely there is enough space in the world to give every nation a state the size of Belgium or Switzerland, or at least the size of East Timor or Luxembourg.

Of course the idea is ridiculous. But it's not ridiculous because of a shortage of space. It's ridiculous because we expect that none of the communities in question would uproot themselves and move to the other side of the world. It's not that every nation needs x amount of space, but that every nation wants a very particular place. And as often

---

[2] Yael Tamir, *Liberal Nationalism*, 86.

as not, two or more nations want the same very particular place. Israel was arguably a nation transplanted to new land, but such a thing has only happened once. Not only did it happen with a diaspora community (rather than transplanting an intact community), not only did it happen in part because of genocide, but it happened because of the image of Palestine as the Jews' ancestral homeland. Herzl thought Argentina was a possible site for a Jewish state; others later thought Madagascar would do. But Zionism would not have been as successful at attracting Jewish migrants without the images and resonances associated with reclaiming Israel.[3] The concern with a particular place is actually central to nationalism. Tamir might have proposed to solve it, to cure nationalism of its concern with place; but instead she simply ignores it. Her account of the possible peaceful coexistence of nationalistic nations with each other and with liberalism is less plausible because of it.

Kymlicka also fails fully to account for the importance of particular places. He argues at one point that native land rights shouldn't really be understood as having to do with the connection between particular persons and particular land. Land rights aren't about discovering whether the Sioux really own the Black Hills or not. They're about giving out resources in accordance with need; land is to be thought of as a kind of welfare payment to make up for the extreme poverty and cultural disadvantage of Indians. Land rights are properly justified, not in terms of compensatory justice or ownership, but in terms of distributive justice.[4] But this is untrue to the way indigenous peoples understand their demands.[5] Like Tamir's landless nationalism, it simplifies the task of reconciling liberalism with ethnic claims by reconceptualizing the ethnic claims as more liberal than they are.

In a number of essays, Charles Taylor has offered an account of the impulses behind nationalism and the quest for cultural recognition.[6] In particular, he has tried to explain the desires and aspirations that have given rise to Quebecois nationalism. He asks 'why nations have to become states,'[7] but does not ask about the borders of those states. His

---

[3] Palestinians, of course, also want Palestine in particular, not just some land somewhere for a national homeland. The conflicts this creates are discussed below, especially in the final section, 'Evaluations and Limitations'.

[4] *Multicultural Citizenship*, 219–21.

[5] It is also an odd kind of mechanism of distributive justice—why not make large cash grants to indigenous people rather than according them land rights which are unequally distributed among them on grounds of entitlement rather than grounds of need, and the burden of which is not widely distributed but rather concentrated on those unfortunates with interests in land which is subject to indigenous claims?

[6] See *Reconciling the Solitudes* and 'The Politics of Recognition.'

[7] 'Why Do Nations Have to Become States?' in *Reconciling the Solitudes*.

writings combine to describe what goals cannot be realized except by an independent Quebec or by one that has a special status within the Canadian federation. But nowhere does he identify a goal whose satisfaction requires that an independent or especially autonomous Quebec be as large as the current province. The expression, realization, and recognition of a linguistic culture may require self-government; but why do they require so much territory? The northern third of Quebec is essentially uninhabited by francophone Quebecois; its residents are Indians and Inuits. The indigenous population of Quebec is overwhelmingly opposed to Quebecois secession, and there has been talk of secession from Quebec if the province leaves the confederation. This is entirely unacceptable to Quebecois nationalists. Taylor gives us no reason to expect such a reaction and no way to explain it.

LAND AND ETHNIC POLITICS

Many ethnic conflicts, nationalist movements, and claims made by indigenous minorities are centrally about land. This is not to deny that they are also about language, religion, a sense of identity, or a way of life; but they are often about how those things relate to possession of, or power over, particular pieces of land.

This is not true of all kinds of ethnic politics. Some ethnic conflicts concern the distribution of wealth, or of jobs, or of positions in the military, or of seats in the legislature. But secessionist, irredentist, and national unification movements are common forms of ethnic politics; so are demands for regional autonomy, indigenous land rights, and restrictions on land purchases by outsiders. From the early days of German and Italian nationalism to the contemporary disputes over Aboriginal land claims in Australia, in attempts to alter the ethnic balance of power with deliberate settlements from Jerusalem to Bosnia, in claims to ethnic priority by the 'sons of the soil' from the Sinhalese in Sri Lanka to Fijians in Fiji, land has always had a special status in ethnic and nationalist politics.[8] For a number of other economic resources which are the subjects of distributive fights, ethnicity may serve as a useful way of coordinating and organizing a distributional coalition, but in disputes about land there is typically something more at stake.[9]

[8] See Donald Horowitz, *Ethnic Groups in Conflict* (Berkeley: University of California Press, 1986), 202–4, 209–11.

[9] On the use of ethnicity as a tool for coordinating and organizing political activity, see Russell Hardin, *One for All: The Logic of Group Conflict* (Princeton: Princeton University Press, 1995) as well as Horowitz, *Ethnic Groups in Conflict*, 291–332.

One rough indicator of the prevalence of disputes over land can be found in Ted Robert Gurr's study of ethnic 'minorities at risk.' Gurr describes five kinds of politicized communal groups, based largely on the kinds of demands made.[10] Thus ethnoclasses are primarily concerned with the distribution of jobs and wealth, communal contenders seek power in the capital, and so on. Two categories, collectively deemed 'national peoples,' are centrally concerned with land. Ethnonationalists are characterized by their separatist or secessionist activities, while indigenous peoples typically seek to retain or regain control over their peripheral lands. Of the 233 groups in the study, 140 fall into one or both of these two categories.

Benedict Anderson characterizes the nation as inherently bounded and limited. 'No nation imagines itself coterminous with mankind. The most messianic nationalists do not dream of a day when all the members of the human race will join their nation in the way that it was possible, in certain epochs, for, say, Christians to dream of a wholly Christian planet.'[11] Although this is correct, it is also true that nations tend to imagine themselves expansively; the boundaries imagined by most nationalists tend to be rather wide. Thus, Mazzini included South Tyrolia, Trieste, Sicily, Sardinia, and Corsica as naturally Italian territories. Chinese nationalists claim that China's natural national territory extends to the farthest reaches of land that the old empire ever controlled, though it was never all controlled at the same time and some of it was only loosely bound to the center. Even the post-colonial nations like Indonesia and India, which Anderson says had their national consciousness shaped by the European maps, have sought to fill out to somewhat larger natural limits than those on the colonial charts; Goa and East Timor were both conquered in that spirit.

This might be seen as simply the unremarkable claim that nationalism, like most things, can be used as a pretext for greed. But there *is* something remarkable about the nationalist urge for limited expansiveness. One strain of nationalism is concerned with the purity of the nation and concerned about the presence of aliens or foreigners of various kinds within a nation. Sometimes we should therefore see the majority or *Staatvolk* of a nation-state seceding from around an unwanted minority. Occasionally we ought to hear a nationalist saying that it would be better to have less territory and a more homogenous

---

[10] Ted Robert Gurr, *Minorities at Risk: A Global View of Ethnopolitical Conflicts* (Washington, DC: US Institute for Peace Press, 1993), 15–23

[11] Benedict Anderson, *Imagined Communities* (2nd edn., London: Verso, 1991), 7.

nation than the reverse. Wouldn't an independent Quebec be better off without all those non-francophone Indians anyway?

But this is almost unheard-of. Other than the expulsion of Singapore from the Malay Federation, nothing of the sort has happened in the postwar world. The (sometimes unrealistic, sometimes all-too-realistic) plan of expelling the minority from the national homeland, but keeping its territory, is common. Even where it is impossible, however, the nationalist program almost never includes the sacrifice of any territory, the declaration that some of the land within current borders isn't really part of the national homeland and is expendable.

LAND IN NATIONALIST THEORY

The links between ethnicity and territory in practice are reflected in theory, in the nationalist and indigenous understandings of land. Herder's nationalism, commonly thought to be more linguistic and cultural than political or economic, includes a proto-Lamarckian notion of human adaptation to climate which leaves people almost biologically bound to their own country.

Some sensitive people feel so intimately close to their native country, are so much attached to its soil, that they can scarcely live if separated from it. The constitution of their body, their way of life, the nature of work and play to which they have become accustomed from their infancy, indeed their whole mentality, are climatic. Deprive them of their country, and you deprive them of everything.[12]

Nationalism celebrates a people's history and culture, but it also celebrates their land. Moreover, it celebrates the link between the two. Here as in much else, Mazzini is typical (in part because he was an example to so many later nationalists).

To you, who have been born in Italy, God has allotted, as if favoring you specially, the best-defined country in Europe . . . God has stretched round you sublime and indisputable boundaries; on one side the highest mountains of Europe, the Alps; on the other the sea, the immeasurable sea . . . As far as this your language is spoken and understood; beyond this you have no rights. Sicily, Sardinia, Corsica, and the smaller islands between them and the mainland belong undeniably to you.[13]

---

[12] J. G. Herder, *Ideas for a Philosophy of the History of Mankind*, bk. VII, chs. 2–5. In F. M. Barnard (ed.), *Herder on Social and Political Culture* (Cambridge: Cambridge University Press, 1969), 285–311. Compare Montesquieu's comments on migration, quoted in Ch. 1.

[13] Mazzini, 'The Duties of Man,' reprinted in Omar Dahbour and Micheline Ishay (eds.), *The Nationalism Reader* (Atlantic Highlands, NJ: Humanities Press, 1995).

Mazzini goes so far as to attribute divine origins to the natural boundaries which keep nations separate; the 'design of God' can be seen 'clearly marked out, as far, at least, as regards Europe, by the courses of the great rivers, by the lines of the lofty mountains, and by other geographical conditions.'

David Miller offers a general characterization of the nationalist view.

[N]ational identity . . . connects a group of people to a particular geographical place, and here again there is a clear contrast with most other group identities that people affirm. For example, ethnic or religious identities often have sacred sites or places of origin, but it is not an essential part of having the identity that you should permanently occupy that place; if you are a good Muslim you should make a pilgrimage to Mecca at least once, but you need not set up house there. A nation, by contrast, must have a homeland.[14]

What's more, nationalism thinks about that homeland in certain recurrent ways. It elides the distinction between sovereignty and owner-ship; all of the land belongs to *this* people, from whom it cannot be taken away. Nationalism typically conceptualizes land as place, not property. *This* piece of land is part of the patrimony of *this* nation. Perhaps it is of particular historical or religious importance. Perhaps the beauty of this spot is a cause for national pride, or perhaps this kind of terrain is taken to embody something about the nation (rugged moun-tains are a particular favorite). Even when the particular piece of land has no such distinctiveness, however, it remains national soil. A people is in some way particularly well-suited to this piece of land. It is where one's ancestors are buried, an important and recurring image. A particu-lar valorization of agriculture is common; the truest sons of the soil are those who work it every day. Indeed this is so common that some nationalists felt a need to create an agricultural sector where none existed.

According to the dominant social-democratic stream in Zionist thought, Jews could become a proper nation only if they became once again a 'normal' people with a normal division of labor, especially in productive activities such as agri-culture.[15]

There is a long-standing tradition, dating at least to Henry Sumner Maine, that disputes the link I am suggesting. It holds territory and ethnicity, contiguity and consanguinity, *jus soli* and *jus sanguinis,* to be opposed and competing methods of organizing a community. In prim-itive or racialist or ethnic nationalist societies, one's loyalty follows

[14] David Miller, *On Nationality* (Oxford: Oxford University Press, 1995), 24.
[15] Milton Esman, *Ethnic Politics* (Ithaca, NY: Cornell University Press, 1993), 112.

blood; in modern or democratic or civic nationalist societies, loyalty follows the soil, and all citizens of the territory are equally one's compatriots.[16] But this distinction accomplishes less than its proponents sometimes believe, and the principles of contiguity and consanguinity are linked as often as they compete. Ethnic nationalism—or cultural nationalism, which is not the same thing—is still, always, nationalism of a place. It is one way to answer the question 'Who belongs to this society in this place?' And in the civic nationalist states—the United States and France are taken as paradigmatic—birth remains by far the most common means of gaining membership.[17]

Indigenous peoples and their political movements articulate an even more intense connection between a people and its land. Even where it is no longer true as a matter of fact, indigenous people commonly speak of themselves as living off, and with, the land. More of the land, sometimes all of it, is understood as having religious or sacred status; the relationship between humans and earth is commonly cast in religious terms. Where nationalism blurs the line between sovereignty and ownership, the indigenous account of land sometimes does away with it altogether. The permanent alienation of land is characterized as impossible or profane.

The political movements of indigenous peoples are about land more than any other issue—about the right to prevent or at least benefit from development on their traditional lands, about the restoration of lands from which they have been dispossessed, and about securing against future losses. A statement of indigenous activists meeting at the United Nations in 1992 stated in the second article of its preamble that '[t]he struggle for our territorial rights is common to all indigenous nations and peoples, and this right is persistently denied by governments and dominant societies.' The first active article of the resolution demanded 'that the United Nations and its member-states . . . recognize indigenous rights to indigenous territories, including the recovery and demarcation of such territories.'[18] Indigenous peoples in New Zealand, Australia,

---

[16] This dichotomy has been put to a variety of crude uses, but for a sophisticated contemporary application, see Rogers Brubaker, *Citizenship and Nationhood in France and Germany* (Cambridge, Mass.: Harvard University Press, 1992).

[17] Steven Grosby, 'Territoriality: The Transcendental, Primordial Feature of Modern Societies,' *Nations and Nationalism* 1 1995, 143–62, quite thoroughly undermines the dichotomy and shows the recurring links between kinship and territorial claims. Jacqueline Stevens discusses the importance of birth to membership in even democratic states in *Reproducing the State* (Princeton: Princeton University Press, 1999).

[18] 'Statement of Indigenous Nations, Peoples, and Organizations,' 11 Dec. 1992, in *Voice of Indigenous Peoples: Native Peoples Address the United Nations* (Santa Fe: Clear Light Press, 1994).

and Canada are currently making considerable progress in their quest for the restitution of traditional lands.

Now, it is important to note what the nationalist and indigenous conception of land is not. For one thing, it is not the happy Rousseaunian vision of pulling up the stakes of the first man to fence off property, with all of humanity continuing to enjoy travel across all the earth. Indigenous statements about land in particular sometimes suggest this image; but on this conception of land there are undoubtedly fences separating *their* territory from *ours,* even if ours is not subsequently divided into yours and mine. Indians, Maori, Aborigines, and others all had strong senses of territoriality, sometimes completely excluding other groups, sometimes permitting them only for certain purposes. The nationalist may wish to establish kibbutzim rather than individual farms, but he or she remains quite clear about the border worth killing and dying for.

Neither is the nationalist/indigenous vision of land simply the civic republican one, although here the commonality is stronger. Non-cultivating indigenous peoples clearly could not make use of the ideology of the citizen-farmer in any straightforward way. To the degree that the republican vision imagines farmers whose love for the land extends to the entire *patrie,* so far is there overlap between the two. But the republican ideology gives no reason for caring about any land beyond the borders of the republic; what counts is not all the land allegedly belonging to a particular people, but the land where one's freedom is situated and realized. Machiavelli, with his concern to liberate and unify Italy, was thus not simply a republican patriot but a nationalist as well, in a way that Cicero in one era and Bolingbroke in another were not.

LIBERALISM

Liberalism has a very different image of what land is. Land is, in general, fungible with other goods. It is alienable—it can be bought, sold, used as collateral for credit, leased, rented, and so on. It is divisible, both in space and in the rights that accrue to it; a plot of land might be divided in half, or its subsurface mineral rights might be owned separately from the surface, and so on. It circulates, as money and other goods circulate; sometimes it is held by one person, sometimes by another. Sometimes it is put to one use, sometimes to another. A piece of land can generally be exchanged for another piece, if not necessarily one of the same size, or exchanged for cash. Moreover, there is no necessary tie between particular persons and particular places. Anyone, from anywhere in the world, can buy a piece of land in the United States, though they may not even be eligible to enter the country. A Parisian can buy a farm in Brittany—or, for that matter, in Western Australia. Land, in short, is property, not place.

One of the earliest liberal projects was the abolition of primogeniture and entail.[19] Jefferson and Burke, Smith and Mill, saw the fungibility of land and other goods, the ability of new people to buy new pieces of land and put them to new use, as critical to a free society.

Burke, characteristically straddling the liberal-conservative divide, considers land a special kind of wealth by virtue of its permanence and the ties it creates to a particular place; but he also sharply criticizes the French *ancien regime* for tying up so much land in entailed estates in part because this prevented new men of ability and wealth from acquiring land and gaining a more stable perspective and loyalty.[20] Despite the conservative tenor to this argument, the prescription is the liberal one: free land up for exchange in the commercial economy. A state in which most land is inalienable fails to meet the needs of a modern society.

Jefferson was similarly critical of the *ancien regime's* allocation of land, if for somewhat different reasons.[21] By keeping land out of commercial circulation, France immunized the estate-owning aristocrats from responding to the needs of others. Land was left unused, or used only as a game reserve, when it would have been far more profitable, as well as more humane, to sell or lease it to the unemployed who might then cultivate it.

Earlier in his career, Jefferson sponsored the bill that abolished entail and primogeniture in Virginia, among the first acts of that state's revolutionary legislature.

The transmission of this property from generation to generation in the same name raised up a distinct set of families who, being privileged by law in the perpetuation of their wealth were thus formed into a Patrician order, distinguished by the splendor and luxury of their establishments . . . [The law was

[19] According to Gordon Wood, '[i]n the decades following the Revolution all the new states abolished the legal devices of primogeniture and entail where they existed, either by statute or by writing the abolition into their constitutions' (Gordon Wood, *The Radicalism of the American Revolution* (New York: Knopf, 1992), 182–3).

[20] See e.g. Edmund Burke, *Reflections on the Revolution in France* (New York: Penguin, 1968 [1790]).

[21] Letter to Madison, 28 Oct. 1785, in Merrill Peterson (ed.), *The Portable Thomas Jefferson* (New York: Penguin, 1975), 396.

intended] to annul this privilege, and instead of an aristocracy of wealth, of more harm and danger, than benefit, to society, to make an opening for the aristocracy of virtue and talent . . .[22]

Even Kant insisted that 'there can be no corporation, class, or order within the state which may as an owner hand down land indefinitely, by appropriate statutes, for the exclusive use of subsequent generations.'[23]

Primogeniture and entail were objects of particular concern to the liberal reformers. This might at first seem odd. The classical liberal view of property in land is commonly discussed as if it were primarily concerned with the natural rights to acquire and possess property. Entail did nothing to impugn past acquisitions or to jeopardize current holdings. Indeed, it promised to extend current holdings indefinitely into the future. Neither did primogeniture deprive anyone of their holdings, or even of their right to dispose of their property as they wished (since it could be pre-empted by a will). Moreover, since the good in question always could have been given to someone else in a will, no one had any right to inherit any particular good that could be said to be violated by primogeniture. Why, then, were liberals from Burke to Jefferson to Mill united in seeking to do away with the feudal inheritance rules?

Michael Walzer has characterized liberal society as importantly marked by four mobilities.[24] Of these, two—geographic and social—are closely related to the flexibility of land (as well as being tied to each other). The ability to sell the piece of land on which one currently lives and go elsewhere and buy a new one has always been tightly related to geographic mobility in liberal societies. Since by social mobility Walzer means not only changes in income but also changes in the way income is earned from one generation to the next, the fungibility of land with other goods has made a tremendous difference here as well. A society in which land could not be exchanged for other goods would tend to keep people in place (since the alternative to staying might be to abandon a valuable piece of land and gain nothing for it); and it would tend to at least rigidify the tendency of the urban to remain urban and the rural to remain rural. That in turn tends to keep the children of farmers as farmers, and so on. Private property in land is one of the institutions that support the liberal mobilities.

Contrast this with the view of a prominent nationalist. In Gandhi's defense of Indian nationalism, the *Hind Swaraj*, he denounces the

---

[22] 'Autobiography,' in Merrill Peterson (ed.), *Thomas Jefferson: Writings* (New York: Library of America, 1984), 32.

[23] Immanuel Kant, *The Metaphysics of Morals*, section 49B.

[24] Michael Walzer, 'The Communitarian Critique of Liberalism,' *Political Theory* 18 (1990), 6–23.

British introduction of railroads to India. The increase in mobility which they allow has not only allowed the bubonic plague to spread more easily; it has actually 'made the holy places of India unholy' because 'formerly, people went to these places with very great difficulty. Generally, therefore, only the real devotees visited such places. Nowadays rogues visit them in order to practice their roguery.'[25] Mobility, moreover, is to blame for tension between Hindus and Muslims; when people could not stray far from home, they could not run into those with whom they differed with the same frequency.

The desire to promote mobility of various kinds lurked beneath the liberal commitment to abolishing entail and primogeniture. A free, democratic, commercial society was thought of as more than simply a state that respected rights of various kinds. It was a society of a particular kind, one characterized by mobility, the rise and fall of elites based on achievement, and a certain fluidity. Certainly Jefferson was motivated by a taste for equality and an antipathy toward the landed aristocracy; but that was not his only motivation, and it was no part of Burke's. For present purposes what is interesting is that there is an important liberal argument against entail that is concerned not with the aristocracy but with the stagnating effect on society of a system that prevents the division, sale, and circulation of land.

This was all seen clearly enough by liberalism's critics. Hegel defended entail, precisely because he feared that the fluid and mobile liberal society would be too little attached to stability and the preservation of the existing order. Polanyi, too, saw the commodification of land as one of the pillars of liberal society (the others being the commodification of labor and money), one that denied the real nature of land.

It should be noted that the liberal conceptualization of land as property is, at least in principle, separable from general questions of liberal ownership and private property. The political economy of Henry George and his followers provides a stark example; George was in general a proponent of economic liberalism, including substantially unconstrained property rights in liquid capital, in industrial capital, and in one's own labor. He denied, however, any possibility of a legitimate proprietary interest in land. But in this the Georgists were and are exceptional.

Note also that it is not only libertarian liberalism that honors property in land. Libertarian and other liberalisms disagree about the absoluteness of property rights in (generally) liquid assets—is it or is it

[25] Mohandas Gandhi, *Hind Swaraj*, in Raghavan Iyer (ed.), *The Moral and Political Writings of Mahatma Gandhi*, v. 1 (Oxford: Clarendon Press, 1986 [1909]).

not morally problematic to tax wealth, income, and the like? But the prohibition against taking land without just compensation is much more widely accepted than is the libertarian position on taxation. Exercising powers of eminent domain or resumption without compensating landowners is thought unfairly to concentrate the burdens of public policy; if the state has a good public reason for needing the land, then the entire public (that is, the taxpayers), not just a handful of landowners, should share the cost. There is serious dispute about which rights over the land, how much control of the land, the government may take before a taking requiring compensation has occurred; but it is mostly uncontroversial that an actual taking of the title to land requires compensation (in a way that taking a portion of someone's income does not). While the prohibition on uncompensated takings shows that respect for landed property is not limited to libertarian liberals, the possibility of compensated takings reinforces the point that land may legitimately be exchanged for money.

CONFLICT

The liberal and nationalist/indigenous conceptions of land have conflicted in a number of ways over the years. It is worth considering two moments of such conflict. The first was the clash between liberal theories of proper land use and indigenous possession in the Americas and the antipodes. Recall Jefferson's indignation at seeing the land of aristocrats go to waste as gardens or game preserves when there were hungry Frenchmen who could cultivate it. He even speculated that there might be a natural right of the unemployed to simply start farming land that another was putting to such frivolous use.

What Jefferson considered with regard to the aristocrats, Locke and Smith (among others) positively affirmed with regard to the Indians. Hunter-gatherers could have property in their game or in what they collected, but they had no right to exclude from the land itself those who would put it to more productive agricultural use. Europeans had a perfect right simply to farm plots of land in the Indian territories. Some liberals argued that, since enclosure and cultivation could feed more people more easily than could hunting and gathering, all would be better off under such an arrangement.[26] This does not mean that Locke

[26] See Andrew Reeve, *Property* (London: Macmillan, 1986), 51–63, on Locke and Smith; and James Tully, *Strange Multiplicities: Constitutionalism in an Age of Diversity* (Cambridge: Cambridge University Press, 1995), 70–82, on Locke and Kant. Kant, at least, is misrepresented in this account, as I discuss below.

or Smith bore any causal responsibility for the history of expropriation that followed. It may well be that the gradual expropriation of Indian—and later Maori and Aboriginal—lands would have proceeded uninterrupted even if Europe's intellectuals had unanimously argued against it. But the fact remains that there was a radical conflict between the Lockean view (that circulation and efficient use were more important than the permanence of holdings) and the indigenous. Those views are not merely different but flatly incompatible. If only cultivation and development generated property rights, then no conceptual space remained for indigenous land rights. If land was properly held collectively in perpetuity, then there was no place for a society of individual cultivators.[27]

This conflict, of course, was not only on the level of ideas. The colonizing states and their succeeding settler states seized vast areas of land and committed extraordinary violence against indigenous peoples in doing so. Not all liberals took the Lockean position; many honorably protested this terrible treatment. But the conflict was in part on the level of ideas; the Lockean and indigenous accounts of property were incompatible. And they were incompatible in a way that sanctioned the use of violence. If indigenous peoples lacked property rights, and settlers had such rights through original acquisition, then the settlers were justified in using force to protect 'their' land.

The second moment of conflict is contemporary, though it has been repeated for centuries. If the liberal legal system *does* acknowledge indigenous land rights, what kinds of rights should those be? One liberal answer has long been to divide tribal land into individual alienable plots, so as to allow indigenous persons the full economic use of their land and an equal opportunity for mobility (either social and economic mobility, gained by using the land as a resource, or geographic mobility, gained by selling the land and getting a fresh start elsewhere). This was frequently done with an eye toward obtaining tribal lands more quickly and cheaply than would otherwise have been possible, but there was still a genuine belief that treating indigenous land this way was the appropriate, fair, non-paternalistic thing to do, that it would benefit the indigenous persons as well as the rest of society.

Indigenous activists and leaders—as well as those, like Kymlicka, concerned to justify their claims—dispute all of this. The land was

---

[27] Moore offers an interesting discussion of the use of similar arguments by Zionists ('The Territorial Dimension,' in Margaret Moore (ed.), *National Self-Determination and Secession* (Oxford: Oxford University Press, 1998) 148.

traditionally held by a tribe, band, clan, or some other collectivity; it is meant to sustain all who belong to that group; and it belongs to them in perpetuity. It can neither be divided nor sold. Alienability of the land is seen as presenting yet another opportunity for the settler society to cheat the group out of what belongs to it. Alienability combined with divisibility is said to create collective action problems making preservation of the culture impossible, to be untrue to the customary law under which the land is held, and openly to invite fraud by having outsiders designate certain friendly or corruptible members of the group as really owning this or that piece of land.

Kymlicka's defense of inalienability notwithstanding, there is a genuine tension between the liberal conception of land and a right to hold land collectively and inalienably. Recall the liberal concern about entail. For some liberals that concern was about inequality and aristocracy, a concern that is inapplicable to the present question. But for all of them it was about mobility, flexibility, fluidity and openness in the society. The inalienability of land both tended to bind the current inhabitants to the land (since they could not sell it, leaving meant simply abandoning a valuable resource) and to shut off an important kind of mobility for those who did not currently own land.[28] As more and more land comes under the laws of indigenous land rights in Canada, the United States, Australia, and New Zealand, the old fears about entail may become relevant. The land held or claimed by indigenous populations in those states is far out of proportion to their fraction of the population (unsurprisingly, since the land held under land rights law tends to be rural and put to non-industrial uses). Some—including Kymlicka—see a potential problem of distributive justice in that disproportion, but that is not my concern here. What does it do to a liberal and mobile society if an ever-growing portion of its land is held under a kind of indigenous entail? The logic of indigenous collective inalienable ownership has been extended the farthest in Fiji; and the mobility of both indigenous Fijians and Indian Fijians has been sharply limited as a result.[29]

---

[28] Collective ownership does not necessarily raise the same barriers to mobility as does inalienability; I return to this point below.

[29] See Joseph Carens, 'Democracy and Respect for Difference: The Case of Fiji,' *University of Michigan Journal of Law Reform* 25:3 (1992), 547–631. Although Carens defends the collective and inalienable ownership of the land by indigenous Fijians, he recognizes that such ownership has restricted the geographic and social mobility of indigenous Fijians as well as the mobility and security available to the Indian minority.

PROPERTY RIGHTS

The remaining question is whether the fact that indigenous peoples and to a lesser extent most ethnic and nationalist movements view land in a way alien to liberalism means that liberal property rights are inappropriate in societies with such peoples or movements.

An analogy with freedom of religion is instructive. From a certain liberal perspective, freedom of religion is valuable because persons can change their minds about religious matters. They can convert from one religion to another, or abandon it altogether. As far as public policy is concerned, religion is treated like a matter of choice. This, of course, is wildly untrue to the self-understanding of many religious people. For them religion is a matter of deep fundamental conviction, something which is believed rather than chosen. They may think that they were divinely called to join their current faith, or that they have an unchosen obligation to hold to the religion of their parents. They may believe that their religions uniquely access the truth, and refuse to see their truth as even belonging to the same category as the various falsehoods believed by many others. How can public policy and common institutions be true to all of those self-understandings?

The answer, of course, is that they can't. Public institutions can respect those beliefs, but they cannot reflect them. At most the institutions could reflect or establish one such set of beliefs, but at the cost of not even respecting the others. Therefore, we instead create those institutions which will allow each their own self-understanding while keeping their aspirations compatible with those of others. Even if we believe that religion is a matter of conviction and not of choice, for certain public purposes we treat it as a matter of choice. In short, we institutionalize freedom of religious practice, freedom to convert, proselytize, and apostatize, and non-establishment. This way the adherents of a plurality of religions can peacefully coexist.

Something of the sort is true for the liberal institutions of property. It will often not be possible simultaneously and publicly to endorse the understandings that different cultures attach to a piece of land. This is most obviously true when two nationalist movements both attach historical or other similar significance to the same piece of earth. Think of the site of the old temple in Jerusalem, now the site of the Dome of the Rock. (Or, for that matter, think of Jerusalem as a whole, or Israel and Palestine as a whole.) But it is also true in settler societies with indigenous populations. The Australian Aborigines traditionally believe that their gods dreamed their land into existence and then dreamed the Aborigines themselves into being born out of the land. How can the laws and institutions of a modern society actually instantiate the belief of that strong a mystical tie between person and place? They can not, and should not try. But nor do they need actually to instantiate the view that such beliefs are false. They can recognize aboriginal ownership of traditional lands, a step which was only taken four years ago in Australia, they can ensure that land is not taken against the will of the owners, and they can allow for the mutual adjustment of ends that is made possible through a price system in land. It is not the case that every acre of traditional land is as sacred as every other acre; and while for some land possibly nothing could induce traditional owners to part with it, for other land the intensity of the preferences of others—as reflected, for example, in the price a mining company is willing to pay for a subdivision of the land—could result in a sale.

The institutions of religious toleration may look somewhat different if they are based on a political overlapping consensus than if they are based on a particular metaphysical view about religion. Is this true of the liberal institutions of property? I think it is. If one does away with the foundational view that cultivation is always the most appropriate use of land, that undeveloped land is wasted, the resulting laws and institutions will differ from those built on such foundations. While inalienability cannot be part of the liberal system, collective ownership could and often should be. A requirement that land be individually owned cannot be justified in terms acceptable to those who hold divergent views on the nature and uses of land, though alienability can be so justified as the measure that allows for the mutual adjustment of projects and uses.

Thus, while the indigenous view of land cannot be reflected by the public institutions of a diverse society, neither can the Lockean. The liberalism of a multiculturalism of fear cannot endorse or incorporate ideas that sanctioned the violent theft of three continents. Kant rather than Locke shows the way toward a liberal political settlement with regard to land, a legal system that both indigenous and non-indigenous inhabitants of the same space might peacefully accept. Kant was no friend to claims of Indian sovereignty, but explicitly and harshly rejected the claim that cultivating Europeans had a right to take the land of the American natives. The 'cultivation or modification of [land] by labour forms nothing more than an external sign' of valid possession, and the contrary argument is nothing but 'a flimsy veil of injustice.'[30]

---

[30] *Philosophy of Right*, 'Private Right,' section 15. In fact, Kant also points the way toward the need for a political settlement in which those with different ideas about justice with regard to land come to terms with those with whom they 'cannot avoid living side by side' (section 12). See Jeremy Waldron, 'Kant's Legal Positivism,' *Harvard Law Review* 109 (1996), 1535–66.

The relationship between, say, the Lockean view of land and the institutions of property appropriate to a liberal multicultural society is similar to the relationship described by Rawls between a comprehensive liberalism and the institutions of religious toleration in a politically liberal multireligious society. The relationship is not, however, identical. Lockeans might accept collective ownership—and indigenous peoples, alienability—despite the fact that such ownership (or alienability) could not really be justified from *within* their respective comprehensive views. The rules that allow both collective ownership and alienability are likely to be accepted *only* for the sorts of 'political' reasons that on Rawls' account stand apart from the various comprehensive views.

This does not mean that the multiculturalism of fear is simply a *modus vivendi*, changed whenever the balance of power changes, which Rawls sees as the alternative to an overlapping consensus in such situations. Some religious persons genuinely endorse the political rules of toleration and separation without considering them to be defensible from within their religions; they endorse the liberal rules for the reasons offered by the stand-alone political justifications. They are outside the range of what Rawls accepts as 'reasonable' comprehensive views without being part of the problem of the unreasonable who actually reject the institutions of political liberalism. The relationship of Lockeans and indigenous persons to the 'political liberalism' of land may well be like the relationship of the 'neither-reasonable-nor-unreasonable' to political liberal toleration.

This is representative of a more general relationship between the moralities and social views of particular cultures, on the one hand, and the social, legal, and political institutions necessary for a common and peaceful coexistence, on the other. It is a way of understanding the problem of developing an adequate framework for intercultural interaction, discussed in Chapter 2. Conventions regarding intercultural exchanges and transactions—including the law of land that will govern different cultural communities—cannot simply codify the traditional internal morality of one group or the other.

James Scott has argued that land tenure standardization is an example of a tendency he calls 'high modernism,' a tendency that culminates in catastrophic socialist and utopian development schemes.[31] High modernism, on Scott's characterization, is a hubristic attitude similar to what F. A.

---

[31] James Scott, 'State Simplifications: Nature, Space, and People,' in Ian Shapiro and Russell Hardin (eds.), *NOMOS XXXVIII: Political Order* (New York: New York University Press, 1996); and *Seeing Like a State* (New Haven: Yale University Press, 1998).

Hayek terms the fatal conceit of rationalist constructivism.[32] It is contemptuous of local or decentralized knowledge, of diversity, of the real complexity of human institutions. The high modernist divides all land into identical units of area and reduces all land rights to identical freehold title. Scott argues that these high modernist projects historically have been undertaken for the convenience of state officials in general and tax collectors in particular, *not* for the convenience or economic advantage of landholders.

On the Hayekian account, the price system incorporates and transmits all of the necessary decentralized and tacit knowledge.[33] If formally identical but substantively different objects are alienable, the differences will be captured in prices. According to Scott, however, the formally identical status of alienable freehold itself necessarily wastes or destroys much of that knowledge. The attempt to make land registrable and taxable tends to disrupt the complex, evolved, overlapping sets of rights and duties to land. This argument seemingly extends insights used by Hayek to defend liberal markets into a criticism of one of the foundations of such markets.

But a system in which land tenure is not formalized depends on the continuity of shared local understandings about the correct uses of particular pieces of land. Such shared understandings are precisely what is not available across cultural boundaries. The demise or lack of such shared understandings is what creates the need for institutions that can try to mediate across different visions of land. Those whose understandings of land differ must acknowledge that a plurality of understandings exist, and endorse such mediating institutions.[34]

SOVEREIGNTY AND ADVERSE POSSESSION

In defending the Palestinian Authority's threat of execution against any Palestinian who sold land to Jews, one official argued that

[32] F. A. Hayek, *The Fatal Conceit* (Chicago: University of Chicago Press, 1988).
[33] See the essays collected in F. A. Hayek, *Individualism and the Economic Order* (Chicago: University of Chicago Press, 1948), esp. 'The Use of Knowledge in Society.'
[34] Scott's argument bears more than a passing resemblance to the arguments of Michael Walzer, Elizabeth Anderson, and Margaret Jane Radin about inalienability and blocked exchanges; and the similarity is telling. All of the arguments, but Walzer's most explicitly, depend on a shared social understanding of a particular good as not a commodity, not appropriately distributed through markets, and the risk that *any* market exchanges of the good will undermine that social understanding, corrupting and commodifying the good throughout society. But what is to be done when the social understanding of a good as non-commodifiable is *not* shared? Compare Jeremy Waldron's commentary on Walzer, 'Money and Complex Equality,' in David Miller and Michael Walzer (eds.), *Pluralism, Justice, and Equality* (Oxford: Oxford University Press, 1995), especially the discussion of land alienability on pp. 168–9.

The problem is that Israel does not distinguish between ownership of land and sovereignty over it. If a certain area is under Jewish ownership, Israel sees it as part of its sovereign territory.[35]

This puts into stark relief another difference between liberal and nationalist conceptions of land, and indeed helps to explain part of the liberal account. Nationalism blurs sovereignty and ownership, while liberalism tries to separate them. The separation, while historically justified on other grounds, can be defended in terms of a multiculturalism of fear, or a need for legal rules peacefully mediating among cultures and ethnic groups. In general, a weaker separation between sovereignty and ownership is a greater invitation to ethnic and nationalist conflict than a stronger one—and this is true whether the potential conflict is between two nationalist claims or between indigenous and liberal claims.

The division of sovereignty and ownership is a characteristic of liberal views of land even before they are modified to take the facts of cultural pluralism into account. The division allows for independence from the state. It is also closely related to alienability; sovereignty is ordinarily not alienable. The more closely tied ownership is to sovereignty, the more land ownership is a public concern, the more difficult it will be for land to change hands freely in the way that encourages mobility.

The Australian High Court thus moved that country's law both in a liberal direction and in a direction more conducive to ethnic harmony when it detached sovereignty from ownership in its 1993 *Mabo* decision. The case concerned Aboriginal land rights, which Britain and Australia had traditionally not recognized. British discovery and settlement had been held to vest title to the entire continent in the British Crown. The High Court ultimately ruled that the Crown acquired sovereignty, 'radical title,' but not straightforward ownership, 'beneficial title.' This allows the position that the Crown (later embodied in the colonial, state, and Commonwealth governments) is the ultimate source for all land titles acquired *since settlement* to coexist with acknowledgment of prior Aboriginal claims to the land which were not simply extinguished when Britain acquired sovereignty.

If ownership ought to be separated from settlers' sovereignty, it also ought to be separated from indigenous sovereignty. Where, as in the United States, indigenous peoples are recognized as sovereign, collective tribal ownership of land becomes less defensible. For the same tribal government to be sovereign over the land of a reservation and to be the

---

[35] Freih Abu Middein, the Palestinian Authority's justice minister, quoted in Joel Greenberg, 'Did This Arab Die for Selling Land to Jews?' *The New York Times*, Monday, 12 May, 1997, A3.

owner of that land would constitute a dangerous concentration of power. If tribal sovereignty expands when tribal ownership does, then the stakes of ordinary intercultural transactions are raised, just as they are by expanding Israeli sovereignty to match Jewish ownership. (The stakes are raised higher still if land becomes inalienable once it is purchased by the tribe or tribe members.)

In fact, in the United States the land over which tribal governments have sovereignty is often owned in trust by the federal government; and more often than not it has been the settler government which expanded its sovereignty based on private land purchases.[36] If every time a non-tribe member purchases a plot of land tribal *sovereignty* is diminished, tribal insistence on collective ownership is an obvious move. Before tribal governments can reasonably be expected to allow individuated land ownership, they need to know that they will continue to have jurisdiction over land sold to outsiders.

The liberal settlement concerning land also includes rules of adverse possession and possession through occupancy. In the interest of contemporary and future peace and stability, there must be a moratorium on the rectification in kind of past dispossessions of land. Here again the place of land in a liberal multiculturalism of fear differs from its place in a libertarian theory based on unfailing respect for property rights.[37] The latter has no space for rules of adverse possession, and no limit to the obligation to redress past wrongs. While any theory of legitimate land holdings will at some point be dependent on an account it should also not be exaggerated to the detriment of the liberal social settlement.

What is the value of adverse possession and related rules? It is sometimes argued that *any* recognition of indigenous land rights, or any such recognition which depends on the validity of indigenous claims to particular pieces of land, logically necessitates giving the whole Australian or American landmass back to indigenous peoples.[38] (An occasional follow-up comment is that one would then be obliged to find

---

[36] Sharon O'Brien, *American Indian Tribal Governments* (Norman Okla: University of Oklahoma Press, 1989), 212–20.

[37] I mean to differentiate an account like Robert Nozick's from any of the utilitarian libertarian theories associated with, for example, the law and economics school. Contrast Nozick, *Anarchy, State, and Utopia* (New York: Basic Books, 1974), with Richard Epstein, *Simple Rules for a Complex World* (Cambridge, Mass.: Havrard University Press, 1995), 63–7.

[38] See Kymlicka, *Multicultural Citizenship*, 219–21; Roger Scruton, 'The Legitimacy of British Civilisation in Australia,' in R. Scruton, F. Brennan, and J. Hyde, *Land Rights and Legitimacy: Three Views*, Perth: Australian Institute for Public Policy, 1985; and David Lyons, 'The New Indian Claims and Original Rights to Land,' in Jeffrey Paul (ed.), *Reading Nozick: Essays on Anarchy, State, and Utopia* (Totowa, NJ: Rowman and Littlefield, 1981).

out which indigenous groups had been dispossessed by others prior to colonization.) The implication to be drawn is that this would require grave injustice to the living in order to rectify injustices to the dead, and that therefore recognition should not be granted. A rule of adverse possession prevents these implications; it allows recognition of land rights without requiring that they be used in an impossible attempt to undo history. Adverse possession can even serve as a foundation for indigenous land rights at the same time that it defines their limitations. The land rights recognized in the Australian *Mabo* decision are primarily those of Aborigines who have continued to occupy their traditional lands which were previously considered government-held 'waste land.' Even without recognition of *prior* Aboriginal possession, for many such groups it should have been held long ago that adverse possession transferred ownership from the Crown to the Aborigines.[39]

Nor is this situation unique to indigenous–settler conflicts. It is unlikely that the current possessor of any piece of land on earth acquired it peacefully and legitimately from someone who acquired it peacefully and legitimately from someone, and so on until original acquisition. Moreover, many of the forceful dispossessions and acquisitions have been ethnic or nationalistic, at least insofar as the dispossessors generally belonged to one national group and the dispossessed to another. As Margaret Moore puts it, most or all land is subject to more than one claim of past possession by some ethnic or national group, and 'it is impossible to develop an adequate principle or mechanism to adjudicate such rival claims to territory; it depends where in history one starts, and whose history one accepts.'[40] If we are to have any of the benefits (economic, social, or political) of several property in land, then current holdings must not be constantly called into question. Monetary compensation will often be appropriate for the victims of past dispossessions or their successors, and if land is often bought and sold then monetary compensation could allow the repurchase of lost land; but a right of actual restitution cannot exist in perpetuity.[41]

At the same time, adverse possession is not without its costs. Knowing in advance that conquest and theft will be legitimated if only the spoils can be held for long enough creates undesirable incentives. Where problems of proof are soluble, restitution in kind for past dispossession might

---

[39] See the excellent discussion in Kent McNeil, *Common Law Aboriginal Title* (Oxford: Oxford University Press, 1989), 6–78 and 196–221, and my discussion of common law incorporation in Chapter 6.

[40] Moore, 'The Territorial Dimension,' 145.

[41] See also Jeremy Waldron, 'Superseding Historic Injustice,' *Ethics* 103:1 (1992), 4–28.

be the right choice. Apartheid land laws resulted in the legalized theft of
land from thousands of blacks; but careful records were kept of who
lost what to whom. The dispossession was not a result of the replace-
ment of one legal or administrative system with another (as in Australia
and, in a very different way, the Communist states of Central Europe).
Blacks and their white successors held titles under the same system, and
that system kept track of the transfers. The current Land Court, charged
with returning land to its former owners or their descendants, has not
been hobbled by evidentiary problems.[42] Even with such favorable
conditions for restitution, however, the cases faced in South Africa are
all less than fifty years old. There is no question of returning to black
ownership (which blacks?) the vast tracts of land taken by English or
Afrikaner conquest in centuries past. Such a course of action would face
the same difficulties as widespread restitution in Australia or the
Americas.

Where evidentiary problems are soluble, a cramped reading of the
rules of evidence should not be allowed to preclude claims for restitution. Oral traditions necessarily make up a significant part of the
evidence for many indigenous land claims. If liberal legal systems
exclude evidence of the kind 'I know this is my land because my father
told me that his father had told him so' as hearsay, then those legal
systems have failed in their responsibility to find a framework which
can mediate cross-cultural disputes over land. In an attempt to forestall
such outcomes, the Australian *Native Title Act* holds that the court
determining Aboriginal land claims must provide a mechanism of determination which is 'informal' and that, in conducting its proceedings, it
'is not bound by technicalities, legal forms, or rules of evidence.'[43] This
seems unnecessary and dangerous overkill. While there is a need to
interpret the rules of evidence broadly enough that land claims are
possible, this can be done without throwing them out altogether.
Indeed, even *Milirrupum v Nabalco*, the 1971 Australia decision which
held that Aborigines had no property interest in their traditional lands,
rejected an attempt by the state to circumvent the land claim by throwing out the evidence which Aborigines presented. That is, the evidence
was held to be valid as evidence even though it allegedly did not bear
out the claim being made.[44] More recently, the Supreme Court of

[42] There have been the expected difficulties of land currently held by an innocent third
party who purchased it from the illegitimate recipient, but monetary compensation to
such persons seems to be a workable solution, not obviously inferior to the alternative of
compensating the blacks and leaving current white posession undisturbed.

[43] Section 82, *Native Title Act,* 1993.

[44] *Milirrupum v Nabalco,* 1971, 17 FLR 141, at 151–165.

Canada has rightly and decisively ruled that oral evidence is valid in Canadian First Nations land rights-claims.[45] Of course, this requires courts to make hard decisions about the reliability of such evidence and how to handle conflicts between different oral traditions; but such accommodation is necessary. Disregarding all such evidence is unfair and not something indigenous peoples could be expected to endorse as part of a political settlement; discarding the rules of evidence entirely is more extreme than the settlement demands.

CONCLUSION

Without a liberal settlement concerning land—including recognition of a variety of kinds of ownership, alienability, a separation of ownership and sovereignty, and rules of adverse possession combined with some compensation for past dispossessions—groups with nationalist or indigenous conceptions of land are extremely likely to come into conflict with one another, the kind of ethnic conflict that a multiculturalism of fear seeks to avoid. Those with comprehensive liberal views of land, such as Lockeans who insist on productive use and individuation of title, offer too little to indigenous peoples to make a liberal settlement worthwhile; they, like the nationalists, ought to limit themselves to something like the settlement described here. Alienability allows for mobility, including mobility between cultural groups. The separation of sovereignty and ownership limits the stakes of the alienation of land; land sales need not lead to the aggrandizement of one group at another's expense. Adverse possession limits the rewards of endlessly reopening old disputes of the kind that cannot be decisively resolved in any event. And a variety of kinds of ownership under a common law of exchange leaves room for collective ethnic aspirations and expressions without unduly jeopardizing intercultural peace.

[45] *Delgamuukw v British Columbia*, S.C.J. No. 108 (Canada 1997).

8

Ethnic Symbolism and Official Apologies[1]

THE STAKES OF SYMBOLISM

In the early part of 1994, Australia was rocked by violence between its Greek and Macedonian communities. Prior to the 1993 election Prime Minister Paul Keating promised leaders of the 300,000 strong Greek Australian community that his government would not recognize the new Macedonian state until its dispute with Greece over its name and national symbols was resolved. In early 1994 Keating's Labor government did recognize 'The Former Yugoslav Republic of Macedonia' following a general international movement toward recognition. Protests from Greek Australians were immediate, and egged on by the Liberal premier of Victoria, the state with the largest Greek population. In an attempt to soothe Greek feelings, the government announced that the 75,000 Macedonians in Australia would henceforth be officially known as 'Slav–Macedonians.' It even attempted (unsuccessfully) to get state-funded radio and television news networks to adopt the name change.

The recognition of Macedonia and the subsequent renaming of Macedonians were followed by tens of thousands of protesters in the streets, and by firebombings of churches, community centers, and private homes and business on both sides. Those involved in a fight at an ethnically charged soccer game in Melbourne threw bricks at each other. A Victoria state senator's office was bombed; bottles were thrown at the federal Immigration Minister.

No one was killed by this conflict, the intense stage of which lasted some two and a half months. Still, the dispute turned remarkably vicious by Australian standards. Cultural organizations in both communities received government funding as part of official multiculturalism. Both Greeks and Macedonians had lived in Australia for decades. No

[1] For a more extended treatment of the topics addressed in this chapter, albeit one that reaches somewhat different conclusions, see Sanford Levinson's *Written In Stone: Public Monuments in Changing Societies* (Durham, NC: Duke University Press, 1998).

decisions about state funding, immigration policy, or language rights were at stake; neither the rights nor the resources of either community was at risk. Yet this dispute over words and names turned acutely violent, in a way that not even the dispute over Aboriginal land rights ever did, despite the massive resources at stake in the latter.

Ethiopian Jews have been coming to Israel since about 1978. Many trekked across the Sudan by foot, and about 8,000 arrived before 1984. During the famine in Ethiopia in 1984, the Israeli government organized a daring airlift operation, called 'Operation Moses,' to bring more than 10,000 Ethiopian Jews to Israel. Over the next few years, 20,000 more were brought to Israel. Finally, in 1991, during the last days of the Ethiopian civil war, Israel staged a thirty-six hour 'Operation Solomon' to fly 11,000 of the Ethiopian Jews to Israel, almost the entire remaining population. By 1995, Israel's Ethiopian community had grown to over 55,000.

For centuries, until this period of mass migration, there had been little contact between Ethiopian and other Jews. Ethiopian Jews do not eat pork, they do circumcise their boys, and they hold the Jewish Bible as their own, but many of their other religious habits have long since diverged from those of other Jews. While the origin of the community—which has also been known as Beta-Israel or as the Falasha, though the latter term is now considered offensive—is a matter of some dispute, the divergence seems to have occurred prior to the writing or adoption of the Talmud, the rabbinical commentaries on the laws of the Torah that have been the foundation of the interpretation of those laws for millennia. In 1973 the Chief Rabbi of Israel's Sephardic Jews ruled that Ethiopians who considered themselves Jews were in fact Jewish; a sixteenth-century rabbi had named them as descendants of one of the lost tribes of Israel. The 1984 and 1991 airlifts were thus widely celebrated in Israel and abroad as a highlight of the Israeli tradition of *aliya*, or the ingathering of the Jews from around the world, regardless of their place of origin. Early successes in integrating the immigrants into the Israeli armed forces, in which membership holds a central place in Israeli culture, were also a source of pride for Ethiopian and other Jews alike.

But after an initial euphoria on both sides, tensions quickly arose concerning the absorption of the Ethiopians into Israeli society. Many disputes centered on whether the Ethiopian Jews were really religiously Jewish. The country's powerful Chief Rabbinate had confirmed that they were genuinely enough Jewish to have an automatic right of immigration to Israel under the so-called Law of Return. But it then issued a somewhat different ruling considering their right to be considered *religiously*

Jews. It insisted that they undergo symbolic reconversions if they were to be considered Jewish. Most rabbis would not perform marriage rites for Ethiopians who had not been so reconverted, and the Ethiopians' own rabbis were not admitted to the official rabbinate.

For several years Ethiopian children were enrolled in state religious boarding schools to speed the convergence of religious traditions. But this meant keeping them out of the state secular schools, generally academically superior and a better route to economic success. It also meant separating them from their families and interrupting the transmission of Ethiopian culture. Moreover, even within those schools, Ethiopian children were often placed in vocational or remedial courses. While there was considerable affirmative action for Ethiopian students who qualified for higher education, few did. By 1995, only 7 per cent of Ethiopian students graduating from high school received the matriculation certificate that paved the way to universities or prestigious positions in the military. By comparison, 60 per cent of the overall population graduated with matriculation certificates.

Other problems included residential segregation, which persisted for many years after the disbanding of most of the refugee camps where the Ethiopians were initially housed. Even the housing subsidies were typically insufficient to allow families to get housing outside of run-down neighborhoods. Israeli officials were aware that there were problems of acculturation and integration, but noted that migration from Ethiopia and the former Soviet bloc had given Israel a recent immigrant population of nearly 10 per cent, saying that some difficulties were inevitable. They argued that the transition was unavoidably more difficult for Ethiopian Jews than for their Russian counterparts. Many of the Ethiopians came from rural villages with no electricity or running water, and illiteracy was the rule; their new country was far stranger for them than for the highly-educated Russians.

Yet despite all these complaints about education and housing, discrimination and opportunity, there was no violent conflict until a newspaper revealed that Magen David Adom (MDA), a nationwide organization equivalent to Red Cross and Red Crescent societies elsewhere, secretly threw away all blood donated by Ethiopian Jews. On 28 January 1996, 10,000 Ethiopian Jews demonstrated outside the Prime Minister's office in Jerusalem. Organizers had predicted only 1,000 participants, and the Ethiopian community had a reputation as being relatively docile and passive, so the Jerusalem police were unprepared. When some protesters tried to climb the fence surrounding the building where the Cabinet was meeting, the police responded with anti-riot tactics including tear gas, billy clubs, and water cannons. In the ensuing riot, more than fifty people were injured, about thirty of them police officers; one officer lost an eye, and another was paralyzed.

Ethiopian Jews suffered from an HIV infection rate of fifty times that of the remaining Israeli population, and rates of hepatitis-B of three times the general rate. When the rate of HIV carriers in the new immigrant population became known in 1991, government authorities were concerned to prevent widespread stigmatization. There seemed to be a tradeoff between educating the Ethiopian Jews about AIDS and preserving acceptance of the immigrants. Officials from the Ministries of Health, Absorption, and Education convened a secret meeting attended by journalists and health reporters from all Israeli mass media; the meeting's existence would only be disclosed years later during the investigation of the blood policy. The journalist group included reporters from Israel Radio's Amharic section, which broadcasts to the Ethiopian community. The purpose of the meeting: to ask that the journalists not publish or report anything about the relatively high prevalence of HIV among Ethiopian immigrants. All the participants were warned to preserve secrecy on this issue so as not to stigmatize the immigrants and thereby undermine their absorption into Israeli society. As Dr Zvi Ben-Yishai, AIDS coordinator in the Health Ministry, remembered it, 'the entire journalistic community joined in the effort' to prevent any widespread knowledge of the infection rate.

The officials at the meeting also asked for suggestions on how to increase awareness of HIV prevention within the community. Those most familiar with the Ethiopian community, the Amharic-speaking radio journalists, asked that any information campaign be 'controlled and careful.' Because, they said, the immigrants were 'not aware of AIDS and that if this fact became known, they would not cooperate.' In the aftermath of this meeting, the government launched vaccination efforts among the Ethiopians for hepatitis-B and a small-scale information campaign concerning the spread of HIV.

Although not discussed openly by government ministers, the health risks among Ethiopian Jews posed a problem for the donation of blood, since transmissions of infected blood pass along HIV and hepatitis to the recipient. Few Ethiopian Jews privately donated blood. Those Ethiopians in the army, however, did so routinely along with their units. The Israel Defense Force has a strong tradition of its members donating blood together. Officials worried that refusing to allow the Ethiopian soldiers to donate blood would set them apart from their units and create an impression that they were unhealthy—an unacceptable situation, given the importance of the IDF as an integrating force in Israeli life.

In the years since 1991 increasingly sophisticated tests have become available for identifying the presence of HIV-antibodies in donated blood. However, testing every unit of blood donated is expensive. More important, if the donor contracted HIV less than six months before the test, the blood may test as 'safe' when it in fact is not.

Given any test that is less than 100 per cent accurate, safety can always be improved by entirely excluding any group with a higher-than-average exposure rate. The American Red Cross, which tests every unit of donated blood for HIV (among other diseases), still excludes higher-risk groups including male homosexuals, intravenous drug users, and those who have recently spent time in a high-risk country. Donors are interviewed about whether they have engaged in any high-risk activity and if they have, they are instructed not to give blood. Donors in the United States also receive a 'confidential unit exclusion' form, which includes bar code stickers to be placed on their donation records. Someone who wants to participate in giving blood and doesn't want to publicly reveal high-risk behavior can place a sticker on their form which a computer scanner will later identify as instructions to discard the blood. Starting in 1983, Haitians entering the United States were prohibited from donating blood because of inexplicably higher rates of AIDS among them. This ban was lifted in 1990 when more was known about the transmission of HIV and epidemiologists determined they could eliminate virtually all infected Haitians by asking donors explicit questions about their sex and drug-use habits.

The fact that the Israeli policy involved blood invoked a number of wider resonances. Blood is often used as a metaphor for descent of various kinds: bloodlines, pure blood, mixed blood, blood feuds, corruption of the blood, and so on. What's more, those metaphors are often linked with the idea of race. Israel avowedly does not identify Jews on the basis of race but only that of ethnicity; Ethiopian Jews officially make up an ethnic category more similar to that of Yemeni Jews or East European Jews than to that of the American category of 'black.' But the image of blood has long been associated with race and racism (e.g. a longstanding American custom of racial identification held that 'one drop' of African blood made a person black rather than white). The fact that it was blood being discarded was bound to aggravate the feeling among some Ethiopians that, contrary to the official view, they were viewed as being of another, and an inferior, race. The discarding of *soldiers'* blood in particular invited the question of why they should be willing to shed blood for a country that considered that blood inferior. Many Ethiopian Jews invoked the memory of the 'blood libel' against medieval European Jews, the story that Jews baked the blood of Christian children into their matzoh, although others sharply denied that there was any relevant similarity to the blood libel.

Perhaps the most significant resonance, however, was with the process of 'reconversion' of the Ethiopian Jews. For thousands of men in the first wave of immigrants, the reconversion took the form of having their penises pricked for the letting of a ceremonial drop of blood, a kind of re-circumcision. This was sometimes done to large numbers of men at once. Sometimes the immigrants were not even told what was happening; the presiding officials claimed that they were performing blood tests on the new arrivals. Although this practice was eventually stopped—subsequent reconversions took the form of ritual immersions in water—it remains a source of bitter complaint for many in the Ethiopian community.

As with the Australian case, the policy of discarding Ethiopian Jewish blood did not affect the distribution of rights or resources in Israeli society. No Ethiopian Jew was disturbed in his or her material possessions or expectations; no one was deprived of legal liberties or powers. Unlike with the recircumcisions, the right to bodily integrity was waived by consenting adults who chose to donate. No person has a right that his or her donation be used; discarding a gift may be ungrateful but it is not unjust. (I set aside the question of whether citizens have a right not to be deceived by their democratic governments, and focus on the policy the deception was intended to hide.)

What's more, the symbolic resonances of the case were just that; the discarding of Ethiopian blood was not actually *about* recircumcision, blood libel, and so on. One could easily imagine a decision by agencies which distribute donated goods to the poor to discard, say, clothing and blankets which were collected in areas with high rates of smallpox infection, but not revealing the policy so that even infected communities could have the experience (and the tax deductions) associated with giving. The differences between the two cases, the factors that made the Ethiopian case more explosive, were mostly symbolic.

Such symbolic ethnocultural disputes are widespread, and at least sometimes are particularly potent and difficult to resolve. Their subjects range from how the state names groups or places to what historical figures are honored with public buildings named after them or statues to special constitutional recognition of founding peoples or official languages.[2] They span developed and developing countries, immigrant, national, and aboriginal minorities; the symbols at stake include official

---

[2] I mean to detach the symbolic question of whether a language is given official or national status from the legal questions of who has the right to use which languages when, and in what language[s] the state does business. The latter are not symbolic in the sense I use that word here. I return to this distinction below.

apologies for centuries-old wrongs and the British Millenium Dome commemorating the year 2000. In his comparative study of ethnic conflict, Donald Horowitz finds that 'symbolic claims are not readily amenable to compromise. In this, they differ from claims deriving wholly from material interest. Whereas material advancement can be measured both relatively and absolutely, the status advancement of one ethnic group is entirely relative to the status of others.'[3] That is to say, conflicts about symbolism are both zero-sum and zero-sum in a particular way that makes them unsuited to compromise. Geoffrey Brennan and Loren Lomasky have argued that voters in large democracies tend to use their votes expressively, as a way of cheering for one kind party, outcome, or principle rather than as an expression of any actual calculation of interest. This, they say, encourages a greater degree of other-regardingness than is the case when each actor thinks that his or her actions bear a substantial relationship to the costs he or she will bear and the benefits he or she will receive. 'Other-regardingness,' though, may be for good or for ill; voters collectively may support more collective altruism in the form of welfare than any of them would if given a decisive vote, but they may also support more racial discrimination. Because individual voters know that their votes are not decisive, that there are no direct consequences of any single vote in almost any large election, some self-interested incentives for moderation are loosened.[4]

This is, in a way, an extension of the idea—at least as old as Montesquieu, Smith, and in a different way Hobbes—that mutual disinterestedness (as opposed to envy, spite, or hatred) and the self-interested pursuit of non-zero-sum goods (material goods as opposed to status and

---

[3] Donald Horowitz, *Ethnic Groups in Conflict* (Berkeley: University of California Press, 1986), 223–4. I do think Horowitz casts the conceptual net of 'symbolism' somewhat too broadly. For instance, whether or not to ban the slaughter of cows in India, and whether to permit, compel, or forbid culturally specific clothing in various circumstances, have concrete effects on the lives of particular persons. Whether to imprison a Muslim woman for contempt of court or whether to expel Muslim schoolgirls for wearing headscarves, both of which have been done in France, for are not merely symbolic questions. And, as noted above (and as Horowitz recognizes), official languages are not only symbolic matters. But under the heading of 'symbolism' Horowitz also includes much of what I regard as genuine symbolism, especially including place-names and national symbols.

[4] Geoffrey Brennan and Loren Lomasky, *Democracy and Decision* (Cambridge: Cambridge University Press, 1993). This is not just the point that political action overcomes collective action problems, so that none of us would give to charity individually or discriminate against a disfavored race individually but all of us favor collective action binding us to a welfare or Jim Crow system. Brennan and Lomasky argue that a voter who knew that his or her vote would be decisive would vote for more moderate policies than do real voters, because the latter do not but the former would calculate the costs of other-regarding policies on themselves.

honor) can moderate, soften, and avoid conflict. If self-interest is not a virtue, it is a moderate and moderating kind of vice. Sometimes both public choice political scientists and their critics talk about sheer individual self-interest as a pessimistic postulate, a kind of worst-case scenario. In fact it is nothing of the kind, as Brennan and Lomasky illustrate, as Montesquieu, Smith, and Hobbes knew. Worst cases in politics can be terrible indeed, and can make mere individual material self-interest seem almost utopian. Ethnic passions and the competition for ethnic status and recognition should remind us of the religious conflicts and of the competition for honor and status which so exercised early modern thinkers.

None the less, many people much of the time do vote with at least some regard for costs and consequences. But extremism regarding purely symbolic issues like those under discussion here is costless. There is no self-interested incentive for moderation. Even if an individual voter knew that his or her vote would be decisive, it is not expensive in any straightforward way to have official symbols which glorify one's own group and denigrate others. So symbolic conflicts are not only zero-sum; there is little natural incentive to avoid extreme demands or resistance to demands. In fact I think that Horowitz is a touch too pessimistic and that not all symbolic disputes are strictly zero-sum; I explain this below. But it is characteristically true that such disputes lack incentives for moderation.

Ethnic conflicts are not always or primarily about symbolism, even when there are words and symbols at stake. The Turkish government's longtime insistence on calling Kurds 'mountain Turks' surely had less to do with the Kurdish resort to armed conflict than did, say the ban on use of the Kurdish language. Place-names, names of groups, flags, and coats of arms often count for much less than concrete matters: who has the right to use which language when? Who controls which land? Which cultural traditions will be banned, which ones tolerated? Some say that questions of recognition and respect, not questions of rights and resources, are at the heart of ethnic politics; but this thought seems to me a luxury of living in largely just and decent liberal states. It may also be a luxury of immersion in educational institutions, which have more direct control over curricula, mottoes, and holidays than over legal liberties and powers.

But neither do such concrete questions of rights and resources make up the whole of ethnic and cultural politics. Issues of identity and recognition, symbolic issues, play an important part as well; and there is no general tendency for symbolic disputes to be less intense, to be taken less seriously by the participants.

Certain styles of political thought are uncomfortable with the importance of symbolic issues. Marxist variants of materialism and the
Lasswellian view of politics as concerning only 'who gets what, how
and when' are obvious cases. But any political theory grounded in
neoclassical economics, Anglo-American jurisprudence, or neo-Kantian
rights theory has some difficulty with the idea that there can be important political questions which do not affect the rights or resources of
individual persons. These methods of analysis play a central part in
contemporary liberalism. Partly for that reason, critics of liberalism,
including Charles Taylor and Iris Marion Young, have both grasped and
endorsed the importance of symbolic issues of identity and recognition.

Liberalism is right to give rights and resources moral priority over
recognition and symbols; but that should not prevent liberals from
seeing the tremendous importance symbolic disputes can have to their
participants. How liberalism, and a liberal state, ought to handle ethnic
symbolism is the topic of this chapter.

RESPONSES TO SYMBOLISM

I now briefly consider several possible approaches to problems of ethnic
symbolism. Some of them are straw-man arguments which could not
fairly be attributed to any particular person; but examining even these
arguments has some use.

The State May Speak and Use Symbols Freely[5]

As children put it, words can never hurt me. Since symbolism does not
affect any rights or resources of any person, there can be nothing to say
about it from the moral point of view. Words, expressions, and symbols
are not the stuff of justice or morality, or even of morally interesting
politics. They are 'only words.' What statues are erected and what holidays are celebrated are inevitably arbitrary, but they fail to meet the
threshold test of warranting moral praise or condemnation; they have
no actual effect on individual persons. The justification would vary a

---

[5] Sanford Levinson characterizes this as the default liberal position, on the grounds
that it is a content-neutral, pro-free-expression view. But even Levinson recognizes that
there is something a bit odd about this, as state expression differs in morally relevant
respects from the expression about which liberals demand content-neutral rules. *Written
In Stone: Public Monuments in Changing Societies* (Durham, NC: Duke University Press,
1998).

bit, but this basic position might be embraced by anyone from a conservative opposed to 'political correctness' to an Old Left socialist who finds symbolic disputes to be distractions from the serious business of economic politics.

To indicate what this position leaves out, return to this example: What if the United States Census Bureau adopted the word 'nigger' as the name for the racial category currently referred to as 'black' or 'African–American'? It is, after all, only a word. But it is a word that is tied up with a long history of violence, public and private. It is a word that is understood, by whites and blacks alike, to exclude blacks not just from full citizenship but from full humanity. The use of the word by a speaker with power or authority is nearly a threat. Leaving aside questions like whether it would be a rights-violation or whether it would be legally justiciable, what reason could we possibly have for declining to say that it would be wrong for the state to adopt this epithet for common use?

As it happens, I think that symbolic wrongs like this are not rights-violations and are probably not be justiciable. American courts might allow a suit to proceed in this particular example, because the Fourteenth Amendment (centrally concerned with the rights and status of free blacks) has been held to prohibit 'badges of slavery.' The rules of standing might be bent in such a case. But in the absence of such a specific tie between a constitutional provision and the symbolic wrong—the other American example being the Establishment Clause of the First Amendment, which has been held to prohibit a variety of state uses of religious symbols—probably no particular person would be held to have suffered an actionable harm. But with or without a court being willing to find it so, a name change like this would be an egregious moral wrong.

Sometimes civil libertarians suggest that words and expressions are immune from political and moral criticism, unlike material harms, in order to defuse the threat of censorship. But the concept of censorship is out of place in a discussion of the state's own speech. When the question is not, 'May the state evaluate our words?' but rather, 'May we evaluate the state's?' then there is no threat of force, no threat to the diversity of expressed ideas, no threat to the democratic process.[6]

Humiliation is not a synonym for cruelty; words associated with violence are not the same as violence. The partial truth in this first approach to symbolism is that symbolism should usually, perhaps

---

[6] I leave aside problems of state-subsidized private speech, such as artwork, scholarship, and (often) museum exhibits, though such issues are related to the ones at hand.

always, be morally subordinate. Words and symbols are not worth violence and coercion. This, I think, is part of the argument against criminal bans on hate speech; even if using a racial slur wrongs someone, it is not a level of wrong that justifies using state force against someone who has only spoken. But (at least) all non-perfectionist political moralities recognize the existence of a category of moral wrongs that cannot rightly be met by force. The hateful and humiliating use of words and symbols falls into that category; and criticizing state speech does not carry even a tacit threat of coercion.

The State May Not Speak

The state should not publicly endorse particular points of view, particular cultural identities, particular visions of the good life. 'Content neutrality' is a concept from the American constitutional jurisprudence of speech regulation, but might be elevated to a general liberal principle of state action and speech. Content neutrality, however, is a principle for evaluating an actor who referees speakers, not a principle for evaluating speech itself. No particular speech, expression, or symbol can be content-neutral, so if the principle of content-neutrality is applicable to state speech, that means the state may not speak. Liberal neutrality requires that the state avoid official symbolism, which necessary elevates some substantive claims about cultural communities and their worth over others.

The seemingly interminable disputes in the post-Dayton Bosnian state about national symbols—a flag, a coat of arms, a national anthem, even license plates—illustrate the appeal of this approach. Symbols which are Muslim, Serbian, avowedly multiethnic, or avowedly non-ethnic are all unacceptable to some constituents and political leaders. None of the symbols are neutral. Both liberal neutrality and prudence might both counsel abandoning the project of adopting *any* symbols of state. Similarly, there is no neutral resolution to the ongoing American disputes over how to commemorate the location of the nineteen-century Battle of Little Big Horn; perhaps justice and prudence both recommend that the US government give up and not commemorate it in any official way at all.

The State Must Recognize Each Cultural Community on its Own Terms

Consider a rule that simply allows each group to define its own labels and symbols. Outsiders, and the state, should accept each group's claims about its own name, symbols, and so on. While this may answer the question of 'who decides?' across a certain range of cases, it does not dampen the conflicts over the decisions. It is just not the case that what another group calls itself is of no concern to my group. The crux of the conflict between Greeks and Macedonians (in Australia as in the Balkans) was that two groups were both laying claim to the word 'Macedonian,' with Greece maintaining that 'Macedonian' described only a subset of 'Greek.' What if white Protestant Americans tried to reserve for themselves the label 'American,' or another like 'God's people?' I do not suggest that either move is likely; but the possibility illustrates that one group's preferred name can easily be an insult to another. A liberal state cannot prevent persons from referring to themselves however they like; but it cannot simply adopt their preferred terms for its own usage. Moreover, cultural groups are too heterogeneous for us to assume that the name chosen by leaders or a majority will not be experienced as an insult by other members of the community.

Finally, the principle of self-definition is silent on most of the subjects of symbolic dispute. It does not, for example, help us decide what a city should be called, or even to decide who shall decide. Flags, official seals, state names, public monuments and holidays, and so on usually preclude a plurality of answers. One could, perhaps, imagine giving each ethnic group a veto right over such decisions; but in practice this might well approximate the rule that the state may not speak at all.

The State Must Exercise Prudence

Symbols cannot hurt anyone, but conflicts over symbolism can. One could take seriously the conflicts while still denying that there is anything morally interesting to say about the symbols themselves. The state, under such a rule, should use those names and symbols which are unlikely to lead to violence or conflict. One cannot say of ethnic symbolism that it is right or wrong, good or evil, but one can say that it is wise or foolish, prudent or imprudent. This would allow criticism of the Australian governments for its actions, at least if the consequences could reasonably have been foreseen.[7]

If some of the other standards do not seem to allow adequate criticism of the state's symbols and speech, this one does not seem to allow adequate criticism of ethnic groups that threaten violence over symbolism.

---

[7] This is the position I endorsed in the 'Symbolic claims' section of 'Classifying Cultural Rights,' in Will Kymlicka and Ian Shapiro (eds.), *NOMOS XXXIX: Ethnicity and Group Rights* (New York: New York University Press 1997). It will become clear that I have changed my mind on this point.

Whenever a sufficiently powerful group objects to a symbol sufficiently strenuously, prudence demands that the symbol be withdrawn or vetoed—regardless of whether the group is right or wrong to object. This standard does not allow us to draw a distinction between the democratic majority in South Africa objecting to retaining the old symbols of the apartheid regime (flag, national anthem, and so on) and a die-hard minority objecting to *changing* those symbols. It falls into the trap of negative consequentialism described in Chapter 2; it is subject to moral blackmail. We must be able to evaluate which objections to symbolism are justified and which are not; and even when objections are justified, we must not provide an incentive to object violently.

Taking the partial truths in these various responses into account, we are left with a standard that treats humiliating public symbols—especially symbolic celebrations of past instances of ethnic violence, cruelty, and injustice—as worthy of moral condemnation, while leaving most cases of symbolism which do not involve state humiliation of any person or group to the considerations of prudence. If a state cannot affirm each group on its own terms, it can at least refrain from symbolically humiliating any of them. Humiliation is a debatable standard but must not be simply a subjective one; we (whoever we are evaluating a particular cultural dispute) must ask whether the person or people are right to feel humiliated. State symbols that celebrate a history of violence and cruelty against a particular group—say, the Confederate battle flag—are legitimately taken to be humiliating. So are the preambular statements in some states' constitutions that the state belongs to a particular ethnic group; the words may not strip anyone of citizenship, but they symbolically exclude from citizenship.

Above I mentioned the argument that symbolic disputes are zero-sum. Many disputes over ethnic and cultural symbolism are strictly zero-sum; but not all of them are. Symbolic status is not *entirely* relative to the status of others. If my culture is routinely degraded and humiliated, if it is pronounced to be primitive and bestial, and then policy changes and it is admitted to be human, is that status gain at anyone's expense? In some sense, maybe; the other groups' *superiority* is diminished. But they are not degraded in turn. It's not as though one group's liberation from humiliation requires another group's humiliation. If it does require some diminution in status, as long as that is only *the other group's sense of superiority* rather than *the other group's sense of its own worth,* then perhaps all is well. Now, none of this is true about the symbolism of national character. A state becomes officially binational only at the expense of its being national. Malays or Fijians gain symbolic priority only at the expense of Chinese–Malaysians or

Indian–Fijians. But minimal symbolic recognition might not be zero-sum in quite the same way.

OFFICIAL LANGUAGES

Official languages are not only or even primarily symbolic. They are often deeply tied up with questions of material advancement, who can get into university, who can get into the civil service, who can defend themselves in court. But the legal right to use one's own language in interactions with the state, even the legal question of what language the state itself uses for communication, is conceptually separate from the question of what languages are deemed official or national languages. The symbolism of that latter status is seen in pure form by the success-ful (in 1938) drive to have Rhaeto-Romansh declared a national language of Switzerland. Rhaeto-Romansh was *not* made a language of state business; German, French, and Italian remained the only languages with that role ('official' languages). Laws did not have to be translated; courts, legislative assemblies, and the army had no new requirement to operate even in part in Rhaeto-Romanic. Native speakers had the right to address courts and authorities in their own language, but they had had that right long before, as well. The constitutional amendment yielded almost no *practical* changes, but it meant that Rhaeto-Romansh speakers were recognized as one of the constituent peoples of Switzerland. This symbolic outcome was what was most desired by peti-tioners, who were indeed at pains to point out that they were *not* requesting that theirs be made a language of state business.[8]

The United States does not have much debate on whether to make any minority languages official languages but has a fierce debate over whether to formally establish English as the official language; the coun-try has never formally declared an official language at the federal level and state provisions for official English are less than two decades old.[9]

---

[8] Bernard Cathamos, 'Rhaeto-Romansh in Switzerland up to 1940,' in Sergij Vilfan *et al.* (eds.), *Ethnic Groups and Language Rights (Comparative Studies on Governments and Non-Dominant Ethnic Groups in Europe, 1850–1940, V.3)* (New York: New York University Press, European Science Foundation, 1993), 98–105. The Swiss approval of the Rhaeto-Romansh petition was probably related to events outside Switzerland in the late 1930s. It was conceivable that two-thirds Germanic Switzerland would be seen as a candid-ate for *Anschluss*, and emphasizing the multilingualism of the Swiss state emphasized, in however minor a way, that the Swiss did not seek inclusion in the pan-German Reich.

[9] The organization US English claims two exceptions to this rule, Hawaii and Louisiana; but it is dishonest to count either as having official English in the sense that US English proposes for the country as a whole. Both have long been officially bilingual; English and Hawaiian are constitutionally entrenched in Hawaii, and English and French

The symbolic aspects of official languages provide much of the motivation for the official English movement in the United States. Even without an official national language, there is no question of the practical dominance of English in American government and law. The First Amendment places sharp constraints on any official language law that has more than symbolic significance, as was seen by the Supreme Court in *Arizona v U.S. English*. Official English is less about the distribution of actual legal language rights than it is about affirming the symbolic priority of English, its status as the unifying language of an immigrant society.

Contrary to what some opponents of official English suggest, that affirmation need not be at all related to an affirmation of non-Hispanic whites as the dominant ethnicity of the country. Indeed, many prominent leaders of the official English movement have been Asian–Americans or Hispanics who believe that linguistic assimilation is the *sine qua non* of a successful society of immigrants. Undoubtedly, some of those who vote for official English referenda are motivated by ethnic bigotry; but we have little reason even to think that such is a general rule.

At least some of the official language laws that have been passed or proposed restricted or eliminated linguistic assistance rights as well as giving English symbolic priority; the Arizona statute struck down by the Supreme Court is certainly a case in point. But bilingual education, the linguistic assistance right that generates the most controversy in the US, has almost never been prohibited by an official English law. California voters declared English the state's official language several years before they eliminated bilingual education in a separate referendum. Even the law in Dade County, Florida, which when passed was the country's most restrictive of linguistic assistance rights, was both supported and opposed on mainly symbolic grounds. The county government lacked the authority to eliminate either bilingual education or bilingual ballots. After it was amended in 1983 to exempt government services related to health and safety, the law mostly restricted bilingual publication of such mundane things as county bus schedules, signs at the county zoo, and notifications of public meetings.

Certainly the bus schedules affected many people's daily lives and the lack of notification of public meetings can limit important access to the democratic process, but the passion surrounding the law's passage, and

both have protected status in Louisiana. That English has been *an* official language in these states for many decades does not make them forerunners of states in which English is *the* official language. See http://www.us-english.org/states.htm.

its eventual repeal as the first action of the county's first Hispanic-majority council, were out of proportion to its practical effects. Supporters and opponents alike knew that the law had greater symbolic than practical importance. A defender of the ordinance at the public meeting preceding its repeal demanded, 'Has it come to this? A divided community where immigrants demand that we learn their language? What an insult.' Chris Doss, a field director for US English who participated in the Miami debate, said that 'Across the United States . . . there are a lot of people who think [the repeal] is a symbolic slap in the face by rejecting our common language.' Opponents of the ordinance said that it insulted and symbolically excluded a majority of the county's population. A representative of the NAACP went so far as to say the ordinance was unconstitutional because it placed 'a badge of slavery' on Haitians, the kind of public insult to blacks that violates the Fourteenth Amendment.[10]

The official entrenchment of one language almost always silently but specifically excludes one or two other languages, and the United States is no exception. The official English movement is specifically concerned with Spanish, and is justified with claims that Hispanic immigrants are not following the path of previous immigrants into mainstream American anglophone society. Official English in the US thus seems to me a milder form of the claim in a constitution that a state belongs to a particular people; it is legitimately perceived as a symbol of exclusion, and so taken to be humiliating.

SLAVERY IN THE UNITED STATES

The debates and disputes over the symbolic legacy of slavery in the United States are widespread and can be bitter. There has been considerable agitation for an official apology for slavery from the United States government. New Orleans has adopted a rule that public schools should not be named for slaveowners; this attracted international attention when a school named for George Washington was renamed. During the battle to integrate the public schools, some southern states resurrected the battle

---

[10] This argument—which was never used in court—runs quickly into the paradox that the ancestors of Haitian–Americans were not slaves in the United States, while those Americans whose ancestors were slaves are virtually all native-English speakers. That is, if official English is a badge of inferiority, it is so for precisely those black Americans whose ancestors were not enslaved in America and so cannot be a badge of *slavery*, the specific kind of badge of inferiority which is arguably prohibited by the Fourteenth Amendment.

flag of the Confederate States of America as a symbol of their defiance; it
flies over some state capitols to this day. Statues of Confederate leaders
and monuments to the Confederate war dead dot the south. A statue of
Queen Catherine of Braganza, which is supposed to stand overlooking
New York's borough of Queens which was named for her, has been the
subject of bitter controversy because some activists have charged her with
profiting from the slave trade. (Historians say this is false, and Catherine
left money in her will to be used to free slaves, but it is undoubtedly true
that the two states of which she was royalty, Portugal and the United
Kingdom, were at that time involved in the slave trade.)

The passage of time matters in symbolic disputes. Retaining the
month-names of July and August does not at all connote official
approval of the millennia-old wrongs committed by the Caesars, and no
one (not republicans, not Jews or Christians, not the descendants of the
Gauls) can reasonably claim to be humiliated or symbolically excluded
from the polity because of it. Slavery was abolished a century and a third
ago. However, American blacks did not attain full legal equality for a
century after that. Violence against blacks was pervasive in the south for
decades after slavery was abolished. This history does not mean that
every symbol at which some African–Americans take offense really is a
humiliating endorsement of past injustice. It seems to me, for example,
that there is a difference between celebrating figures who fought a war
to defend slavery (Robert E. Lee, Jefferson Davis) and celebrating figures
who owned slaves but who are being celebrated for other reasons
(George Washington). The dispute over Queen Catherine shows even
more clearly that simply invoking a history of injustice does not make the
claim correct; a statue of Catherine cannot rightly be interpreted as a
celebration of slavery or of the slave trade. On the other hand, the
emphasis on slavery, and on not symbolically endorsing it, is justified.
The questions are right even if the answers are wrong, as it were.

OFFICIAL APOLOGIES

If symbolism is often particularly troublesome in ethnic politics, there
are symbolic moves that can be made that promote peace and reconciliation. An increasingly prominent part of multicultural politics involves
official apologies to minority groups for past wrongs or injustices.[11]

---

[11] Although neither of these discussions is limited to official apologies or to apologies
to ethnic groups, see Michael Cunningham, 'Saying Sorry: The Politics of Apology,'
Political Quarterly 70:3 1999, 285–93, and Donald Shriver, Jr., *An Ethic For Enemies:
Forgiveness in Politics* (Oxford: Oxford University Press, 1995).

These are the mirror image of many symbolic disputes, which are often about the commemoration and celebration of past instances of violence, cruelty, and injustice. But some state symbols and symbolic expression seek specifically to reconcile old disputes, to atone in some way for past evils. If too often symbolism provides a cheap opportunity for extremism, perhaps it can sometimes provide an affordable means of reconciliation. Brennan and Lomasky, it should be remembered, argue that when we act expressively we may promote greater good as well as greater evil than when we act decisively and self-interestedly. Official apologies are not the only kind of such possibly beneficent symbolism, but they are probably the most prominent and the most widely discussed.

More than a decade ago, the United States government officially apologized to, as well as offering compensation to, Japanese–Americans interned during World War II. In recent years, some African–Americans have lobbied for an official government apology for slavery. The Canadian government has formally apologized to Canadian First Nations for injustices against them by the Canadian government and the British Crown. Queen Elizabeth II, in her capacity as monarch of New Zealand, apologized to the Maori for the unjust taking of Maori lands and for other breaches of the Treaty of Waitangi. There is much debate in Australia about whether the federal government ought to formally apologize to 'the stolen generation' of Aboriginal children, thousands of whom were taken away from Aboriginal homes in order to be placed into white homes where they might acculturate and assimilate. A government commission recommended a formal apology; Prime Minister John Howard decisively refused to follow the recommendation and instead issued a personal statement of regret. There is talk in Ireland of demanding an official apology from Britain for the potato famine. Even the Cajun descendants of francophone Acadians, illegally expelled from New Brunswick by the British government in the late 1700s, have filed legal action against Britain in search of an official apology.[12]

Official apologies are not always matters of pure symbolism. The apology to Japanese–Americans included a package of financial compensation, and Queen Elizabeth's apology to the Maori was part of a process of returning taken lands. But, to the degree that an apology is demanded or offered *in addition* to such compensation or restitution, to the degree that (e.g.) money alone is taken to be insufficient, thus far does the dispute involve symbolism. And in several of these cases the symbolic demand or offer is detached from material considerations,

---

[12] 'An old British crime. Cajuns' belated counter-attack' *The Economist*, 31 Jan. 1998.

either because there is no financial demand being made or because it is being pursued separately.

One proponent of an apology to Australia's stolen generation, the leader of a parents' organization which has itself apologized for its past complicity with the policy, said that 'If you don't speak up you are almost in the same category as the people who perpetuated the policy.'[13] Whatever the merits of an apology, in the first place it must be made clear that this isn't so. Even leaving aside for the moment the problem of one generation apologizing for the faults of a past one, the gap between symbol and reality is larger than this. Those who imposed the policy were actually guilty of trying to deliberately destroy a culture; and they were responsible for the breakup of thousands of families, itself a gross violation of liberty and privacy. Those who fail to apologize do no harm, even if they also fail to do good.

This, too, marks apologies as a distinctive kind of symbolism. In some symbolic disputes inaction does not seem to be an option. Failing to take down the Confederate flag from an American state capitol building isn't much different from putting it up in the first place. Both affirm the flag as a legitimate symbol of the state; if this is a harm to the descendants of slaves, then it is a harm committed by those who maintain it as well as by those who initiated it. But official apologies are not like that. Presumably by the time an apology becomes an option the harmful policy itself has been stopped; failing to apologize for it is not equivalent to perpetuating it. Similarly, apologies are not zero-sum, at least not in the same way that the symbolism of national character is. An apology to one group does not preclude (though perhaps it dilutes?) an apology to another.

The case against official apologies is that they misidentify the perpetrators and, sometimes, the victims of wrongs; they suppose that guilt can be both collective and intergenerational. An entire nation, state, or ethnic group (usually a state) admits to a wrong which only a minority actually committed. The living apologize instead of the dead who committed the wrong; the living receive an apology instead of the dead.

It is said that it is unjust to expect the living to apologize for the sins of the dead. If the government of Great Britain, speaking on behalf of all British citizens, apologizes to the Maori, does it not unjustly implicate innocent people in a guilty action? Perhaps; but even if there is a wrong it is only symbolic. The harm done to innocent Britons is

---

[13] Ros Brennan, president of the Federation of Parents and Citizens' Associations of New South Wales, quoted in Debra Jopson, 'Parents plan an apology to stolen children,' *The Australian*, Wednesday 6 Aug. 1997.

certainly no more real than is the benefit to the Maori. In any event, the living are expected to pay the debts of the dead all the time; how else do public bonds and other forms of state debt work? The living are taxed to repay the debt, as are recent migrants, as are those who opposed incurring the debt in the first place. Certainly no greater harm is done to the innocent person in whose name an apology is issued than to the innocent person whose wealth is taken to pay an old state debt or (even more apposite) compensation to someone who was long ago financially wronged by the state.

More interesting, perhaps, is the question of whether the living are entitled to an apology for a wrong that was done to the dead. The Aboriginal children taken from their homes are still alive; American slaves are not. Of course, many living African–Americans have experienced discrimination of various kinds and disadvantage traceable in various ways to slavery; but they have not experienced *slavery*. Does it make sense to apologize to living African–Americans, many of whom count dead slaveholders as well as dead slaves among their ancestors, for slavery?

Overall, the passage of time does matter, and the case for an official apology is stronger the more recent the injustice. With very recent wrongs, for example if the offending government is still in office, the case is strongest (even if an apology is most unlikely at such moments). When many of the immediate victims are still alive— Japanese–Americans, the stolen generation—there are still good grounds for an apology, even if there has been a change in government.

When an ancient wrong is ongoing, or has been until very recently, there is in some sense still a living class of victims. Land taken from the Maori more than a century ago was not restored to their descendants until the last decade; an apology to the Maori was therefore more legitimate and appropriate than would be (to imagine an absurd example) an Italian apology to France for the Roman conquest of Gaul. The descendants of Acadians, trying to appeal to considerations like these, point out that they are still legally forbidden from returning to New Brunswick under penalty of death. They are right to draw attention to this provision, but plainly no one has dreamed of enforcing it within living memory. It is difficult to plausibly claim that living Cajuns—or even their parents or grandparents—have been harmed by the British action, and to that degree the case for an apology is diminished. Aftereffects of an ancient wrong—as with the continuing effects of chattel slavery in the United States—are a different and difficult problem to which I return below. But in general, the less recent the wrong, the less case there is for an official apology, as even advocates of official apologies recognize.

An apology depends on some distance between the class of offenders and the class of victims. That is, when the victims or their descendants are now full members of the government, it seems odd for the government to apologize to them. When they are [still] excluded, formally or informally, an apology is to that degree more sensible. It would be very strange for the current South African government to apologize to black South Africans for the wrongs of apartheid. The new government is thought to *belong* to apartheid's victims and their descendants; it is legally but not morally the successor to the apartheid regime. It still services the financial debts accumulated by its predecessor, but it does not seem to have any moral debt to blacks rolled over from before 1993. By contrast, neither the British government nor its Canadian counterpart belongs to the Louisiana Cajuns in any sense. There is a wide range of intermediate cases. Maori, Aborigines, the Canadian First Nations, and African–Americans are now formally full members of their respective democratic communities but can claim to varying degrees that the government still belongs predominantly to the groups that wronged them, that they are still excluded from the societies whose apologies they seek.

It is common to invoke the fact of immigration as an argument against official apologies, one that combines worries about collective guilt with those about intergenerational guilt. Australia, Canada, the United States, Britain, and New Zealand have all had considerable immigration since the wrongs began or occurred. Why should Pakistani–Britons be held morally accountable for the expulsion of the Acadians? Why should Vietnamese–Americans apologize for slavery? But I doubt that this objection has nearly as much force as does the objection to asking the current South African government to apologize for apartheid, namely that it would constitute black South Africans apologizing to themselves.

An official apology, even in a democratic state, does *not* constitute an apology by all the citizens of the state, and it does not impute collective guilt. Citizens do not own the actions of their governments that directly. Of course, many citizens choose to take pride in the praiseworthy actions of their state, their compatriots, and their forbears. Once citizens have chosen to identify with their political communities in that way, they have little room for complaint if they are also urged to feel shame for the blameworthy acts of their state, their compatriots, and their forbears. But whether or not individual citizens feel ashamed is not quite the point. When Queen Elizabeth and the New Zealand government apologized for past injustices to the Maori, they did *not* do so in the name of all Britons or all Anglo-New Zealanders. The Queen is the head of state, apologizing for a past act of state. There was no pretense that each individual Briton owed each individual Maori an apology, and that the Queen was only acting as their proxy; what was offered was an official apology, *not* a collective apology. This case represents an extreme: the apology of a foreign-born unelected head of state for the acts of her ancestor does not at all morally implicate the people of New Zealand. But even democratic states are *states,* not mere stand-ins for their citizens. They have a discrete corporate existence, one which both endures across generations and stands apart from their citizens taken as a collective. Thus, the apologies to interned Japanese–Americans and the African–American victims of the Tuskegee experiments were in the name of the government of the United States but not in the name of all Americans.

Of course, democratic citizens bear some responsibility for the actions of their governments; they have a duty to try to prevent their governments from committing injustices. But sometimes injustices are committed nevertheless. Clearly those who vigorously and actively opposed an unjust policy of their governments do not share in any actual *guilt,* and it would not be appropriate of them to personally apologize to victims of the policy as though they had committed the wrong. Yet if financial compensation is owed the victims, opponents as well as supporters of the policy will be taxed to provide it. An official apology does not even demand this much of those who are innocent of the wrong.

The case is somewhat different when an apology is demanded of, or guilt is attributed to, an ethnic group or a nation rather than a state. A collectivity without a corporate existence cannot claim the same sort of moral separateness from its members that a state can. On the other hand, a collectivity without a corporate existence cannot usually issue an 'official' apology or pay compensation, either.

After World War II, the West German state paid reparations of a sort to the state of Israel, in a case that famously illustrates the problem of misidentification of both villains and victims. The German state had undergone a radical discontinuity; the *Bundesrepublik* was in no moral sense an heir to the Nazi regime. For the *Bundesrepublik* to be morally or financially responsible for the wrongs of Nazism, both the wartime and the postwar state must be seen as agents of a continuous underlying nation or populace. That is, the German nation must be seen as responsible for the acts of the Nazi regime, and the *Bundesrepublik* government for the acts of the (by then politically-divided) German nation. The latter is dubious, and the former is of course hotly contested.

It is interesting—and appropriate—that a limited range of wrongs have been invoked as calling for apologies. Slavery, internment, expulsion, the taking of land, the breaking up of families—these are all very concrete wrongs, which were committed either by the state or with its close collaboration against persons under the state's own jurisdiction. The supposed victims of symbolic and expressive harms ask that the harms be ended, but they do not ask for official apologies for their past misnaming, misrecognition, or mischaracterization. This, I think, gives lie to the idea that status and recognition are more important to persons and to peoples than are violence and deprivation of rights.

But even when the wrong was monstrous, after too much time has passed, sometimes the requirements for an apology to make sense are no longer present. I doubt, for example, that it makes much sense for Spain to apologize for the conquest of the Americas. There's just not sufficient continuity between the Spanish state of 1500–1600 and that of today. Too many of the victims of the colonization don't have descendants, as they were killed off. The vast majority of the descendants of the indigenous peoples of 1500 are also descendants of Spanish settlers and colonizers; the *mestizo* populations of much of Latin America have as ancestors both victims and victimizers. The creole or *mestizo* republics are neither the institutional successors to the Spanish crown nor, certainly, the institutional successors to destroyed Indian nations. They rebelled against the Spanish Empire, but in turn some of them have too often continued brutal imperial policies against surviving indigenous peoples.

Public commemoration of past wrongs need not take the form of an apology. When the circumstances of an apology do not pertain (no institutional continuity, no ready way to distinguish descendants of victims, no continuing separation between victims and offending institution), that does not mean that nothing can be done. The new South African government is commemorating the wrongs of apartheid in public statues, holidays, and the renaming of public places. A state that came to repent a thoroughly successful genocide—that is, a state that had no one left to apologize *to*—could still seek public remembrance of its wrongs, in ways ranging from an official institutional admission of guilt to physical symbols like public monuments. In this case the state isn't seeking reconciliation, but memory for its own sake; it's trying to remind future generations of citizens and the world at large of what happened, and that it was wrong. One effect might be to build into the public culture a strong prohibition against such acts in the future, as West Germany did in its own public culture in the decades after the war.

Sometimes official apologies may be like that, too. In personal apologies, that an apology be *accepted* is a part of the process. 'Forgive and forget' is a common refrain when a friend or family member apologizes to us. But forgiveness may be inappropriate, and forgetting is positively wrongheaded, when a state apologizes for genocide, slavery, expropriation, or conquest. The 'Draft Declaration for Reconciliation' between Aboriginal or Torres Strait Islander Australians and other Australians is unusual in holding that 'as one part of the nation expresses its sorrow and profoundly regrets the injustices of the past, so the other part accepts the apology and forgives.'[14] A public official apology has as part of its purpose the official memorialization, the committing to public memory, of the wrong. This is important in its own right, even when there is no one who could, or wishes to, 'accept' the apology.

Politicians of the right are generally more opposed to official apologies than are those of the left; but this is odd. As I noted above, the more willing one is to bask in the reflected glory of one's forbears, the more one is obliged to accept blame for their wrongs. If society is, as Burke put it, a contract among the living, the dead, and the yet-to-be-born; if conservatives take seriously some of their arguments about the reverence due to written constitutions and their long-dead authors; if conservatives truly believe that it is hubristic to try to remake the moral world anew every generation; then why are so many of them so resistant to taking on blame for their ancestors' injustices? Indeed, many conservatives in these states purport to take Christianity seriously as a source of moral knowledge; but central to Christianity are the twin ideas that an original sin can taint those who did not commit it, and that an act of redemption can redeem those who did not perform it. Those who refer to slavery and dispossession of indigenous peoples as 'original sins' of the founding of the United States, Canada, Australia, and New Zealand fully intend to evoke the Christian idea that an original sin taints not just the sinners but those who come after. The distaste that conservatives show for what Liberal (that is, center-right) Australian Prime Minister John Howard calls 'the black armband view of history' seems to be motivated by nationalist pride rather than by principle. On the other hand, liberalism ordinarily rejects collective, transgenerational responsibilities. Even before the inclusion of a Bill of Rights, the US Constitution rejected the old idea of 'corruption of the blood'; under a liberal regime the crimes of the fathers are not to be considered the crimes of the sons.

---

[14] By the time this book sees print there will be a final rather than a draft Declaration for Reconciliation; the wording of that document might differ.

But if what I've suggested above is true, official apologies don't necessarily violate liberal principles. A state that can act in its own name, a state that has a corporate existence, can commit wrongs in its own name—and can legitimately apologize in its own name. This is not even only true of states. The Catholic Church—which both legally and as a matter of its own self-understanding has a corporate, institutional existence and is not merely the sum of its faithful at any moment—has apologized for some of its failures during the Holocaust. That this means some persons who hold church offices today, and who were not yet born at the time of the Holocaust, have apologized for the actions of others long dead, is neither a conceptual nor a moral problem. There would have been a problem had Catholic prelates apologized in their capacities as natural persons for the actions of other natural persons; but this is not what they did. And it is not what state officials do when they properly apologize for past actions of the state, either. Australian Prime Minister Howard thus got matters precisely backward when he resisted an official apology to the 'stolen generation' of Aboriginal children but issued a personal statement of regret. That personal statement could be no more than the expression of sorrow of an onlooker to a tragedy; Howard had had no hand in the policy. It was the Australian state, not the person of the head of government, that owed (and still owes) an apology.

This view does not require endorsing anything like the British pluralists' account of real group personality.[15] We may hold that states and other corporate bodies are purely artificial creations, that their 'personhood' is purely a legal fiction, and still accept the appropriateness of official apologies. The entire point of allowing such legal fictions is to create a means whereby projects of various kinds can outlive their creators, can endure stably from one generation to the next. Their assets and their debts survive. They routinely claim a kind of survival of moral assets as well. That a state, a church, or a corporation committed some good act generations ago is treated as an object of pride or celebration today. As long as all of this is true, there is no reason why moral debts should not survive as well.

Based on the criteria described here, whether the United States government ought to apologize for slavery in the United States is a hard question. Much time has passed, but the aftereffects of the injustice are still very much with us. African–Americans are formally full members of the

---

[15] See F. W. Maitland, 'Moral Personality and Legal Personality,' reprinted in David Nicholls, *The Pluralist State* (London: Macmillan Press, 1975).

polity, but there is clearly still some distance between them and it. Moreover, the corporate moral responsibility of the United States government is difficult to determine. After all, the United States of America fought a long, bloody, costly war against the Confederacy, a war that had the effect—and, in the minds of many of the participants on both sides, the intent—of abolishing slavery. It then subjected the former Confederacy to a military occupation for some decades in order to protect the rights of African–Americans. If it then allowed the long years of Jim Crow and segregation, these were sins of omission rather than of commission. When the federal government has *acted* and not merely allowed the states to act, it has usually acted to protect African–Americans (however partially and haltingly). To ascribe to the federal government—the legal continuation of Lincoln's Union government—moral responsibility for slavery and the injustices that followed it seems a mistake. The mistake is not merely the sort that always accompanies official apologies to the living for crimes the dead committed against the dead. There seems to be a mistake in holding *this* corporate body, *this* institution, responsible for the crimes at all. If the Confederacy had survived then it would owe an apology (at the very least); and perhaps some of the existing state governments owe official apologies to African–Americans. But the federal government, so it would seem, does not.

As I said, the case is a hard one. The preceding argument is plausible, and might be correct. But I do not think that it is complete. The United States government is not only the continuation of the government of 1865, 1954, and 1964. It is also the continuation of the government of *Dred Scott,* the Fugitive Slave Act, the Compromises, and the three-fifths-of-a-person proviso. Slavery was a creation of the colonial and state governments; but from 1789 until 1865, it was in part sustained by the federal government as well. It was not merely tolerated; it was endorsed, protected, and preserved by the government in Washington. To think this it is not necessary to think the Constitution a hopelessly racist document, or to think the Founders evil men. But for the first eighty years of the republic, the federal government was an active participant in the evil of slavery.

Perhaps partly in recognition of these facts, Abraham Lincoln declined to attribute all of the guilt of slavery to the South and the Confederacy. In a famous passage of his Second Inaugural Address, he said

If we shall suppose that American slavery is one of those offenses which, in the providence of God, must needs come, but which, having continued through His appointed time, He now wills to remove, and that He gives to both North and

South this terrible war as the woe due to those by whom the offense came, shall we discern therein any departure from those divine attributes which the believers in a living God always ascribe to Him? Fondly do we hope, fervently do we pray, that this mighty scourge of war may speedily pass away. Yet, if God wills that it continue until all the wealth piled by the bondsman's two hundred and fifty years of unrequited toil shall be sunk, and until every drop of blood drawn with the lash shall be paid by another drawn with the sword, as was said three thousand years ago, so still it must be said 'the judgments of the Lord are true and righteous altogether.'

It was not only southern blood of which he spoke; it was all of the blood being shed on both sides in the Civil War. Perhaps there is some larger sense in which the sins of the United States were paid for, the moral debt extinguished, with the blood shed in those four years. But we do not have secular access to that kind of truth. What we do have access to is the knowledge that, even in the position Lincoln was in, he refused to absolve the United States of its share of culpability for slavery. Thirteen decades later, there is no longer any question of paying that debt in blood. But we remain well within the statute of limitations Lincoln described; and it is not too late for a formal recognition of, and apology for, the federal government's role in sustaining slavery.

Afterword

This is not a cheerful book. Slavery, genocide, civil wars, expulsions, forced assimilation, expropriations, and mutilations are not the subjects one would emphasize in celebrating the beauty of human diversity. I have emphasized the dangers of ethnic politics and the difficulties of coexistence, not because they are the only or even the most important facts about life in a multiethnic world, but because I think they are the most important for politics and for political theory. For many, the crucial questions about ethnicity and culture on an ongoing basis are those that have to do with living life within them. How shall I understand my identity? Which traditions of my culture do I wish to endorse, to preserve, to pass on to my children? How do I wish to shape my community, and how am I shaped by it? How should we best understand our culture's rules, norms, and standards? But I have argued that these should not be, must not be, the sorts of questions that are central to our thought about politics in multicultural states or in a multicultural world. Instead, we have to think about the terms of our coexistence, the institutions and norms that can help us prevent the worst outcomes of that coexistence.

Hannah Arendt described as part of the human condition *plurality*, 'the fact that men, not Man, live on the earth and inhabit the world.'[1] It seems to me that the same must be true of our thought about culture, nation, and the like. It is irresponsible to theorize about why a nation deserves to be a state without thinking about a world in which nations seek to become states. It is incomplete to discuss special state action to preserve a culture without thinking about the fact that the state encompasses cultures. The laws, rules, and norms of coexistence under conditions of cultural plurality will not be the same as the laws, rules, and norms of cultural preservation without such conditions. Moreover, the cultures in the world have histories of interaction which have often been histories of radical injustice, violence, and cruelty, histories which themselves have to be taken into account in the politics of today.

If this is not a cheerful book, it is none the less a hopeful one. If the possibility of grave evils is always with us, the evils themselves are not.[2]

---

[1] Hannah Arendt, *The Human Condition* (Chicago: University of Chicago Press, 1958), 7.

[2] See James Fearon and David Laitin, 'Explaining Interethnic Cooperation,' *American Political Science* 90:4 (1996), 715–35.

Fear and hope are in this sense compatible. If there were no way to avoid catastrophe, then the cautions of a fearful political theory would serve no purpose. Laws and political institutions can be arranged in ways that give due recognition to histories of injustice, that encourage long-lived peaceful coexistence, that let the plurality of cultures increase the options of those seeking to escape their own community without encouraging the state to stamp any community out, and so on. I have given only a few examples of such arrangements. But they may serve to show the possibilities, some of the ways in a multiculturalism of fear can be put into practice.

BIBLIOGRAPHY

Acton, Lord, (Sir John Emerich Edward Dalberg), 'Nationality,' in *Selected Writings of Lord Acton*, i: *Essays in the History of Liberty* (Indianapolis: Liberty Fund, 1985 [1862]).

Allen, Jonathan, review of Isaiah Berlin, *The Sense of Reality*, *South African Journal of Philosophy* 17:2 (1998), 173–177.

—— 'Political Theory and Negative Morality,' *Political Theory* (forthcoming).

Anderson, Benedict, *Imagined Communities: Reflections on the Origin and Spread of Nationalism* (2nd edn., London: Verso, 1991).

Arendt, Hannah, *The Origins of Totalitarianism* (New York: Harcourt Brace and Co., 1973 [1950]).

—— *The Human Condition* (Chicago: University of Chicago Press, 1958).

Australian Law Reform Commission, *The Recognition of Aboriginal Customary Law* (Canberra: AGPS, 1986).

Baker, Ken (ed.), *A Treaty With the Aborigines?* (Melbourne: Institute of Public Affairs, 1988).

Barber, Benjamin, 'Muticulturalism Between Individuality and Community: Chasm or Bridge?' in Dana Villa and Austin Sarat (eds.), *Liberal Modernism and Democratic Individuality: George Kateb and the Practices of Politics* (Princeton: Princeton University Press, 1996).

Barry, Brian, *An Egalitarian Critique of Multiculturalism* (Cambridge: Polity Press, 2000).

Benhabib, Seyla, ' "Nous" et "Les Autres," ' in Christian Joppke and Steven Lukes (eds.), *Multicultural Questions* (Oxford: Oxford University Press, 1999).

Bennett, T. W., 'The Equality Clause and Customary Law,' *South African Journal on Human Rights* 10 (1994), 122–30.

—— *Human Rights and African Customary Law* (Cape Town: Juta & Co. and University of the Western Cape, 1995).

Beran, Harry, 'A Liberal Theory of Secession,' *Political Studies* 32 (1984), 21–31.

Berlin, Isaiah, *Vico and Herder: Two Studies in the History of Ideas* (London, Hogarth Press, 1976).

—— *Against The Current* (New York: Viking Press, 1980).

—— *The Crooked Timber of Humanity* (New York: Vintage Books, 1992).

—— *The Magus of the North: J. G. Hamman and the Origins of Modern Irrationalism* (New York: Farrar, Straus, and Giroux, 1993).

—— *The Sense of Reality* (New York: Farrar, Straus and Giroux, 1996).

—— 'My Intellectual Path,' *The New York Review of Books*, 14 May 1998, 53–60.

Berlin, Isaiah, 'In Conversation with Steven Lukes,' *Salmagundi* 120 (1998), 52–134.

Bhattacharjee, A. M., *Muslim Law and the Constitution* (2nd edn., Calcutta: Eastern Law House, 1994).

Birch, Anthony, 'Another Liberal Theory of Secession,' *Political Studies* 32 (1984), 596–602.

Brennan, Geoffrey, and Lomasky, Loren, *Democracy and Decision: The Pure Theory of Electoral Preference* (Cambridge: Cambridge University Press, 1993).

Brubaker, Rogers, *Citizenship and Nationhood in France and Germany* (Cambridge, Mass.: Harvard University Press, 1992).

—— *Nationalism Reframed* (Cambridge: Cambridge University Press, 1996).

Brune, Tom, 'Refugees' Beliefs Don't Travel Well; Compromise Plan on Circumcision of Girls Gets Little Support,' *The Chicago Tribune*, Monday 28 Oct. 1996, 11.

Buchanan, Allen, 'Assessing the Communitarian Critique of Liberalism,' *Ethics* 99 (1989), 852–82.

—— *Secession: The Morality of Political Divorce from Fort Sumpter to Lithuania and Quebec* (Boulder, Colo.: Westview Press, 1991).

Burke, Edmund, *Reflections on the Revolution in France* (New York: Penguin, 1968 [1790]).

Calhoun, Craig, *Nationalism* (Minneapolis: The Open University Press, 1998).

Caney, Simon, 'Self-Government and Secession: The Case of Nations,' *Journal of Political Philosophy* 5 (1997), 351–72.

Canovan, Margaret, *Nationhood and Political Theory* (Cheltenham: Edward Elgar, 1996).

Carens, Joseph H., 'Difference and Domination: Reflections on the Relations Between Pluralism and Equality,' in J. W. Chapman and Alan Wertheimer (eds.), *NOMOS XXXII: Majorities and Minorities* (New York: New York University Press, 1990).

—— 'Democracy and Respect for Difference: The Case of Fiji,' *University of Michigan Journal of Law Reform* 25:3 (1992), 547–631.

—— 'Realistic and Idealistic Approaches to the Ethics of Immigration,' XXX (1) *International Migration Review* 30:1 (1996), 156–70.

—— 'Dimensions of Citizenship and National Identity in Canada,' *The Philosophical Forum* 28 (1996–7), 111–24.

Cathamos, Bernard, 'Rhaeto-Romansh in Switzerland up to 1940,' in Sergij Vilfan *et al.* (eds.), *Comparative Studies on Governments and Non-Dominant Ethnic Groups in Europe, 1850–1940*, iii: *Ethnic Groups and Language Rights* (New York: New York University Press, European Science Foundation, 1993).

Chang, Ruth, 'Introduction,' in Ruth Chang (ed.), *Incommensurability, Incomparability, and Practical Reason* (Cambridge, Mass.: Harvard University Press, 1997).

Clark, Bruce, *Native Liberty, Crown Sovereignty: The Existing Aboriginal*

Right of Self-Government in Canada (Montreal: McGill-Queen's University Press, 1990).

Connor, Walker, *Ethnonationalism: The Quest for Understanding* (Princeton: Princeton University Press, 1994).

Coulombe, Pierre, *Language Rights in French Canada* (New York: Peter Lang Publishing, 1995).

Crawford, James, 'Legal Pluralism and the Indigenous Peoples of Australia,' in Oliver Mendelsohn and Upendra Baxi (eds.), *The Rights of Subordinated Peoples* (Oxford: Oxford University Press, 1994).

Cunningham, Michael, 'Saying Sorry: The Politics of Apology,' *Political Quarterly* 70:3 (1999), 285–93.

D'Alembert, Jean Le Rond, 'The Analysis of the Spirit of the Laws,' in *The Complete Works of M. de Montesquieu*, iv (London: Evans and Davis, 1777).

Danley, John, 'Liberalism, Aboriginal Rights, and Cultural Minorities,' *Philosophy and Public Affairs* 20 (1991), 168–85.

Das, Veena, 'Cultural Rights and the Definition of Community,' in Oliver Mendelsohn and Upendra Baxi (eds.), *The Rights of Subordinated Peoples* (Oxford: Oxford University Press, 1994).

Denis, Claude, *We Are Not You: First Nations and Canadian Modernity* (Peterborough, Ont.: Broadview Press, 1997).

Denitch, Bogdan, *Ethnic Nationalism: The Tragic Death of Yugoslavia* (Minneapolis: University of Minnesota Press, 1994).

Department of the Prime Minister and Cabinet [of Australia], *Aboriginal Reconciliation: An Historical Perspective* (Canberra: AGPS, 1991).

De Witte, Bruno, 'Conclusion: Alegal Perspective,' in Sergij Vilfan, Gudmund Sandvik, and Lode Wils. (eds.), *Comparative Studies on Governments and Non Dominant Ethnic Groups in Europe, 1850–1940*, iii: *Ethnic Groups and Language Rights* (New York: New York University Press, European Science Foundation, 1993).

Drinnon, Richard, *Keeper of Concentration Camps: Dillon S. Myer and American Racism* (Berkeley: University of California Press, 1987).

Dugger, Celia, 'Tug of Taboos: African Genital Rite vs. U.S. Law,' *The New York Times*, Saturday 28 Dec. 1996, A1.

Economist, 'An old British crime. Cajuns' belated counter-attack,' *The Economist*, 31 Jan. 1998, 32–3.

Edwards, John R., *Multilingualism* (London: Routledge, 1994).

Eisenberg, Avigail, 'The Politics of Individual and Group Difference in Canadian Jurisprudence,' *Canadian Journal of Political Science* 27:1 (1994), 3–21.

Epstein, Richard, *Simple Rules for a Complex World* (Cambridge, Mass.: Harvard University Press, 1995).

Eriksen, Knut, *et al.* 'Governments and the Education of Non-Dominant Ethnic Groups in Comparative Perspective,' in Janusz Tomiak *et al.* (eds.), *Comparative Studies on Governments and Non-Dominant Ethnic Groups in*

Europe, 1850–1940, i: *Schooling, Educational Policy, and Ethnic Identity* (New York: New York University Press, European Science Foundation, 1991).

Esman, Milton J., *Ethnic Politics* (Ithaca, NY: Cornell University Press, 1993).

Fearon, James, and Laitin, David, 'Explaining Interethnic Cooperation,' *American Political Science* 90:4 (1996), 715–35.

Ferrara, Peter J., 'Social Security and Taxes,' in Donald Kraybill (ed.), *The Amish and the State* (Baltimore: Johns Hopkins University Press, 1993).

Fletcher, George, 'The Case for Linguistic Self-Defense,' in Robert McKim and Jeff McMahan (eds.), *The Morality of Nationalism* (Oxford: Oxford University Press, 1997).

Forbes, H. D., *Ethnic Conflict: Commerce, Culture, and the Contact Hypothesis* (New Haven: Yale University Press, 1997).

Foster, David, 'Bloody Justice,' *The Independent Monthly*, May 1994, 30–6.

Gandhi, Mohandas, *Hind Swaraj*, in Raghavan Iyer (ed.), *The Moral and Political Writings of Mahatma Gandhi*, v. 1. (Oxford: Clarendon Press, 1986 [1909]).

Gaspard, Françoise, and Khorokhavar, Farhad, *Le Foulard et la République* (Paris: Éditions La Découverte, 1995).

Gellner, Ernest, *Nations and Nationalism* (Ithaca, NY: Cornell University Press, 1983).

—— 'Reply to Critics,' in J. A. Hall and I. C. Jarvie (eds.), *The Social Philosophy of Ernest Gellner* (Amsterdam: Rodopi Publishers, 1996).

—— 'Reply: Do Nations Have Navels?' *Nations and Nationalism* 2:3 (1996) 366–70.

Gilbert, Paul, *The Philosophy of Nationalism* (Boulder, Colo.: Westview Press, 1998).

Glazer, Nathan, *We Are All Multiculturalists Now* (Cambridge: Harvard University Press, 1997).

Goodin, Robert E., 'Conventions and Conversions, or, Why Is Nationalism Sometimes So Nasty?' in Robert McKim and Jeff McMahan (eds.), *The Morality of Nationalism* (Oxford: Oxford University Press, 1997).

Gray, John, *Liberalism* (Minneapolis: University of Minnesota Press, 1986).

—— 'The Politics of Cultural Diversity,' in *Post-Liberalism: Studies in Political Thought* (London: Routledge, 1993).

—— 'After the New Liberalism,' *Social Research* 61:3 (1994), 719–35.

—— *Isaiah Berlin* (Princeton: Princeton University Press, 1996).

—— 'From Post-Liberalism to Pluralism,' in Russell Hardin and Ian Shapiro (eds.), *NOMOS XXXLVIII: Political Order* (New York: New York University Press, 1996).

Green, Leslie, 'Internal Minorities and Their Rights,' in Judith Baker (ed.), *Group Rights* (Toronto: University of Toronto Press, 1994).

Greenberg, Joel, 'Did This Arab Die for Selling Land to Jews?' *The New York Times*, Monday 12 May 1997, A3.

Grosby, Steven, 'Territoriality: The Transcendental, Primordial Feature of Modern Societies,' *Nations and Nationalism* 1 (1995), 143–62.

Guinier, Lani, *The Tyranny of the Majority: Fundamental Fairness in Representative Democracy* (New York: Free Press, 1994).

Gurr, Ted Robert, *Minorities at Risk* (Washington, DC: United States Institute of Peace, 1993).

Gutmann, Amy, 'The Challenge of Multiculturalism in Political Ethics, *Philosophy and Public Affairs* 22:3 (1993), 171–206.

—— 'How Limited is Liberal Government?' in Bernard Yack (ed.), *Liberalism without Illusions: Essays on Liberal Theory and the Political Vision of Judith N. Shklar* (Chicago: University of Chicago Press, 1996).

Hardin, Russell, *One for All: The Logic of Group Conflict* (Princeton: Princeton University Press, 1995).

Hartney, Michael, 'Some Confusions Concerning Collective Rights,' *Canadian Journal of Law and Jurisprudence* 4 (1991), 293–314.

Havel, Vaclav, 'In A Time of Transition,' in Paul Wilson (trans.), *Summer Meditations* (New York: Vintage Books, 1993).

Hayek, F. A., *Individualism and the Economic Order* (Chicago: University of Chicago Press, 1948).

—— *The Fatal Conceit* (Chicago: University of Chicago Press, 1988).

Hazlitt, William, 'Race and Class,' in *Selected Writings* (New York: Penguin, 1982).

Herder, J. G., *Ideas for a Philosophy of the History of Mankind*, in F. M. Barnard (ed.), *J. G. Herder on Social and Political Culture* (Cambridge: Cambridge University Press, 1969).

Hobsbawm, Eric J., *Nations and Nationalism Since 1780* (Cambridge: Cambridge University Press, 1990).

Hollis, Martin, 'Is Universalism Ethnocentric?' in Christian Joppke and Steven Lukes (eds.), *Multicultural Questions* (Oxford: Oxford University Press, 1998).

Horowitz, Donald L., *Ethnic Groups in Conflict* (Berkeley: University of California Press, 1986).

—— *A Democratic South Africa? Constitutional Engineering in a Divided Society* (Berkeley: University of California Press, 1991).

—— *The Deadly Ethnic Riot* (forthcoming).

Huntington, Gertrude Enders, 'Health Care,' in Donald Kraybill (ed.), *The Amish and the State* (Baltimore: Johns Hopkins University Press, 1993).

Huntingon, Samuel, *The Clash of Civilizations and the Remaking of World Order* (New York: Simon & Shuster, 1996).

Hurka, Thomas, 'The Justification of National Partiality,' in Robert McKim and Jeff McMahan (eds.), *The Morality of Nationalism* (Oxford: Oxford University Press, 1997).

Isaac, Thomas, 'Individual versus Collective Rights: Aboriginal People and the Significance of *Thomas v Norris*,' *Manitoba Law Journal* 21:2 (1992), 618–30.

Jamrozik, Wanda, 'White Law, Black Lore,' *The Independent Monthly,* May 1994, 37–8.

Jefferson, Thomas, Letter to Madison, 28 Oct. 1785, in Merrill Peterson (ed.), *The Portable Thomas Jefferson* (New York: Penguin, 1975).

——— 'Autobiography,' in Merrill Peterson (ed.), *Thomas Jefferson: Writings* (New York: Library of America, 1984).

Johnston, Darlene, 'Native Rights as Collective Rights: A Question of Self-Preservation,' *Canadian Journal of Law and Jurisprudence* 2 (1989), 19–34.

Jopson, Debra, 'Parents Plan an Apology to Stolen Children,' *The Australian*, Wednesday 6 Aug. 1997.

Kant, Immanuel, *The Metaphysics of Morals*, in Hans Reiss (ed.), *Kant's Political Writings* (Cambridge: Cambridge University Press, 1970 [1797]).

Kateb, George, 'Notes on Pluralism,' *Social Research* 61 (1994), 571–37.

Kekes, John, 'Cruelty and Liberalism,' *Ethics* 106 (1996), 834–44.

Keon-Cohen, B. A., 'Some Problems of Proof: The Admissibility of Traditional Evidence,' in M. A. Stephenson and Suri Ratnapala (eds.), *Mabo: A Judicial Revolution* (Brisbane: University of Queensland Press, 1993).

Kernohan, Andrew, *Liberalism, Equality, and Cultural Oppression* (Cambridge: Cambridge University Press, 1998).

Kiss, Elizabeth, 'Five Theses on Nationalism,' in Ian Shapiro and Russell Hardin (eds.), *NOMOS XXXVII: Political Order* (New York: New York University Press, 1996).

Chandran, Kukathas, 'Are There Any Cultural Rights?' *Political Theory* 20 (1992), 105–39.

——— 'Cultural Rights Again: A Rejoinder to Kymlicka,' *Political Theory* 20 (1992), 674–80.

——— 'Liberalism, Communitarianism, and Political Community,' *Social Philosophy and Policy* 13 (1996), 80–104.

——— 'Cultural Toleration,' in Will Kymlicka and Ian Shapiro (eds.), *NOMOS XXXIX: Ethnicity And Group Rights* (New York: New York University Press, 1997).

——— *The Liberal Archipelago* (Oxford: Oxford University Press (forthcoming)).

Kuran, Timur, 'Ethnic Norms and their Transformation through Reputational Cascades,' *Journal of Legal Studies* 27:2 (1998), 623–59.

Kymlicka, Will, *Liberalism, Community, and Culture* (Oxford: Oxford University Press, 1989).

——— *Multicultural Citizenship: A Liberal Theory of Minority Rights* (Oxford: Oxford University Press, 1995).

Lackey, Douglas, 'Self-Determination and Just War,' *The Philosophical Forum* 28 (1996–7), 100–10.

Laitin, David, *Identity in Formation: the Russian-Speaking Populations in the Near Abroad* (Ithaca, NY: Cornell University Press, 1998).

Las Casas, Bartolomé de, *The Devastation of the Indies*, trans. Bill Donovan (Baltimore: Johns Hopkins University Press, 1992 [1552]).

Levine, Andrew, 'Electoral Power, Group Power, and Democracy,' in J. W. Chapman and Alan Wertheimer (eds.), *NOMOS XXXII: Majorities and Minorities* (New York: New York University Press, 1990).

Levinson, Sanford, *Constitutional Faith* (Princeton: Princeton University Press, 1988).

—— 'Is Liberal Nationalism an Oxymoron? An Essay for Judith Shklar,' *Ethics* 105 (1995), 626–45.

—— *Written In Stone: Public Monuments in Changing Societies* (Durham, NC: Duke University Press, 1998).

Levy, Jacob T., 'Reconciliation and Resources: Mineral Rights and Aboriginal Land Rights as Property Rights,' *Policy* 10:1 (1994), 11–15.

—— 'The Value of Property Rights: Rejoinder to Brennan and Ewing,' *Policy* 10:2 (1994), 44–6.

Lind, Michael, *The Next American Nation* (New York: Free Press, 1995).

Lijphart, Arend, *Democracy in Plural Societies* (New Haven: Yale University Press, 1979).

Lyons, David, 'The New Indian Claims and Original Rights to Land,' in Jeffrey Paul (ed.), *Reading Nozick: Essays on Anarchy, State, and Utopia* (Totowa, NJ: Rowman and Littlefield, 1981).

Lyons, James, 'Islamic Court Condemns Author Who Depicts Jesus as a Homosexual,' *The Independent* Saturday, 30 Oct. 1999, 3.

MacIntyre, Alasdair, *After Virtue: A Study on Moral Theory* (Notre Dame: University of Notre Dame Press, 1984).

McKim, Robert, and McMahan, Jeff (ed.), *The Morality of Nationalism* (Oxford: Oxford University Press, 1997).

McMahan, Jeff, 'The Limits of National Partiality,' in Robert McKim and Jeff McMahan (eds.), *The Morality of Nationalism* (Oxford: Oxford University Press, 1997).

McNeil, Kent, *Common Law Aboriginal Title* (Oxford: Oxford University Press, 1989).

Madison, James, 'Federalist #10,' in Clinton Rossiter (ed.), *The Federalist Papers* (New York: Mentor Books, 1961).

Maitland, F. W., 'Moral Personality and Legal Personality,' reprinted in David Nicholls, *The Pluralist State* (London: Macmillan Press, 1975).

Margalit, Avishai, *The Decent Society* (Cambridge, Mass.: Harvard University Press, 1996).

—— 'The Moral Psychology of Nationalism,' in Robert McKim and Jeff McMahan (eds.), *The Morality of Nationalism* (Oxford: Oxford University Press, 1997).

—— and Raz, Joseph, 'National Self-Determination,' *Journal of Philosophy* 87 (1990), 439–61.

—— and Habertal, Moshe, 'Liberalism and the Right to Culture,' *Social Research* 64 (1994), 491–510.

Matson, J. N., 'The Common Law Abroad: English and Indigenous Laws in the British Commonwealth,' *International and Comparative Law Quarterly* 42 (1993), 753–79.

Mayerfeld, Jamie, 'The Myth of Benign Group Identity: A Critique of Liberal Nationalism,' *Polity* 30:4 (1998), 555–78.

Mazzini, Giuseppe, 'The Duties of Man,' in Omar Dahbour and Micheline Ishay (eds.), *The Nationalism Reader* (Atlantic Highlands, NJ: Humanities Press International, 1995).

Meyers, Thomas, 'Education and Schooling,' in Donald Kraybill (ed.), *The Amish and the State* (Baltimore: Johns Hopkins University Press, 1993).

Mill, John Stuart, *Utilitarianism, Liberty, and Representative Government*, ed. A. D. Lindsay (New York: E. P Dutton and Company, 1951 [1861]).

Miller, David, *On Nationality* (Oxford: Oxford University Press, 1995).

—— review of Paul Gilbert, *The Philosophy of Nationalism*, 16(2) *Journal of Applied Philosophy* 16:2 (1999), 191–2.

—— *Citizenship and National Identity* (Cambridge: Polity Press, 2000).

Modood, Tariq, 'Anti-Essentialism, Multiculturalism and the "Recognition" of Religious Groups,' in Will Kymlicka and Wayne Norman (eds.), *Citizenship in Diverse Societies* (Oxford: Oxford University Press, 2000).

Montesquieu, Charles Louis de Secondat, Baron de, *Les Lettres persanes*, ed. Laurent Versini (Paris: Garnier-Flammarion, 1995 [1721]).

—— *Considérations sur les causes de la grandeur des Romains et de leur décadence* (Paris: Garnier-Flammarion, 1968 [1748]).

—— *De l'esprit des lois* (Paris: Garnier-Flammarion, 1979 [1758]).

—— 'Montesquieu on the Effects of Laws on Population,' *Population and Development Review*, 17:4 (1991), 717–29.

Moore, Margaret, 'The Territorial Dimension of Self-Determination,' in Margaret Moore (ed.), *National Self-Determination and Secession* (Oxford: Oxford University Press, 1998).

Morse, Bradford W., and Woodman, Gordon R., 'Introductory Essay: The State's Options,' in Morse and Woodman (eds.), *Indigenous Law and the State* (Providence: Foris Publications, 1988).

Mulqueeny, K. E., 'Folk-law or Folklore: When a Law is Not a Law. Or is it?' in M. A. Stephenson and Suri Ratnapala (eds.), *Mabo: A Judicial Revolution* (Brisbane: University of Queensland Press, 1993).

Myburgh, A. C., *Papers on Indigenous Law in Southern Africa*, (Pretoria: J. L. van Schaik, 1985).

Narain, Vrinda, 'Women's Rights and the Accommodation of 'Difference:' Muslim Women In India,' Southern California Review of Law and Women's Studies 8 (1998), 43.

Narveson, Jan, 'Collective Rights?' *Canadian Journal of Law and Jurisprudence* 4 (1991), 329–45.

Neate, Graeme, 'Looking After Country: Legal Recognition of Traditional Rights To and Responsibilities For Land,' *University of New South Wales Law Journal* 16:1 (1993), 161–222.

Nehru, Jawaharlal, *The Discovery of India* (New Delhi: Oxford University Press, 1985[1946]).

Nettheim, Garth, 'Mabo and Legal Pluralism: The Australian Aboriginal Justice Experience,' in Kayleen Hazlehurst (ed.), *Legal Pluralism and the Colonial Legacy* (Brookfield, Vt: Avebury Press, 1995).

Nielsen, Kai, 'Cultural Nationalism, Neither Ethnic nor Civic,' *The Philosophical Forum* 28 (1996–7), 42–50.

—— 'Liberal Nationalism, Liberal Democracies, and Secession,' *University of Toronto Law Journal* 48 (1998) 253–95.

Norman, Wayne, 'Toward a Philosophy of Federalism,' in Judith Baker (ed.), *Group Rights* (Toronto: University of Toronto Press, 1994).

Nozick, Robert, *Anarchy, State, and Utopia* (New York: Basic Books, 1974).

O'Brien, Sharon, *American Indian Tribal Governments* (Norman, Okla.: University of Oklahoma Press, 1989).

Offe, Claus, *Ethnic Politics in Eastern European Transitions* (Bremen: Center for European Law and Policy, Papers on East European Constitution Building No. 1, 1993).

Okin, Susan Moller, 'Is Multiculturalism Bad For Women?,' *The Boston Review* 22:5 (Oct./Nov. 1997), 25–8.

—— 'Feminism and Multiculturalism: Some Tensions,' *Ethics* 108:4 (1998), 661–84.

Ostrom, Carol, 'Harborview Debates Issue of Circumcision of Muslim Girls,' *The Seattle Times,* Friday 13 Sept. 1996, A1.

Parekh, Bhikhu, 'Superior People: The Narrowness of Liberalism From Mill to Rawls,' *Times Literary Supplement,* 25 Feb. 1994, 11–13.

Place, Elizabeth, 'Land Use,' in Donald Kraybill (ed.), *The Amish and the State* (Baltimore: Johns Hopkins University Press, 1993).

Puri, Kamal, 'Copyright Protection for Australian Aborigines in the Light of *Mabo*,' in M. A. Stephenson and Suri Ratnapala (eds.), *Mabo: A Judicial Revolution* (Brisbane: University of Queensland Press, 1993).

Raz, Joseph, *The Morality of Freedom* (Oxford: Oxford University Press, 1986).

—— 'Value Incommensurability: Some Preliminaries,' *Proceedings of the Aristotelian Society* 86 (1985–6), 117–34.

—— *Ethics in the Public Domain* (Oxford: Oxford University Press, 1994).

—— 'Moral Change and Social Relativism,' in E. F. Paul, F. D. Miller, and J. Paul (eds.), *Cultural Pluralism and Moral Knowledge* (Cambridge: Cambridge University Press, 1994).

Reaume, Denise G., 'The Group Right to Linguistic Security,' in Judith Baker (ed.), *Group Rights* (Toronto: University of Toronto Press, 1994).

Reeve, Andrew, *Property* (London: Macmillan, 1986).

Reno, Janet, 'U.S. Department Of Justice Commitment To American Indian Tribal Justice Systems,' *Judicature* 79 (Nov.–Dec. 1995), 113–17.

Reynolds, Henry, *Aboriginal Sovereignty* (Sydney: Allen & Unwin, 1996).

Rosenblum, Nancy, 'The Democracy of Everyday Life,' in Bernard Yack (ed.), *Liberalism without Illusions: Essays on Liberal Theory and the Political Vision of Judith N. Shklar* (Chicago: University of Chicago Press, 1996).

—— *Membership and Morals: The Personal Uses of Pluralism in America* (Princeton: Princeton University Press, 1997).

Shachar, Ayelet, 'Group Identity and Women's Rights in Family Law: The Perils of Multicultural Accommodation,' *Journal of Political Philosophy* 6:3 (1998), 285–305.

—— 'The Paradox of Multicultural Vulnerability: Individual Rights, Identity Groups, and the State,' in Christian Joppke and Steven Lukes (eds.), *Multicultural Questions* (Oxford: Oxford University Press, 1999).

Schlesinger, Arthur, Jr., *The Disuniting of America* (New York: W. W. Norton, 1990).

Scott, James C., 'State Simplifications: Nature, Space, and People,' in Ian Shapiro and Russell Hardin (eds.), *NOMOS XXXVIII: Political Order* (New York: New York University Press, 1996).

—— *Seeing Like a State* (New Haven: Yale University Press, 1998).

Scruton, Roger, 'The Legitimacy of British Civilisation in Australia,' in R. Scruton, F. Brennan, and J. Hyde, *Land Rights and Legitimacy: Three Views* (Perth: Australian Institute for Public Policy, 1985).

Shepherd, John R., *Statecraft and Political Economy on the Taiwan Frontier 1600–1800* (Stanford: Stanford University Press, 1993).

Shklar, Judith, *Ordinary Vices* (Cambridge: Harvard University Press, 1984).

—— 'The Liberalism of Fear,' in Nancy L. Rosenblum (ed.), *Liberalism and the Moral Life* (Cambridge, Mass.: Harvard University Press, 1989).

—— *The Faces of Injustice* (New Haven: Yale University Press, 1990).

—— *American Citizenship: The Quest for Inclusion* (Cambridge, Mass.: Harvard University Press, 1991).

—— *Political Thought and Political Thinkers*, ed. Stanley Hoffman (Chicago: University of Chicago Press, 1998).

Shriver, Donald W. Jr., *An Ethic For Enemies: Forgiveness in Politics* (Oxford: Oxford University Press, 1995).

Simon, Robert, 'Pluralism and Equality: The Status of Minority Values in a Democracy,' in J. W. Chapman and Alan Wertheimer (eds.), *NOMOS XXXII: Majorities and Minorities* (New York: New York University Press, 1990).

Simon, Thomas W., 'Prevent Harms First: Minority Protection in International Law,' *International Legal Perspectives* 9 (1997), 129–66.

Smith, Anthony, *National Identity* (Reno: University of Nevada Press, 1991).

—— 'Opening Statement: Nations and their Pasts,' *Nations and Nationalism* 2:3 (1996), 359–65.

—— 'Memory and Modernity: Reflections on Ernest Gellner's Theory of Nationalism,' *Nations and Nationalism* 2:3 (1996), 371–88.

Sowell, Thomas, *Preferential Policies* (New York: Basic Books, 1991).

Spinner-Halev, Jeff, 'Land, Culture and Justice: A Framework for Collective Recognition,' *Journal of Political Philosophy* (forthcoming).

'Statement of Indigenous Nations, Peoples, and Organizations,' 11 Dec. 1992, in *Voice of Indigenous Peoples: Native Peoples Address the United Nations*. (Santa Fe: Clear Light Publisher, 1994).

Stevens, Jacqueline, *Reproducing the State* (Princeton: Princeton University Press, 1999).

Sunstein, Cass, 'Constitutionalism and Secession,' *University of Chicago Law Review* 58 (1991), 633–70.

Svensson, Frances, 'Liberal Democracy and Group Rights: The Legacy of Individualism and its Impact on American Indian Tribes,' *Political Studies* 27 (1979), 421–39.

Tamir, Yael, *Liberal Nationalism* (Princeton: Princeton University Press, 1993).

—— 'The Land of the Fearful and the Free,' *Constellations* 3:3 (1997), 296–314.

—— 'Pro Patria Mori!: Death and the State' in Robert McKim and Jeff McMahan (eds.), *The Morality of Nationalism* (Oxford: Oxford University Press, 1997).

Taylor, Charles, 'The Diversity of Social Goods,' in *Philosophy and the Human Sciences* (Cambridge: Cambridge University Press, 1985).

—— *Reconciling the Solitudes: Essays on Canadian Federalism and Nationalism*, ed. Guy Laforest (Montreal: McGill-Queens University Press, 1993).

—— 'Multiculturalism and the 'Politics of Recognition,' " in Amy Gutmann (ed.), *Multiculturalism and the 'Politics of Recognition'* (Princeton: Princeton University Press, 1993).

—— *Philosophical Arguments* (Cambridge: Harvard University Press, 1997).

—— 'Leading a Life,' in Ruth Chang (ed.), *Incommensurability, Incomparability, and Practical Reason* (Cambridge, Mass.: Harvard University Press, 1997).

—— 'Nationalism and Modernity,' in Robert McKim and Jeff McMahan (eds.), *The Morality of Nationalism* (Oxford: Oxford University Press, 1997).

Thompson, Dennis L., 'Canadian Government Relations,' in Donald Kraybill (ed.), *The Amish and the State* (Baltimore: Johns Hopkins University Press, 1993).

Todorov, Tzvetan, *On Human Diversity* (Cambridge, Mass.: Harvard University Press, 1993).

Tomasi, John, 'Kymlicka, Liberalism, and Respect for Aboriginal Cultures,' *Ethics* 105:3 (1995), 580–603.

Tomiak, Janusz, *et al.* (eds.), *Comparative Studies on Governments and Non-dominant Ethnic Groups in Europe, 1850–1940*, i: *Schooling, Educational Policy, and Ethnic Identity* (New York: New York University Press, European Science Foundation, 1991).

—— and Kazarnias, Andreas, 'Introduction,' in Janusz Tomiak *et al.* (eds.), *Comparative Studies on Governments and Non Dominant Ethnic Groups, 1850–1940*, i: *Schooling, Education Policy, and Ethnic Identity* (New York: New York University Press, European Science Foundation, 1991).

Toronto Sun, 'Memory Lapses,' *The Toronto Sun* Opinion/Editorial section p. 1, Wednesday 31 May 1995.

Tully, James, 'Aboriginal Property and Western Theory: Recovering a Middle Ground,' *Social Philosophy and Policy* 11 (1994), 153–80.

—— *Strange Multiplicities: Constitutionalism in an Age of Diversity* (Cambridge: Cambridge University Press, 1997).

Van Dyke, Vernon, 'The Individual, the State, and Ethnic Communities in Political Theory,' *World Politics* 29 (1979), 343–69.

—— 'Collective Entities and Moral Rights: Problems in Liberal-Democratic Thought,' *Journal of Politics* 44 (1982), 21–40.

Vilfan, Sergij, 'Introduction,' in Sergij Vilfan, Gudmund Sandvik, and Lode Wils (eds.), *Comparative Studies on Governments and Non Dominant Ethnic Groups in Europe, 1850–1940*, iii: *Ethnic Groups and Language Rights* (New York: New York University Press, European Science Foundation, 1993).

—— Sandvik, Gudmund, and Wils, Lode (eds.), *Comparative Studies on Governments and Non-Dominant Ethnic Groups in Europe, 1850–1940*, iii: *Ethnic Groups and Language Rights* (New York: New York University Press, European Science Foundation, 1993).

Viroli, Maurizio, *For Love of Country: An Essay on Patriotism and Nationalism* (Oxford: Oxford University Press, 1995).

Vitoria, Francisco de, 'On the American Indians,' in Anthony Pagden and Jeremy Lawrance (eds.), *Political Writings* (1991 [1539]).

Jeremy Waldron, 'Minority Cultures and the Cosmopolitan Alternative,' 25 *University of Michigan Journal of Law Reform* 25 (1992), 751–93.

—— 'Superseding Historic Injustice,' *Ethics* 103:1 (1992), 4–28.

—— 'When Justice Replaces Affection,' in *Liberal Rights* (Cambridge: Cambridge University Press, 1993).

—— 'Money and Complex Equality,' in David Miller and Michael Walzer (eds.), *Pluralism, Justice, and Equality* (Oxford: Oxford University Press, 1995).

—— 'Kant's Legal Positivism,' *Harvard Law Review* 109 (1996), 1535–66.

—— 'What is a Human Right? Universals and the Challenge of Cultural Relativism,' *Pace International Law Review* 11 (1999), 129–38.

—— 'Citizenship and Identity,' in Will Kymlicka and Wayne Norman (eds.), *Citizenship in Diverse Societies* (Oxford: Oxford University Press, 2000).

Walzer, Michael, *Spheres of Justice* (New York: Basic Books, 1983).

—— 'The Communitarian Critique of Liberalism,' *Political Theory* 18 (1990), 6–23.

—— *Thick and Thin* (Notre Dame: University of Notre Dame Press, 1993).

—— 'On Negative Politics,' in Bernard Yack (ed.), *Liberalism Without Illusions: Essays on Liberal Theory and the Political Vision of Judith N. Shklar* (Chicago: University of Chicago Press, 1996).

—— *On Toleration* (New Haven: Yale University Press, 1997).

Weber, Eugene, *Peasants Into Frenchmen: the Modernization of Rural France, 1870–1914* (Stanford: Stanford University Press, 1979).

Williams, Bernard, *Ethics and the Limits of Philosophy* (London: Fontana Books, 1985).

Williams, Melissa S., 'Group Inequality and the Public Culture of Justice,' in Judith Baker (ed.), *Group Rights* (Toronto: University of Toronto Press, 1994).

Wils, Lode, 'Belgium on the Path to Equal Language Rights up to 1939,' in Sergij Vilfan, Gudmund Sandvik, and Lode Wils (eds.), *Comparative Studies on Governments and Non Dominant Ethnic Groups in Europe, 1850–1940*, iii: *Ethnic Groups and Language Rights* (New York: New York University Press, European Science Foundation, 1993).

Wood, Gordon S., *The Radicalism of the American Revolution* (New York: Knopf, 1992).

Woodman, Gordon, 'How State Courts Create Customary Law in Ghana and Nigeria,' in Bradford Morse and Gordon Woodman (eds.), *Indigenous Law and the State* (Providence: Foris Publications, 1988).

Yack, Bernard, 'The Myth of the Civic Nation,' *Critical Review* 10:2 (1996), 193–211.

Young, Crawford, *The Politics of Cultural Pluralism* (Madison: University of Wisconsin Press, 1976).

Young, Iris Marion, *Justice and the Politics of Difference* (Princeton: Princeton University Press, 1990).

CASES CITED

Baker Lake v Minister of Indian Affairs, 107 DLR (3rd) 513 (Canada 1979).
Coe v Commonwealth, 118 ALR 193 (Australia 1993).
Connolly v Woolrich, 17 RJRQ 75 (Quebec, Canada 1867).
Connolly v Woolrich, 1 RLOS 253 (Quebec, Canada 1869).
Delgamuukw v British Columbia, S.C.J. No. 108 (Canada 1997).
Oregon v Smith, 494 US 872 (USA 1990).
Goldman v Weinberger, 475 US 503 (USA 1986).
Johnson v M'Intosh, 21 US 543 (USA 1823).
Mabo v Queensland (no. 2), 175 CLR 1 (Australia 1992).
Milirrpum v Nabalco, 17 FLR 141 (Australia 1971).
Minnesota v Hershberger, 110 S. Ct. 1918 (USA 1990).
Oliphant v Suquamish Tribe, 435 U.S. 191 (USA 1978)
Re Southern Rhodesia, AC 211 (House of Lords UK 1919).
Reynolds v United States, 98 US 145 (USA 1878).
Simon v R, 24 DLR (4th) 390 (Canada 1985).
State v Hershberger (II), 462 NW2d 393 (Minn., USA, 1990).
Thomas v Norris, 2 CNLR 139 (British Columbia, Canada 1992).
United States v Lee, 455 US 252 (USA 1982).
Walker v NSW, 126 ALR 195 (Australia 1994).
Wik Peoples v State of Queensland, ALR 129 (Australia 1996).
Wisconsin v Yoder, 406 US 205 (USA 1972).
Worcester v State of Georgia, 31 US 515 (USA 1832).

INDEX